Sources of Constitutional Law

Constitutions and Fundamental Legislative Provisions from the United States, France, Germany, the Netherlands and the United Kingdom, Including the ECHR and the EU Charter of Fundamental Rights

Editors:

Sascha Hardt
Aalt Willem Heringa

Sources of Constitutional Law

Constitutions and Fundamental Legislative Provisions from the United States, France, Germany, the Netherlands and the United Kingdom, Including the ECHR and the EU Charter of Fundamental Rights

Q MONTESQUIEU INSTITUTE

Editors:
Sascha Hardt
Aalt Willem Heringa

Sources of Constitutional Law
Constitutions and Fundamental Legislative Provisions from the United States, France, Germany, the Netherlands and the United Kingdom, Including the ECHR and the EU Charter of Fundamental Rights

Intersentia Ltd
Sheraton House | Castle Park
Cambridge | CB3 0AX | United Kingdom
Tel.: +44 1223 370 169 | Email: mail@intersentia.co.uk

ISBN 978-1-78068-267-9
D/2014/7849/135
NUR 823

© 2014 Intersentia
Cambridge – Antwerp – Portland
www.intersentia.com | www.intersentia.co.uk

Cover photo: © Zagorskid – dreamstime.com

British Library Cataloguing in Publication Data. A catalogue record for this book is available from the British Library.

No part of this book may be reproduced in any form, by print, photo copy, microfilm or any other means, without written permission from the editors.

PREFACE

The present volume contains a selection of constitutional and fundamental legislative provisions from the United States, France, Germany, the Netherlands and the United Kingdom. In addition, it provides the full text of the European Convention on Human Rights and the Charter of Fundamental Rights of the European Union.

This compilation is addressed to students of comparative constitutional law. It is intended to help them compare and refer to written sources of constitutional law and to understand the constitutional structure of the five jurisdictions represented. Moreover, this volume functions as the ideal companion to the textbook *Constitutions Compared* (Heringa & Kiiver, Intersentia, 2012).

While the British and American instruments are reproduced in the original English, most of the French, German, and Dutch sources are rendered as new English translations under critical editorship (only the French Declaration of Rights of Man and of the Citizen and the Preamble to the Constitution of the Fourth Republic are reproduced in the much-quoted and widely accepted translation provided by the *Conseil Constitutionnel*). Instead of attempting to turn old-fashioned or ambiguous original language into modern and elegant English, the translations contained in this volume remain true to the content, style and syntax of the original. This allows the reader to appreciate not only the substance but also the authentic form and style of constitutional sources. For easy reference, key legal terms and proper names are added in the original language as in-text citations between square brackets. Enactment formulas are always omitted, preambles are retained unless indicated otherwise.

The editors are grateful to their colleagues and former colleagues from the Maastricht Law Faculty who have contributed to the work on the present volume. In particular, we would like to thank Dr. Philipp Kiiver, who edited the predecessors of this compilation.

Preface

The editors,

Dr. Sascha Hardt, Assistant Professor of Comparative Constitutional Law, and
Prof. Dr. Aalt Willem Heringa, Professor of (Comparative) Constitutional and Administrative Law, Maastricht University

Maastricht, July 2014

TABLE OF CONTENTS

PREFACE v

CONTENTS vii

UNITED STATES 1

Constitution of the United States of America of 17 September 1787 [including Amendments] 1

FRANCE 17

Declaration of the Rights of Man and of the Citizen of 26 August 1789 17

Preamble to the Constitution of 27 October 1946 20

Constitution (of the Fifth Republic) of 4 October 1958 22

Electoral Code as last amended in its relevant parts by Statute No. 2013-702 of 2 August 2013. 49

GERMANY 55

Basic Law for the Federal Republic of Germany of 23 May 1949 55

Federal Elections Act 111

THE NETHERLANDS 115

Charter for the Kingdom of the Netherlands of 28 October 1954 115

Constitution for the Kingdom of the Netherlands of 24 August 1815. 129

Elections Act of 28 September 1989 149

United Kingdom 153
Bill of Rights 1689 153
Parliament Act 1911. 157
Fixed-term Parliaments Act 2011 160
Constitutional Reform Act 2005. 163
Constitutional Reform and Governance Act 2010 169
Scotland Act 1998 172
Government of Wales Act 2006 181
Northern Ireland Act 1998 188
Human Rights Act 1998 199

European Fundamental Rights 207
Convention for the Protection of Human Rights and Fundamental Freedoms 207
Protocols to the Convention for the Protection of Human Rights and Fundamental Freedoms 220
Charter of Fundamental Rights of the European Union 224

UNITED STATES

Constitution of the United States of America of 17 September 1787 [including Amendments]

Preamble
We the People of the United States, in Order to form a more perfect Union, establish Justice, insure domestic Tranquility, provide for the common defence, promote the general Welfare, and secure the Blessings of Liberty to ourselves and our Posterity, do ordain and establish this Constitution for the United States of America.

Article I.

Section 1. All legislative Powers herein granted shall be vested in a Congress of the United States, which shall consist of a Senate and House of Representatives.
Section 2. The House of Representatives shall be composed of Members chosen every second Year by the People of the several States, and the Electors in each State shall have the Qualifications requisite for Electors of the most numerous Branch of the State Legislature.
No Person shall be a Representative who shall not have attained to the Age of twenty five Years, and been seven Years a Citizen of the United States, and who shall not, when elected, be an Inhabitant of that State in which he shall be chosen.
Representatives and direct Taxes shall be apportioned among the several States which may be included within this Union, according to their respective Numbers, which shall be determined by adding to the whole Number of free Persons, including those bound to Service for a Term of Years, and excluding Indians not taxed, three fifths of all other Persons. The actual Enumeration shall be made within three Years after the first Meeting of the Congress of the United States, and within every subsequent Term of ten Years, in such Manner as they shall by Law direct. The Number of Representatives shall not exceed one for every thirty Thousand, but each State shall have at Least one Representative; and until such enumeration shall be made, the State of New Hampshire shall be entitled to chuse three, Massachusetts eight, Rhode-Island and Providence Plantations one, Connecticut five, New-York

six, New Jersey four, Pennsylvania eight, Delaware one, Maryland six, Virginia ten, North Carolina five, South Carolina five, and Georgia three.

When vacancies happen in the Representation from any State, the Executive Authority thereof shall issue Writs of Election to fill such Vacancies.

The House of Representatives shall chuse their Speaker and other Officers; and shall have the sole Power of Impeachment.

Section 3. The Senate of the United States shall be composed of two Senators from each State, chosen by the Legislature thereof for six Years; and each Senator shall have one Vote.

Immediately after they shall be assembled in Consequence of the first Election, they shall be divided as equally as may be into three Classes. The Seats of the Senators of the first Class shall be vacated at the Expiration of the second Year, of the second Class at the Expiration of the fourth Year, and of the third Class at the Expiration of the sixth Year, so that one third may be chosen every second Year; and if Vacancies happen by Resignation, or otherwise, during the Recess of the Legislature of any State, the Executive thereof may make temporary Appointments until the next Meeting of the Legislature, which shall then fill such Vacancies.

No Person shall be a Senator who shall not have attained to the Age of thirty Years, and been nine Years a Citizen of the United States, and who shall not, when elected, be an Inhabitant of that State for which he shall be chosen.

The Vice President of the United States shall be President of the Senate, but shall have no Vote, unless they be equally divided.

The Senate shall chuse their other Officers, and also a President pro tempore, in the Absence of the Vice President, or when he shall exercise the Office of President of the United States.

The Senate shall have the sole Power to try all Impeachments. When sitting for that Purpose, they shall be on Oath or Affirmation. When the President of the United States is tried, the Chief Justice shall preside: And no Person shall be convicted without the Concurrence of two thirds of the Members present.

Judgment in Cases of Impeachment shall not extend further than to removal from Office, and disqualification to hold and enjoy any Office of honor, Trust or Profit under the United States: but the Party convicted shall nevertheless be liable and subject to Indictment, Trial, Judgment and Punishment, according to Law.

Section 4. The Times, Places and Manner of holding Elections for Senators and Representatives, shall be prescribed in each State by the Legislature thereof; but the Congress may at any time by Law make or alter such Regulations, except as to the Places of chusing Senators.

The Congress shall assemble at least once in every Year, and such Meeting shall be on the first Monday in December, unless they shall by Law appoint a different Day.

Section 5. Each House shall be the Judge of the Elections, Returns and Qualifications of its own Members, and a Majority of each shall constitute a Quorum to do Business; but a smaller Number may adjourn from day to day, and may be authorized to compel the Attendance of absent Members, in such Manner, and under such Penalties as each House may provide.

Each House may determine the Rules of its Proceedings, punish its Members for disorderly Behaviour, and, with the Concurrence of two thirds, expel a Member.

Each House shall keep a Journal of its Proceedings, and from time to time publish the same, excepting such Parts as may in their Judgment require Secrecy; and the Yeas and Nays of the Members of either House on any question shall, at the Desire of one fifth of those Present, be entered on the Journal.

Neither House, during the Session of Congress, shall, without the Consent of the other, adjourn for more than three days, nor to any other Place than that in which the two Houses shall be sitting.

Section 6. The Senators and Representatives shall receive a Compensation for their Services, to be ascertained by Law, and paid out of the Treasury of the United States. They shall in all Cases, except Treason, Felony and Breach of the Peace, be privileged from Arrest during their Attendance at the Session of their respective Houses, and in going to and returning from the same; and for any Speech or Debate in either House, they shall not be questioned in any other Place.

No Senator or Representative shall, during the Time for which he was elected, be appointed to any civil Office under the Authority of the United States, which shall have been created, or the Emoluments whereof shall have been encreased during such time; and no Person holding any Office under the United States, shall be a Member of either House during his Continuance in Office.

Section 7. All Bills for raising Revenue shall originate in the House of Representatives; but the Senate may propose or concur with Amendments as on other Bills.

Every Bill which shall have passed the House of Representatives and the Senate, shall, before it become a Law, be presented to the President of the United States: If he approve he shall sign it, but if not he shall return it, with his Objections to that House in which it shall have originated, who shall enter the Objections at large on their Journal, and proceed to reconsider it. If after such Reconsideration two thirds of that House shall agree to pass the Bill, it shall be sent, together with the Objections, to the other House, by which it shall likewise be reconsidered, and if approved by two thirds of that House, it shall become a Law. But in all such Cases the Votes of both Houses shall be determined by yeas and Nays, and the Names of the Persons voting for and against the Bill shall be entered on the Journal of each House respectively. If any Bill shall not be returned by the President within ten Days (Sundays excepted) after it shall have been presented to him, the Same shall be a Law, in like Manner as if he had signed it, unless the Congress by their Adjournment prevent its Return, in which Case it shall not be a Law.

Every Order, Resolution, or Vote to which the Concurrence of the Senate and House of Representatives may be necessary (except on a question of Adjournment) shall be presented to the President of the United States; and before the Same shall take Effect, shall be approved by him, or being disapproved by him, shall be repassed by two thirds of the Senate and House of Representatives, according to the Rules and Limitations prescribed in the Case of a Bill.

Section 8. The Congress shall have Power To lay and collect Taxes, Duties, Imposts and Excises, to pay the Debts and provide for the common Defence and general Welfare of the United States; but all Duties, Imposts and Excises shall be uniform throughout the United States;

To borrow Money on the credit of the United States;

To regulate Commerce with foreign Nations, and among the several States, and with the Indian Tribes;

To establish an uniform Rule of Naturalization, and uniform Laws on the subject of Bankruptcies throughout the United States;

To coin Money, regulate the Value thereof, and of foreign Coin, and fix the Standard of Weights and Measures;

To provide for the Punishment of counterfeiting the Securities and current Coin of the United States;

To establish Post Offices and post Roads;

To promote the Progress of Science and useful Arts, by securing for limited Times to Authors and Inventors the exclusive Right to their respective Writings and Discoveries;

To constitute Tribunals inferior to the supreme Court;

To define and punish Piracies and Felonies committed on the high Seas, and Offences against the Law of Nations;

To declare War, grant Letters of Marque and Reprisal, and make Rules concerning Captures on Land and Water;

To raise and support Armies, but no Appropriation of Money to that Use shall be for a longer Term than two Years;

To provide and maintain a Navy;

To make Rules for the Government and Regulation of the land and naval Forces;

To provide for calling forth the Militia to execute the Laws of the Union, suppress Insurrections and repel Invasions;

To provide for organizing, arming, and disciplining, the Militia, and for governing such Part of them as may be employed in the Service of the United States, reserving to the States respectively, the Appointment of the Officers, and the Authority of training the Militia according to the discipline prescribed by Congress;

To exercise exclusive Legislation in all Cases whatsoever, over such District (not exceeding ten Miles square) as may, by Cession of particular States, and the Acceptance of Congress, become the Seat of the Government of the United States, and to exercise like Authority over all Places purchased by the Consent of the Legislature of the State in which the Same shall be, for the Erection of Forts, Magazines, Arsenals, dock-Yards, and other needful Buildings;--And

To make all Laws which shall be necessary and proper for carrying into Execution the foregoing Powers, and all other Powers vested by this Constitution in the Government of the United States, or in any Department or Officer thereof.

Section 9. The Migration or Importation of such Persons as any of the States now existing shall think proper to admit, shall not be prohibited by the Congress prior to the Year one thousand eight hundred and eight, but a Tax or duty may be imposed on such Importation, not exceeding ten dollars for each Person.

The Privilege of the Writ of Habeas Corpus shall not be suspended, unless when in Cases of Rebellion or Invasion the public Safety may require it.

No Bill of Attainder or ex post facto Law shall be passed.

No Capitation, or other direct, Tax shall be laid, unless in Proportion to the Census or enumeration herein before directed to be taken.

No Tax or Duty shall be laid on Articles exported from any State.

No Preference shall be given by any Regulation of Commerce or Revenue to the Ports of one State over those of another; nor shall Vessels bound to, or from, one State, be obliged to enter, clear, or pay Duties in another.

No Money shall be drawn from the Treasury, but in Consequence of Appropriations made by Law; and a regular Statement and Account of the Receipts and Expenditures of all public Money shall be published from time to time.

No Title of Nobility shall be granted by the United States: And no Person holding any Office of Profit or Trust under them, shall, without the Consent of the Congress, accept of any present, Emolument, Office, or Title, of any kind whatever, from any King, Prince, or foreign State.

Section 10. No State shall enter into any Treaty, Alliance, or Confederation; grant Letters of Marque and Reprisal; coin Money; emit Bills of Credit; make any Thing but gold and silver Coin a Tender in Payment of Debts; pass any Bill of Attainder, ex post facto Law, or Law impairing the Obligation of Contracts, or grant any Title of Nobility.

No State shall, without the Consent of the Congress, lay any Imposts or Duties on Imports or Exports, except what may be absolutely necessary for executing it's inspection Laws: and the net Produce of all Duties and Imposts, laid by any State on Imports or Exports, shall be for the Use of the Treasury of the United States; and all such Laws shall be subject to the Revision and Controul of the Congress.

No State shall, without the Consent of Congress, lay any Duty of Tonnage, keep Troops, or Ships of War in time of Peace, enter into any Agreement or Compact with another State, or with a foreign Power, or engage in War, unless actually invaded, or in such imminent Danger as will not admit of delay.

Article II.

Section 1. The executive Power shall be vested in a President of the United States of America. He shall hold his Office during the Term of four Years, and, together with the Vice President, chosen for the same Term, be elected, as follows:

Each State shall appoint, in such Manner as the Legislature thereof may direct, a Number of Electors, equal to the whole Number of Senators and Representatives to which the State may be entitled in the Congress: but no Senator or Representative, or Person holding an Office of Trust or Profit under the United States, shall be appointed an Elector.

The Electors shall meet in their respective States, and vote by Ballot for two Persons, of whom one at least shall not be an Inhabitant of the same State with themselves. And they shall make a List of all the Persons voted for, and of the Number of Votes for each; which List they shall sign and certify, and transmit sealed to the Seat of the Government of the United States, directed to the President of the Senate. The President of the Senate shall, in the Presence of the Senate and House of Representatives, open all the Certificates, and the Votes shall then be counted. The Person having the greatest Number of Votes shall be the President, if such Number be a Majority of the whole Number of Electors appointed; and if there be more than one who have such Majority, and have an equal Number of Votes, then the House of

Representatives shall immediately chuse by Ballot one of them for President; and if no Person have a Majority, then from the five highest on the List the said House shall in like Manner chuse the President. But in chusing the President, the Votes shall be taken by States, the Representation from each State having one Vote; A quorum for this purpose shall consist of a Member or Members from two thirds of the States, and a Majority of all the States shall be necessary to a Choice. In every Case, after the Choice of the President, the Person having the greatest Number of Votes of the Electors shall be the Vice President. But if there should remain two or more who have equal Votes, the Senate shall chuse from them by Ballot the Vice President.

The Congress may determine the Time of chusing the Electors, and the Day on which they shall give their Votes; which Day shall be the same throughout the United States.

No Person except a natural born Citizen, or a Citizen of the United States, at the time of the Adoption of this Constitution, shall be eligible to the Office of President; neither shall any Person be eligible to that Office who shall not have attained to the Age of thirty five Years, and been fourteen Years a Resident within the United States.

In Case of the Removal of the President from Office, or of his Death, Resignation, or Inability to discharge the Powers and Duties of the said Office, the Same shall devolve on the Vice President, and the Congress may by Law provide for the Case of Removal, Death, Resignation or Inability, both of the President and Vice President, declaring what Officer shall then act as President, and such Officer shall act accordingly, until the Disability be removed, or a President shall be elected.

The President shall, at stated Times, receive for his Services, a Compensation, which shall neither be increased nor diminished during the Period for which he shall have been elected, and he shall not receive within that Period any other Emolument from the United States, or any of them.

Before he enter on the Execution of his Office, he shall take the following Oath or Affirmation:--"I do solemnly swear (or affirm) that I will faithfully execute the Office of President of the United States, and will to the best of my Ability, preserve, protect and defend the Constitution of the United States."

Section 2. The President shall be Commander in Chief of the Army and Navy of the United States, and of the Militia of the several States, when called into the actual Service of the United States; he may require the Opinion, in writing, of the principal Officer in each of the executive Departments, upon any Subject relating to the Duties of their respective Offices, and he shall have Power to grant Reprieves and Pardons for Offences against the United States, except in Cases of Impeachment.

He shall have Power, by and with the Advice and Consent of the Senate, to make Treaties, provided two thirds of the Senators present concur; and he shall nominate, and by and with the Advice and Consent of the Senate, shall appoint Ambassadors, other public Ministers and Consuls, Judges of the supreme Court, and all other Officers of the United States, whose Appointments are not herein otherwise provided for, and which shall be established by Law: but the Congress may by Law vest the Appointment of such inferior Officers, as they think proper, in the President alone, in the Courts of Law, or in the Heads of Departments.

The President shall have Power to fill up all Vacancies that may happen during the Recess of the Senate, by granting Commissions which shall expire at the End of their next Session.

Section 3. He shall from time to time give to the Congress Information of the State of the Union, and recommend to their Consideration such Measures as he shall judge necessary and expedient; he may, on extraordinary Occasions, convene both Houses, or either of them, and in Case of Disagreement between them, with Respect to the Time of Adjournment, he may adjourn them to such Time as he shall think proper; he shall receive Ambassadors and other public Ministers; he shall take Care that the Laws be faithfully executed, and shall Commission all the Officers of the United States.

Section 4. The President, Vice President and all civil Officers of the United States, shall be removed from Office on Impeachment for, and Conviction of, Treason, Bribery, or other high Crimes and Misdemeanors.

Article III.

Section 1. The judicial Power of the United States shall be vested in one supreme Court, and in such inferior Courts as the Congress may from time to time ordain and establish. The Judges, both of the supreme and inferior Courts, shall hold their Offices during good Behaviour, and shall, at stated Times, receive for their Services a Compensation, which shall not be diminished during their Continuance in Office.

Section 2. The judicial Power shall extend to all Cases, in Law and Equity, arising under this Constitution, the Laws of the United States, and Treaties made, or which shall be made, under their Authority;--to all Cases affecting Ambassadors, other public Ministers and Consuls;--to all Cases of admiralty and maritime Jurisdiction;--to Controversies to which the United States shall be a Party;--to Controversies between two or more States;-- between a State and Citizens of another State;--between Citizens of different States;--between Citizens of the same State claiming Lands under Grants of different States, and between a State, or the Citizens thereof, and foreign States, Citizens or Subjects.

In all Cases affecting Ambassadors, other public Ministers and Consuls, and those in which a State shall be Party, the supreme Court shall have original Jurisdiction. In all the other Cases before mentioned, the supreme Court shall have appellate Jurisdiction, both as to Law and Fact, with such Exceptions, and under such Regulations as the Congress shall make.

The Trial of all Crimes, except in Cases of Impeachment, shall be by Jury; and such Trial shall be held in the State where the said Crimes shall have been committed; but when not committed within any State, the Trial shall be at such Place or Places as the Congress may by Law have directed.

Section 3. Treason against the United States, shall consist only in levying War against them, or in adhering to their Enemies, giving them Aid and Comfort. No Person shall be convicted of Treason unless on the Testimony of two Witnesses to the same overt Act, or on Confession in open Court.

The Congress shall have Power to declare the Punishment of Treason, but no Attainder of Treason shall work Corruption of Blood, or Forfeiture except during the Life of the Person attainted.

Article IV.

Section 1. Full Faith and Credit shall be given in each State to the public Acts, Records, and judicial Proceedings of every other State. And the Congress may by general Laws prescribe the Manner in which such Acts, Records and Proceedings shall be proved, and the Effect thereof.
Section 2. The Citizens of each State shall be entitled to all Privileges and Immunities of Citizens in the several States.
A Person charged in any State with Treason, Felony, or other Crime, who shall flee from Justice, and be found in another State, shall on Demand of the executive Authority of the State from which he fled, be delivered up, to be removed to the State having Jurisdiction of the Crime.
No Person held to Service or Labour in one State, under the Laws thereof, escaping into another, shall, in Consequence of any Law or Regulation therein, be discharged from such Service or Labour, but shall be delivered up on Claim of the Party to whom such Service or Labour may be due.
Section 3. New States may be admitted by the Congress into this Union; but no new State shall be formed or erected within the Jurisdiction of any other State; nor any State be formed by the Junction of two or more States, or Parts of States, without the Consent of the Legislatures of the States concerned as well as of the Congress.
The Congress shall have Power to dispose of and make all needful Rules and Regulations respecting the Territory or other Property belonging to the United States; and nothing in this Constitution shall be so construed as to Prejudice any Claims of the United States, or of any particular State.
Section 4. The United States shall guarantee to every State in this Union a Republican Form of Government, and shall protect each of them against Invasion; and on Application of the Legislature, or of the Executive (when the Legislature cannot be convened), against domestic Violence.

Article V.

The Congress, whenever two thirds of both Houses shall deem it necessary, shall propose Amendments to this Constitution, or, on the Application of the Legislatures of two thirds of the several States, shall call a Convention for proposing Amendments, which, in either Case, shall be valid to all Intents and Purposes, as Part of this Constitution, when ratified by the Legislatures of three fourths of the several States, or by Conventions in three fourths thereof, as the one or the other Mode of Ratification may be proposed by the Congress; Provided that no Amendment which may be made prior to the Year One thousand eight hundred and eight shall in any Manner affect the first and fourth Clauses in the Ninth Section of the first Article; and that no State, without its Consent, shall be deprived of its equal Suffrage in the Senate.

Article VI.

All Debts contracted and Engagements entered into, before the Adoption of this Constitution, shall be as valid against the United States under this Constitution, as under the Confederation.
This Constitution, and the Laws of the United States which shall be made in Pursuance thereof; and all Treaties made, or which shall be made, under the Authority of the United States, shall be the supreme Law of the Land; and the Judges in every State shall be bound thereby, any Thing in the Constitution or Laws of any State to the Contrary notwithstanding.
The Senators and Representatives before mentioned, and the Members of the several State Legislatures, and all executive and judicial Officers, both of the United States and of the several States, shall be bound by Oath or Affirmation, to support this Constitution; but no religious Test shall ever be required as a Qualification to any Office or public Trust under the United States.

Article VII.

The Ratification of the Conventions of nine States, shall be sufficient for the Establishment of this Constitution between the States so ratifying the Same.

Done in Convention by the Unanimous Consent of the States present the Seventeenth Day of September in the Year of our Lord one thousand seven hundred and Eighty seven and of the Independence of the United States of America the Twelfth. In Witness whereof We have hereunto subscribed our Names

[The names and signatures are omitted.]

Amendments to the US Constitution

[The preamble to the Bill of Rights is omitted.]

Amendment I. Congress shall make no law respecting an establishment of religion, or prohibiting the free exercise thereof; or abridging the freedom of speech, or of the press; or the right of the people peaceably to assemble, and to petition the Government for a redress of grievances.

Amendment II. A well regulated Militia, being necessary to the security of a free State, the right of the people to keep and bear Arms, shall not be infringed.

Amendment III. No Soldier shall, in time of peace be quartered in any house, without the consent of the Owner, nor in time of war, but in a manner to be prescribed by law.

Amendment IV. The right of the people to be secure in their persons, houses, papers, and effects, against unreasonable searches and seizures, shall not be violated, and no Warrants shall issue, but upon probable cause, supported by Oath or affirmation, and particularly describing the place to be searched, and the persons or things to be seized.

Amendment V. No person shall be held to answer for a capital, or otherwise infamous crime, unless on a presentment or indictment of a Grand Jury, except in cases arising in the land or naval forces, or in the Militia, when in actual service in time of War or public danger; nor shall any person be subject for the same offence to be twice put in jeopardy of life or limb; nor shall be compelled in any criminal case to be a witness against himself, nor be deprived of life, liberty, or property, without due process of law; nor shall private property be taken for public use, without just compensation.

Amendment VI. In all criminal prosecutions, the accused shall enjoy the right to a speedy and public trial, by an impartial jury of the State and district wherein the crime shall have been committed, which district shall have been previously ascertained by law, and to be informed of the nature and cause of the accusation; to be confronted with the witnesses against him; to have compulsory process for obtaining witnesses in his favor, and to have the Assistance of Counsel for his defence.

Amendment VII. In Suits at common law, where the value in controversy shall exceed twenty dollars, the right of trial by jury shall be preserved, and no fact tried by a jury, shall be otherwise re-examined in any Court of the United States, than according to the rules of the common law.

Amendment VIII. Excessive bail shall not be required, nor excessive fines imposed, nor cruel and unusual punishments inflicted.

Amendment IX. The enumeration in the Constitution, of certain rights, shall not be construed to deny or disparage others retained by the people.

Amendment X. The powers not delegated to the United States by the Constitution, nor prohibited by it to the States, are reserved to the States respectively, or to the people.

Amendment XI. The Judicial power of the United States shall not be construed to extend to any suit in law or equity, commenced or prosecuted against one of the United States by Citizens of another State, or by Citizens or Subjects of any Foreign State.

Amendment XII. The Electors shall meet in their respective states and vote by ballot for President and Vice-President, one of whom, at least, shall not be an inhabitant of the same state with themselves; they shall name in their ballots the person voted for as President, and in distinct ballots the person voted for as Vice-President, and they shall make distinct lists of all persons voted for as President, and of all persons voted for as Vice-President, and of the number of votes for each, which lists they shall sign and certify, and transmit sealed to the seat of the government of the United States, directed to the President of the Senate; -- the President of the Senate shall, in the presence of the Senate and House of Representatives, open all the certificates and the votes shall then be counted; -- The person having the greatest number of votes for President, shall be the President, if such number be a majority of the whole number of Electors appointed; and if no person have such majority, then from the persons having the highest numbers not exceeding three on the list of those voted for as President, the House of Representatives shall choose immediately, by ballot, the President. But in choosing the President, the votes shall be taken by states, the representation from each state having one vote; a quorum for this purpose shall consist of a member or members from two-thirds of the states, and a majority of all the states shall be necessary to a choice. And if the House of Representatives shall not choose a President whenever the right of choice shall devolve upon them, before the fourth day of March next following, then the Vice-President shall act as President, as in case of the death or other constitutional disability of the President. The person having the greatest number of votes as Vice-President, shall be the Vice-President, if such number be a majority of the whole number of Electors appointed, and if no person have a majority, then from the two highest numbers on the list, the Senate shall choose the Vice-President; a quorum for the purpose shall consist of two-thirds of the whole number of Senators, and a majority of the whole number shall be necessary to a choice. But no person constitutionally ineligible to the office of President shall be eligible to that of Vice-President of the United States.

Amendment XIII. Section 1. Neither slavery nor involuntary servitude, except as a punishment for crime whereof the party shall have been duly convicted, shall exist within the United States, or any place subject to their jurisdiction.
Section 2. Congress shall have power to enforce this article by appropriate legislation.

Amendment XIV. Section 1. All persons born or naturalized in the United States, and subject to the jurisdiction thereof, are citizens of the United States and of the State wherein they reside. No State shall make or enforce any law which shall abridge the privileges or immunities of citizens of the United States; nor shall any State deprive any person of life, liberty, or property, without due process of law; nor deny to any person within its jurisdiction the equal protection of the laws.
Section 2. Representatives shall be apportioned among the several States according to their respective numbers, counting the whole number of persons in each State, excluding Indians not taxed. But when the right to vote at any election for the choice of electors for President and Vice-President of the United States, Representatives in Congress, the Executive and Judicial officers of a State, or the members of the

Legislature thereof, is denied to any of the male inhabitants of such State, being twenty-one years of age, and citizens of the United States, or in any way abridged, except for participation in rebellion, or other crime, the basis of representation therein shall be reduced in the proportion which the number of such male citizens shall bear to the whole number of male citizens twenty-one years of age in such State.

Section 3. No person shall be a Senator or Representative in Congress, or elector of President and Vice-President, or hold any office, civil or military, under the United States, or under any State, who, having previously taken an oath, as a member of Congress, or as an officer of the United States, or as a member of any State legislature, or as an executive or judicial officer of any State, to support the Constitution of the United States, shall have engaged in insurrection or rebellion against the same, or given aid or comfort to the enemies thereof. But Congress may by a vote of two-thirds of each House, remove such disability.

Section 4. The validity of the public debt of the United States, authorized by law, including debts incurred for payment of pensions and bounties for services in suppressing insurrection or rebellion, shall not be questioned. But neither the United States nor any State shall assume or pay any debt or obligation incurred in aid of insurrection or rebellion against the United States, or any claim for the loss or emancipation of any slave; but all such debts, obligations and claims shall be held illegal and void.

Section 5. The Congress shall have the power to enforce, by appropriate legislation, the provisions of this article.

Amendment XV. Section 1. The right of citizens of the United States to vote shall not be denied or abridged by the United States or by any State on account of race, color, or previous condition of servitude--

Section 2. The Congress shall have the power to enforce this article by appropriate legislation.

Amendment XVI. The Congress shall have power to lay and collect taxes on incomes, from whatever source derived, without apportionment among the several States, and without regard to any census or enumeration.

Amendment XVII. The Senate of the United States shall be composed of two Senators from each State, elected by the people thereof, for six years; and each Senator shall have one vote. The electors in each State shall have the qualifications requisite for electors of the most numerous branch of the State legislatures.

When vacancies happen in the representation of any State in the Senate, the executive authority of such State shall issue writs of election to fill such vacancies: Provided, That the legislature of any State may empower the executive thereof to make temporary appointments until the people fill the vacancies by election as the legislature may direct.

This amendment shall not be so construed as to affect the election or term of any Senator chosen before it becomes valid as part of the Constitution.

Amendment XVIII. Section 1. After one year from the ratification of this article the manufacture, sale, or transportation of intoxicating liquors within, the importation thereof into, or the exportation thereof from the United States and all territory subject to the jurisdiction thereof for beverage purposes is hereby prohibited.
Section 2. The Congress and the several States shall have concurrent power to enforce this article by appropriate legislation.
Section 3. This article shall be inoperative unless it shall have been ratified as an amendment to the Constitution by the legislatures of the several States, as provided in the Constitution, within seven years from the date of the submission hereof to the States by the Congress.

Amendment XIX. The right of citizens of the United States to vote shall not be denied or abridged by the United States or by any State on account of sex.
Congress shall have power to enforce this article by appropriate legislation.

Amendment XX. Section 1. The terms of the President and the Vice President shall end at noon on the 20th day of January, and the terms of Senators and Representatives at noon on the 3d day of January, of the years in which such terms would have ended if this article had not been ratified; and the terms of their successors shall then begin.
Section 2. The Congress shall assemble at least once in every year, and such meeting shall begin at noon on the 3d day of January, unless they shall by law appoint a different day.
Section 3. If, at the time fixed for the beginning of the term of the President, the President elect shall have died, the Vice President elect shall become President. If a President shall not have been chosen before the time fixed for the beginning of his term, or if the President elect shall have failed to qualify, then the Vice President elect shall act as President until a President shall have qualified; and the Congress may by law provide for the case wherein neither a President elect nor a Vice President shall have qualified, declaring who shall then act as President, or the manner in which one who is to act shall be selected, and such person shall act accordingly until a President or Vice President shall have qualified.
Section 4. The Congress may by law provide for the case of the death of any of the persons from whom the House of Representatives may choose a President whenever the right of choice shall have devolved upon them, and for the case of the death of any of the persons from whom the Senate may choose a Vice President whenever the right of choice shall have devolved upon them.
Section 5. Sections 1 and 2 shall take effect on the 15th day of October following the ratification of this article.
Section 6. This article shall be inoperative unless it shall have been ratified as an amendment to the Constitution by the legislatures of three-fourths of the several States within seven years from the date of its submission.

Amendment XXI. Section 1. The eighteenth article of amendment to the Constitution of the United States is hereby repealed.

Section 2. The transportation or importation into any State, Territory, or Possession of the United States for delivery or use therein of intoxicating liquors, in violation of the laws thereof, is hereby prohibited.

Section 3. This article shall be inoperative unless it shall have been ratified as an amendment to the Constitution by conventions in the several States, as provided in the Constitution, within seven years from the date of the submission hereof to the States by the Congress.

Amendment XXII. Section 1. No person shall be elected to the office of the President more than twice, and no person who has held the office of President, or acted as President, for more than two years of a term to which some other person was elected President shall be elected to the office of President more than once. But this Article shall not apply to any person holding the office of President when this Article was proposed by Congress, and shall not prevent any person who may be holding the office of President, or acting as President, during the term within which this Article becomes operative from holding the office of President or acting as President during the remainder of such term.

Section 2. This article shall be inoperative unless it shall have been ratified as an amendment to the Constitution by the legislatures of three-fourths of the several States within seven years from the date of its submission to the States by the Congress.

Amendment XXIII. Section 1. The District constituting the seat of Government of the United States shall appoint in such manner as Congress may direct:

A number of electors of President and Vice President equal to the whole number of Senators and Representatives in Congress to which the District would be entitled if it were a State, but in no event more than the least populous State; they shall be in addition to those appointed by the States, but they shall be considered, for the purposes of the election of President and Vice President, to be electors appointed by a State; and they shall meet in the District and perform such duties as provided by the twelfth article of amendment.

Section 2. The Congress shall have power to enforce this article by appropriate legislation.

Amendment XXIV. Section 1. The right of citizens of the United States to vote in any primary or other election for President or Vice President, for electors for President or Vice President, or for Senator or Representative in Congress, shall not be denied or abridged by the United States or any State by reason of failure to pay poll tax or other tax.

Section 2. The Congress shall have power to enforce this article by appropriate legislation.

Amendment XXV. Section 1. In case of the removal of the President from office or of his death or resignation, the Vice President shall become President.

Section 2. Whenever there is a vacancy in the office of the Vice President, the President shall nominate a Vice President who shall take office upon confirmation by a majority vote of both Houses of Congress.

Section 3. Whenever the President transmits to the President pro tempore of the Senate and the Speaker of the House of Representatives his written declaration that he is unable to discharge the powers and duties of his office, and until he transmits to them a written declaration to the contrary, such powers and duties shall be discharged by the Vice President as Acting President.

Section 4. Whenever the Vice President and a majority of either the principal officers of the executive departments or of such other body as Congress may by law provide, transmit to the President pro tempore of the Senate and the Speaker of the House of Representatives their written declaration that the President is unable to discharge the powers and duties of his office, the Vice President shall immediately assume the powers and duties of the office as Acting President.

Thereafter, when the President transmits to the President pro tempore of the Senate and the Speaker of the House of Representatives his written declaration that no inability exists, he shall resume the powers and duties of his office unless the Vice President and a majority of either the principal officers of the executive department or of such other body as Congress may by law provide, transmit within four days to the President pro tempore of the Senate and the Speaker of the House of Representatives their written declaration that the President is unable to discharge the powers and duties of his office. Thereupon Congress shall decide the issue, assembling within forty-eight hours for that purpose if not in session. If the Congress, within twenty-one days after receipt of the latter written declaration, or, if Congress is not in session, within twenty-one days after Congress is required to assemble, determines by two-thirds vote of both Houses that the President is unable to discharge the powers and duties of his office, the Vice President shall continue to discharge the same as Acting President; otherwise, the President shall resume the powers and duties of his office.

Amendment XXVI. Section 1. The right of citizens of the United States, who are eighteen years of age or older, to vote shall not be denied or abridged by the United States or by any State on account of age.

Section 2. The Congress shall have power to enforce this article by appropriate legislation.

Amendment XXVII. No law, varying the compensation for the services of the Senators and Representatives, shall take effect, until an election of representatives shall have intervened

FRANCE

Declaration of the Rights of Man and of the Citizen
[Déclaration des Droits de l'Homme et du Citoyen] of 26 August 1789[1]

The representatives of the people of France, formed into a National Assembly, considering that ignorance, neglect, or contempt of human rights, are the sole causes of public misfortunes and corruptions of Government, have resolved to set forth in a solemn declaration, these natural, imprescriptible, and inalienable rights: that this declaration being constantly present to the minds of the members of the body social, they may be for ever kept attentive to their rights and their duties; that the acts of the legislative and executive powers of government, being capable of being every moment compared with the end of political institutions, may be more respected; and also, that the future claims of the citizens, being directed by simple and incontestable principles, may tend to the maintenance of the Constitution, and the general happiness.

For these reasons, the National Assembly doth recognize and declare, in the presence of the Supreme Being, and with the hope of his blessing and favour, the following sacred rights of men and of citizens:

I. Men are born, and always continue, free and equal in respect of their rights. Civil distinctions, therefore, can be founded only on public utility.

II. The end of all political associations, is the preservation of the natural and imprescriptible rights of man; and these rights are liberty, property, security, and resistance of oppression.

III. The nation is essentially the source of all sovereignty; nor can any individual, or any body of men, be entitled to any authority which is not expressly derived from it.

---

[1] Translation: Conseil Constitutionnel.

IV. Political liberty consists in the power of doing whatever does not injure another. The exercise of the natural rights of every man, has no other limits than those which are necessary to secure to every other man the free exercise of the same rights; and these limits are determinable only by the law.

V. The law ought to prohibit only actions hurtful to society. What is not prohibited by the law, should not be hindered; nor should any one be compelled to that which the law does not require.

VI. The law is an expression of the will of the community. All citizens have a right to concur, either personally, or by their representatives, in its formation. It should be the same to all, whether it protects or punishes; and all being equal in its sight, are equally eligible to all honours, places, and employments, according to their different abilities, without any other distinction than that created by their virtues and talents.

VII. No man should be accused, arrested, or held in confinement, except in cases determined by the law, and according to the forms which it has prescribed. All who promote, solicit, execute, or cause to be executed, arbitrary orders, ought to be punished, and every citizen called upon, or apprehended by virtue of the law, ought immediately to obey, and renders himself culpable by resistance.

VIII. The law ought to impose no other penalties but such as are absolutely and evidently necessary; and no one ought to be punished, but in virtue of a law promulgated before the offence, and legally applied.

IX. Every man being presumed innocent till he has been convicted, whenever his detention becomes indispensable, all rigour to him, more than is necessary to secure his person, ought to be provided against by the law.

X. No man ought to be molested on account of his opinions, not even on account of his religious opinions, provided his avowal of them does not disturb the public order established by law.

XI. The unrestrained communication of thoughts and opinions being one of the most precious rights of man, every citizen may speak, write, and publish freely, provided he is responsible for the abuse of this liberty, in cases determined by law.

XII. A public force being necessary to give security to the rights of men and of citizens, that force is instituted for the benefit of the community and not for the particular benefit of the persons to whom it is intrusted.

XIII. A common contribution being necessary for the support of the public force, and for defraying the other expenses of government, it ought to be divided equally among the members of the community, according to their abilities.

XIV. Every citizen has a right, either by himself or his representative, to a free voice in determining the necessity of public contributions, the appropriation of them, and their account, mode of assessment, and duration.

XV. Every community has had a right to demand of all its agents an account of their conduct.

XVI. Every community in which a separation of powers and a security of rights is not provided for, wants a constitution.

XVII. The right to property being inviolable and sacred, no one ought to be deprived of it, except in cases of evident public necessity, legally ascertained, and on condition of a previous just indemnity.

Preamble to the Constitution (of the Fourth Republic)
[Préambule de la Constitution (de la IVe République)] of 27 October 1946[1]

In the morrow of the victory achieved by the free peoples over the regimes that had sought to enslave and degrade humanity, the people of France proclaim anew that each human being, without distinction of race, religion or creed, possesses sacred and inalienable rights. They solemnly reaffirm the rights and freedoms of man and the citizen enshrined in the Declaration of Rights of 1789 and the fundamental principles acknowledged in the laws of the Republic.

They further proclaim, as being especially necessary to our times, the political, economic and social principles enumerated below:

1. The law guarantees women equal rights to those of men in all spheres.
2. Any man persecuted in virtue of his actions in favour of liberty may claim the right of asylum upon the territories of the Republic.
3. Each person has the duty to work and the right to employment. No person may suffer prejudice in his work or employment by virtue of his origins, opinions or beliefs.
4. All men may defend their rights and interests through union action and may belong to the union of their choice.
5. The right to strike shall be exercised within the framework of the laws governing it.
6. All workers shall, through the intermediary of their representatives, participate in the collective determination of their conditions of work and in the management of the work place.
7. All property and all enterprises that have or that may acquire the character of a public service or de facto monopoly shall become the property of society.
8. The Nation shall provide the individual and the family with the conditions necessary to their development.
9. It shall guarantee to all, notably to children, mothers and elderly workers, protection of their health, material security, rest and leisure. All people who, by virtue of their age, physical or mental condition, or economic situation, are incapable of working, shall have to the right to receive suitable means of existence from society.
10. The Nation proclaims the solidarity and equality of all French people in bearing the burden resulting from national calamities.
11. The Nation guarantees equal access for children and adults to instruction, vocational training and culture. The provision of free, public and secular education at all levels is a duty of the State.
12. The French Republic, faithful to its traditions, shall respect the rules of public international law. It shall undertake no war aimed at conquest, nor shall it ever employ force against the freedom of any people.

---

[1] Translation: Conseil Constitutionnel.

13. Subject to reciprocity, France shall consent to the limitations upon its sovereignty necessary to the organisation and preservation of peace.
14. France shall form with its overseas peoples a Union founded upon equal rights and duties, without distinction of race or religion.
15. The French Union shall be composed of nations and peoples who agree to pool or coordinate their resources and their efforts in order to develop their respective civilisations, increase their well-being, and ensure their security.
16. Faithful to its traditional mission, France desires to guide the peoples under its responsibility towards the freedom to administer themselves and to manage their own affairs democratically; eschewing all systems of colonisation founded upon arbitrary rule, it guarantees to all equal access to public office and the individual or collective exercise of the rights and freedoms proclaimed or confirmed herein.

Constitution (of the Fifth Republic)
[Constitution (de la Vᵉ République)] of 4 October 1958 as last amended by constitutional statute 2008-724 of 23 July 2008[1]

Preamble

The French people solemnly proclaim their attachment to human rights and the principles of national sovereignty as they are defined by the Declaration of 1789, confirmed and complemented by the Preamble to the Constitution of 1946, as well as to the rights and obligations as defined in the Charter on the Environment of 2004. By virtue of these principles and that of the self-determination of peoples, the Republic offers to the overseas territories that express the will to adhere to them, new institutions founded on the common ideal of liberty, equality and fraternity and conceived with a view to their democratic development.

Article 1. France is an indivisible, secular, democratic and social Republic. It ensures the equality of all citizens before the law, without distinction of origin, race or religion. It respects all beliefs. Its organization is decentralized.
Statute promotes equal access of women and men to elected offices and electoral functions as well as to professional and social positions.

Title I. On sovereignty

Article 2. The language of the Republic is French.
The national emblem is the tricolour flag of blue, white, red.
The national anthem is the Marseillaise.
The motto of the Republic is Liberty, Equality, Fraternity.
Its principle is: government of the people, by the people and for the people.

Article 3. National sovereignty belongs to the people, who exercise it through their representatives and by means of referendum.
No part of the population nor any individual may arrogate the exercise thereof.
Suffrage may be direct or indirect in accordance with the condition of the Constitution. It is always universal, equal and secret.
All French nationals of the age of majority and of both sexes, who enjoy their civil and political rights, have the right to vote, under the conditions provided by statute.

Article 4. Political parties and groups contribute to the expression of suffrage. They establish themselves and carry out their activity freely. They must respect the principles of national sovereignty and of democracy.

---

[1] Translation by Ph. Kiiver, S. Hardt and G. Kristoferitsch. The entry into force of the amended wording of Articles 11, 13, 25 (last paragraph), 34-1, 39, 44, 56, 61-1, 65, 69, 71-1 and 73 as rendered here were, when it was adopted in July 2008, made subject to the entry into force of organic statutes necessary for the amendments' application.

They contribute to the giving effect to the principle enshrined in the second paragraph of Article 1 under the conditions provided by statute.

Statute guarantees pluralist expressions of opinions and the fair participation of political parties and groups in the democratic life of the Nation.

Title II. The President of the Republic

Article 5. The President of the Republic sees that the Constitution is respected. He ensures, by his arbitration, the proper functioning of the public authorities as well as the continuity of the State.

He is the guarantor of national independence, territorial integrity and observance of treaties.

Article 6. The President of the Republic is elected for five years by direct universal suffrage.

No-one may serve more than two consecutive terms.

The details of the implementation of this Article are determined by an organic statute.

Article 7. The President of the Republic is elected by the absolute majority of votes cast. If this is not obtained in the first round of elections, a second round is held on the fourteenth day thereafter. Only the two candidates may run who, after the withdrawal of candidates with more votes where applicable, find themselves having obtained the largest number of votes in the first round.

The elections are opened by a call of the Government.

The election of a new President takes place at least twenty days and, at most, thirty-five days before the expiry of the powers of the incumbent President.

In case of a vacancy of the Presidency of the Republic for whatever reason, or in case the President is prevented from exercising his functions as declared by the Constitutional Council [Conseil Constitutionnel] by absolute majority of its members upon request by the Government, the functions of the President of the Republic, with the exception of those provided by Articles 11 and 12 below, are provisionally exercised by the president of the Senate and, if he in turn is prevented from exercising his functions, by the Government.

In case of a vacancy or when the prevention from the exercise of functions is declared definitive by the Constitutional Council, a vote for an election of a new President takes place, except in cases of force majeure established by the Constitutional Council, at least twenty days and at most thirty-five days after the opening of the vacancy or the declaration of the definitive character of the prevention.

If within seven days prior to the deadline for the filing of candidacies, one of the persons who has publicly announced his decision to be a candidate less than thirty days before that date, dies or finds himself prevented from running, the Constitutional Council may decide to postpone the elections.

If before the first round one of the candidates dies or finds himself prevented from running, the Constitutional Council declares the postponement of the elections.

In the case of death or prevention of one of the two candidates with the largest number of votes in the first round before any withdrawals, the Constitutional Council declares that the election procedure must start entirely anew; the same applies in the case of death or prevention of one of the two remaining candidates for the second round.

In all cases, the Constitutional Council is seized under the conditions prescribed by the second paragraph of Article 61 below or under those provided for the running as a candidate by the organic statute stipulated by Article 6 above.

The Constitutional Council may extend the periods provided by the third and fifth paragraph as long as the vote does not take place any later than thirty-five days after the date of the decision of the Constitutional Council. If the application of the provisions of the present paragraph has as an effect that elections are postponed to a date after the expiry of the powers of the incumbent President, he remains in office until the proclamation of his successor.

Neither Articles 49 and 50 nor Article 89 of the Constitution may be applied during a vacancy of the Presidency of the Republic or during the period between the declaration of the definitive character of the prevention of the President of the Republic from exercising his functions and the election of his successor.

Article 8. The President of the Republic appoints the Prime Minister. He terminates the functions of the Prime Minister when the latter tenders the resignation of the Government.

On the proposal of the Prime Minister, he appoints the other members of the Government and terminates their functions.

Article 9. The President of the Republic presides over the Council of Ministers.

Article 10. The President of the Republic promulgates statutes within fifteen days following the transmission to the Government of the statute finally adopted.

He may, before the expiry of this period, ask Parliament to deliberate anew on the statute or certain provisions of it. Such new deliberation may not be refused.

Article 11. The President of the Republic, on proposal of the Government during sessions or on joint proposal of the two chambers, which are published in the Official Journal [Journal Officiel], may submit to a referendum any government bill [projet de loi] regarding the organization of public authorities, reforms relating to the economic, social or environmental policy of the nation and the public services which contribute to it, or proposing the authorization of the ratification of a treaty which, while not being contrary to the Constitution, would have an effect on the functioning of the institutions.

Where a referendum is organized on the proposal of the Government, it makes a declaration before each chamber, which is followed by a debate.

A referendum regarding a subject mentioned in the first paragraph may be organized on the initiative of one-fifth of the members of Parliament, supported by one-tenth of the voters registered in the electoral lists. Such initiative takes the form of a private member's bill and may not have as its subject the repeal of a statutory provision promulgated less than one year earlier.

The conditions of its submission and those under which the Constitutional Council controls the compliance with the provisions of the preceding paragraph are established by an organic statute.

If the private member's bill has not been considered by the two chambers within a period determined by organic statute, the President of the Republic submits it to referendum.

Where the private member's bill has not been adopted by the French people, no new proposal for referendum regarding the same subject may be submitted before the expiry of a period of two years following the date of the vote.

Where a referendum has resulted in the adoption of a government bill or private member's bill, the President of the Republic promulgates the statute within fifteen days following the proclamation of the results of the referendum.

Article 12. The President of the Republic may, after consultations with the Prime Minister and the presidents of the chambers, declare the dissolution of the National Assembly.

General elections take place at least twenty days and at the latest forty days after the dissolution.

The National Assembly reconvenes by operation of law on the second Thursday following its election. If this convention takes place outside the period envisaged for an ordinary session, a session is opened by operation of law for a period of fifteen days.

No new dissolution may take place during the year following these elections.

Article 13. The President of the Republic signs ordinances [ordonnances] and decrees [décrets] debated in the Council of Ministers.

He appoints civil servants and military personnel of the State.

The members of the Council of State [conseillers d'État], the grand chancellor of the Legion of Honour, the ambassadors and special envoys, the magistrates of the Court of Auditors [Cour des Comptes], the prefects, the representatives of the State in overseas entities governed by Article 74 and in New Caledonia, generals, the rectors of the academies and the directors of the central administration are appointed in the Council of Ministers.

An organic statute determines the other posts to be filled in the Council of Ministers as well as the conditions under which the power of the President of the Republic to make appointments may be delegated by him to be exercised in his name.

An organic statute determines the posts or functions, other than those mentioned in the third paragraph, for which, by reason of their importance to the guarantee of rights and freedoms or the economic and social life of the Nation, the power of appointment of the President of the Republic is exercised on public advice by the competent permanent committee of each chamber. The President of the Republic may not proceed with an appointment where the added negative votes in each committee represent at least three-fifths of votes cast in the two committees. Statute determines the competent permanent committees for the posts or functions concerned.

Article 14. The President of the Republic accredits ambassadors and special envoys to foreign states; foreign ambassadors and special envoys are accredited before him.

Article 15. The President of the Republic is the commander-in-chief of the armies. He presides over the supreme councils and committees of National Defence.

Article 16. Where the institutions of the Republic, the independence of the Nation, the integrity of its territory or the execution of its international commitments is jeopardized in a serious and immediate manner and the regular functioning of the constitutional public authorities is interrupted, the President of the Republic takes measures as the circumstances demand, after official consultation with the Prime Minister, the presidents of the chambers as well as the Constitutional Council.
He informs the Nation in an address.
These measures must be inspired by the will to ensure the constitutional public authorities, in the shortest of periods, of the means to accomplish their mission. The Constitutional Council is consulted regarding their subject.
Parliament convenes by operation of law.
The National Assembly may not be dissolved during the exercise of exceptional powers.
After thirty days of exercise of exceptional powers, the Constitutional Council may be seized by the president of the National Assembly, the president of the Senate, sixty deputies or sixty senators, with a view to examining whether the conditions provided in the first paragraph remain met. It decides within the shortest of periods by a public advice. It commences such examination by operation of law and decides under the same conditions after a period of sixty days of exercise of exceptional powers and at any further moment after that period.

Article 17. The President of the Republic has the right to grant pardons in individual cases.

Article 18. The President of the Republic communicates with the two chambers of Parliament by addresses which he orders to be read out and which are not followed by any debate.
He may speak before Parliament assembled for that purpose in Congress. His statement may, in his absence, be followed by a debate which may not be the object of any vote.
Outside sessions, the parliamentary chambers convene especially for that purpose.

Article 19. The acts of the President of the Republic other than those stipulated in Articles 8 (first paragraph), 11, 12, 16, 18, 54, 56 and 61 are countersigned by the Prime Minister and, where appropriate, the competent ministers.

Title III. The Government

Article 20. The Government determines and conducts the policy of the Nation.
It has at its disposal the administration and the armed forces.
It is responsible before Parliament under the conditions and following the procedures stipulated in Articles 49 and 50.

Article 21. The Prime Minister directs the actions of the Government. He is responsible for the National Defence. He ensures the execution of statutes. Save for the provisions of Article 13, he exercises the power of regulation [pouvoir réglementaire] and appoints civilian and military personnel.
He may delegate some of his powers to the ministers.
He substitutes, where appropriate, the President of the Republic in the presidency over the councils and committees stipulated in Article 15.
He may, by way of exception, substitute him in the presidency over a Council of Ministers by virtue of an express delegation and for a fixed agenda.

Article 22. The acts of the Prime Minister are countersigned, where appropriate, by the ministers who are charged with the execution thereof.

Article 23. The functions of a member of the Government are incompatible with the exercise of any parliamentary mandate, any function of professional representation at national level and any public employment or any professional activity.
An organic statute determines the conditions under which a replacement of the holders of such mandates, functions or employments is provided for.
The replacement of members of Parliament takes place in accordance with the provisions of Article 25.

Title IV. Parliament

Article 24. Parliament adopts statutes [loi]. It controls the action of the government. It evaluates public policies.
It comprises the National Assembly [Assemblée Nationale] and the Senate [Sénat].
The deputies of the National Assembly, whose number may not exceed five hundred seventy-seven, are elected by direct suffrage.
The Senate, the number of whose members may not exceed three hundred forty-eight, is elected by indirect suffrage. It ensures the representation of the territorial entities of the Republic.
The French established outside France are represented in the National Assembly and in the Senate.

Article 25. An organic statute determines the length of the powers of each chamber, the number of its members, their remuneration, the conditions of eligibility, the regime regarding disqualification and incompatibilities.

It equally determines the conditions under which the persons are elected who are called upon to ensure, in case of a vacancy of a seat, the replacement of deputies or senators until new general or partial elections of the chamber to which they belonged or their temporary replacement in case of the acceptance by them of governmental functions.

An independent commission, the composition and rules of organization and functioning of which are determined by statute, pronounces itself in a public advice on government proposals for texts and private member's bills for statutes delimiting the districts for the election of deputies or modifying the distribution of seats of deputies or senators.

Article 26. No member of Parliament may be prosecuted, investigated, arrested, detained or tried based on the opinions or votes expressed by him in the exercise of his functions.

No member of Parliament may be subject to an arrest or any other measure of a criminal or correctional nature depriving him of or restricting his liberty, except with the authorization of the Bureau of the chamber to which he belongs. Such authorization is not required in case of a crime or misdemeanour in flagrante or in case of a final conviction.

The detention, the measures depriving of or restricting liberty or the prosecution of a member of Parliament are suspended for the period of the session if the chamber to which he belongs so demands.

The affected chamber convenes by operation of law for supplementary meetings in order to allow, where appropriate, the application of the preceding paragraph.

Article 27. Any binding mandate is void. The right to vote of the members of Parliament is personal. An organic statute may authorize, by way of exception, the delegation of a vote. In such case, no-one may receive the delegation of more than one mandate.

Article 28. Parliament convenes by operation of law in an ordinary session [session ordinaire] which starts on the first working day of October and ends on the last working day of June.

The number of meeting days [jours de séance] which each chamber may hold during an ordinary session may not exceed one hundred and twenty. The meeting weeks are determined by each chamber.

The Prime Minister, after consultations with the president of the chamber concerned, or the majority of the members of each chamber may decide on holding additional meeting days.

The meeting days and hours are determined by the rules of procedure [règlement] of each chamber.

Article 29. Parliament convenes in an extraordinary session upon the demand of the Prime Minister or of the majority of the members composing the National Assembly, under a fixed agenda.

Where the extraordinary session is held upon the demand of the members of the National Assembly, a decree of closure intervenes as soon as Parliament has exhausted the agenda for which it has been convened and, at the latest, twelve days from its convention.
Only the Prime Minister may demand a new session before the expiry of the month that follows the decree of closure.

Article 30. Outside the cases where Parliament convenes by operation of law, the extraordinary sessions are opened and closed by decree from the President of the Republic.

Article 31. The members of the Government have access to the two chambers. They are heard when they so demand.
They may be assisted by Government agents [commissaires].

Article 32. The president of the National Assembly is elected for the legislative term. The president of the Senate is elected after each partial elections.

Article 33. The meetings of the two chambers are public. The complete minutes of the debates are published in the Official Journal [Journal officiel].
Each chamber may meet in closed committee upon the demand of the Prime Minister or of a tenth of its members.

Title V. The relations between Parliament and the Government

Article 34. Statute determines the rules regarding:
- the civil rights and fundamental guarantees granted to citizens for the exercise of the civil liberties; the freedom, pluralism and independence of the media; the duties imposed on the person and property of citizens by the National Defence;
- the nationality, the status and capacity of persons, the matrimonial regime, inheritance and gifts;
- the determination of crimes and misdemeanours as well as the penalties applicable to them; criminal procedure; amnesty; the establishment of new court systems and the status of magistrates;
- the basis, rate and method of collection of taxes and charges of any nature; the regime for the issuing of currency.
Statute equally determines the rules regarding:
- the electoral system for the parliamentary chambers and local assemblies and the representative bodies for the French established outside France as well as the conditions for the exercise of elected offices and electoral functions for members of the deliberative assemblies of the territorial entities;
- the establishment of categories of public bodies;
- the fundamental guarantees granted to civil servants and members of the armed forces of the State;

- the nationalization of enterprises and the transfer of property of enterprises from the public to the private sector.

Statute determines the fundamental principles:
- of the general organization of the National Defence;
- of the self-administration of territorial entities, their competences and their revenue;
- of education;
- of the preservation of the environment;
- of the property system, real rights and civil and commercial obligations;
- of labour law, trade union law and social security law.

Financial statutes [lois de finances] determine the revenue and the expenditure of the State subject to the conditions and with the reservations provided for by an organic statute.

Social security financing statutes determine the general conditions of their financial equilibrium and, taking into account anticipated revenue, set expenditure objectives subject to the conditions and with the reservations provided for by an organic statute.

Programming statutes [lois des programmation] determine the objectives of the action of the State.

The multiannual directions for public finances are defined by programming statutes. They are in line with the objective of a balance of accounts of the public administration.

The provisions of the present Article may be specified and completed by an organic statute.

Article 34-1. The chambers may pass resolutions under the conditions set by an organic statute [loi organique].

Bills for resolutions of which the Government considers that their adoption or rejection would become a matter of its responsibility or that they contain injunctions against it are inadmissible and may not be included in the agenda.

Article 35. A declaration of war is authorized by Parliament.

The Government informs Parliament of its decision to have the Armed Forces intervene abroad, at the latest three days after the start of the intervention. It specifies the objectives pursued. This information may lead to a debate which is not followed by any vote.

Where the length of the intervention exceeds four months, the Government submits its extension to Parliament for authorization. It may ask the National Assembly to decide in final instance.

If Parliament is not in session after four months have expired, it decides at the opening of the following session.

Article 36. A state of siege is decreed in the Council of Ministers.

Its extension beyond twelve days may only be authorized by Parliament.

Article 37. Matters other than those falling under the scope of statute [loi] are of regulatory nature [réglementaire].

Texts of statutory form enacted with regard to these matters may be modified by decree issued after an opinion by the Council of State [Conseil d'État]. Of these texts, those enacted after the entry into force of the present Constitution may not be modified by decree except if the Constitutional Council [Conseil Constitutionnel] has declared that they are of a regulatory nature pursuant to the foregoing paragraph.

Article 37-1. Statute and regulation may contain, for a limited purpose and time, provisions of an experimental nature.

Article 38. The Government may, in order to implement its programme, request Parliament to authorize, for a limited period of time, the taking of measures by ordinances [ordonnances] which normally fall under the scope of statute.

Ordinances are issued in the Council of Ministers after an opinion by the Council of State. They enter into force upon their publication but become ineffective if the government bill for their ratification is not submitted to Parliament before the date set by the enabling statute. They may only be ratified in an explicit manner.

Upon the expiry of the period of time referred to in the first paragraph of the present Article, ordinances may not be modified except by statute in matters within the scope of statute.

Article 39. The right of initiative for statutes rests both with the Prime Minister and the members of Parliament.

Government bills [projets de loi] are discussed in the Council of Ministers after an opinion by the Council of State and submitted to the bureau of one of the two chambers. Government bills for financial statutes and social security financing statutes are submitted to the National Assembly first. Without prejudice to the first paragraph of Article 44, government bills having as their primary object the organization of the territorial entities are submitted to the Senate first.

The presentation of government bills [projets de loi] submitted to the National Assembly or the Senate meets the conditions set by an organic statute [loi organique].

Government bills may not be included in the agenda if the conference of the presidents of the first chamber seized declares that the rules set by the organic statute have been disregarded. In case of disagreement between the conference of presidents and the Government, the president of the chamber concerned or the Prime Minister may refer the matter to the Constitutional Council which decides within eight days.

Under the conditions stipulated by statute, the president of a chamber may submit to the Council of State [Conseil d'État] a private member's bill submitted by one of the members of that chamber, before its examination in a committee, for its opinion, unless that member objects.

Article 40. Private member's bills [propositions] and amendments formulated by members of Parliament are not admissible if their adoption would have as a consequence either a diminution of public revenue or the creation or aggravation of public expenditure.

Article 41. If it appears, during the legislative process, that a private member's bill or amendment is not a matter of statute or is contrary to a delegation granted by virtue of Article 38, the Government or the president of the chamber seized may oppose it as inadmissible.
In case of disagreement between the Government and the president of the chamber concerned, the Constitutional Council, at the request of either party, rules within a period of eight days.

Article 42. Debate on government bills [projets] and private member's bills [propositions de loi] in the meeting takes place on the basis of the text adopted by the committee seized by application of Article 43 or, by default, the text referred to the chamber.
However, the debate in the meeting on government bills for constitutional amendment statutes [projets de révision constitutionnelle], financial statutes [projets de loi de finances] and social security financing statutes [projets de loi de financement de la sécurité sociale] takes place, in the first reading in front of the first chamber seized, on the basis of the text presented by the Government and, in the other readings, the text transmitted by the other chamber.
The debate in the meeting, in the first reading, of a government bill or a private member's bill may only take place before the first chamber seized after the expiry of a period of six weeks after its submission. It may only take place before the second chamber seized after the expiry of a period of four weeks from the moment of its transmission.
The previous paragraph does not apply if the accelerated procedure has been initiated under the conditions stipulated in Article 45. Nor does it apply to government bills for financial statutes, social security financing statutes and to government bills relating to a state of crisis [états de crise].

Article 43. Government and private member's bills are sent for examination to one of the permanent committees, the number of which is limited to eight in each chamber.
Upon the demand of the Government or the chamber seized, government or private member's bills are sent for examination to a committee set up especially for that purpose.

Article 44. Members of Parliament and the Government have the right of amendment. This right is exercised in the meeting or in a committee under the conditions prescribed in the rules of procedure of the chambers, within the framework determined by an organic statute.
After the opening of the debate, the Government may object to the consideration of any amendment which has not previously been submitted to a committee.

If the Government so demands, the chamber seized decides by a single vote on the whole or part of the debated text, containing only the amendments proposed or accepted by the Government.

Article 45. Every government or private member's bill is considered successively in the two chambers of Parliament with a view to the adoption of an identical text. Without prejudice to the application of Articles 40 and 41, any amendment that has a link, even an indirect one, with the text submitted or transmitted is admissible in the first reading.

Where, as a result of a disagreement between the two chambers, a government or private member's bill could not be adopted after two readings by each chamber or, if the Government has decided to apply the accelerated procedure without the conference of presidents being jointly opposed, after one reading by each of them, the Prime Minister or, for a private member's bill, the presidents of the two chambers acting jointly, have the right to convene a joint committee, composed of an equal number of members of each chamber, charged with the task to propose a text on the provisions still under debate.

The text drafted by the joint committee may be submitted by the Government to the two chambers for adoption. No amendment is admissible except with the consent of the Government.

If the joint committee does not succeed in agreeing on a common text or if this text is not adopted under the conditions provided for by the foregoing paragraph, the Government may, after a new reading by the National Assembly and by the Senate, request the National Assembly to adopt a definitive decision. In that case, the National Assembly may reconsider either the text drafted by the joint committee or the last text adopted by itself, modified, where appropriate, by one or more amendments adopted by the Senate.

Article 46. Statutes which the Constitution defines as organic statutes [lois organiques] are adopted and amended under the following conditions.

The government or private member's bill may not be subjected to deliberation and to a vote of the chambers in the first reading until the expiry of the period fixed in the third paragraph of Article 42. However, if the accelerated procedure has been applied under the conditions stipulated in Article 45, the government or private member's bill may not be subjected to deliberation in the first chamber seized until the expiry of a period of fifteen days after its submission.

The procedure of Article 45 applies. However, failing agreement between the two chambers, the text may be adopted by the National Assembly in final reading only by an absolute majority of its members.

Organic statutes relating to the Senate must be adopted in the same terms by the two chambers.

Organic statutes may not be promulgated until the Constitutional Council has declared their conformity with the Constitution.

Article 47. Parliament adopts government bills for financial statutes under the conditions provided by an organic statute.

If the National Assembly has not reached a decision in the first reading within a period of forty days after the submission of a government bill, the Government seizes the Senate which must reach a decision within a period of fifteen days. Thereafter the procedure of Article 45 is applied.

If Parliament has not reached a decision within a period of seventy days, the provisions of the government bill may be enacted by ordinance.

If a financial statute setting revenues and expenditure for a financial year has not been submitted in time for promulgation before the beginning of that financial year, the Government requests from Parliament, as a matter of urgency, the authorization to collect taxes and make available by decree the funds needed for measures already adopted. The time limits set by the present Article are suspended when Parliament is not in session.

Article 47-1. Parliament adopts government bills for social security financing statutes under the conditions provided by an organic statute. If the National Assembly has not reached a decision in the first reading within a period of twenty days after the submission of a government bill, the Government seizes the Senate which must reach a decision within a period of fifteen days. Thereafter the procedure of Article 45 is applied. If Parliament has not reached a decision within a period of fifty days, the provisions of the government bill may be put into effect by ordinance.

The time limits set by the present Article are suspended when Parliament is not in session and, with respect to each chamber, during the weeks during which it has decided not to meet in conformity with the second paragraph of Article 28.

Article 47-2. The Court of Auditors [Cour des Comptes] assists Parliament with the control of the action of the Government. It assists the Parliament and the Government with the control of the execution of financial statutes and the implementation of social security financing statutes as well as with the assessment of public policies. With its public reports, it contributes to the informing of the citizens.

The accounts of the public administration are regular and sincere. They provide a picture that faithfully shows the results of their management, their assets and their financial situation.

Article 48. Without prejudice to the application of the last three paragraphs of Article 28, the agenda is fixed by each chamber.

Two weeks of meetings out of four are reserved with priority, in the order that the Government has fixed, for the examination of texts and for debates which it requests to be included in the agenda.

Furthermore, the examination of government bills for financial statutes, social security financing statutes and, subject to the provisions of the following paragraph, texts transmitted by the other chamber at least six weeks earlier, government bills relating to a state of crisis and requests for authorization envisaged by Article 35, is, upon request of the Government, included in the agenda with priority.

One week of meetings out of four is reserved, with priority and in the order fixed by each assembly, for the control of the action of the Government and for the assessment of public policies.

One day of meeting per month is reserved for an agenda determined by each chamber upon the initiative of opposition groups of the chamber concerned, as well as of minority groups.

At least one meeting per week, including during extraordinary sessions provided for in Article 29, is reserved, with priority, for questions of members of Parliament and answers by the Government.

Article 49. The Prime Minister, after deliberation by the Council of Ministers, ties the responsibility of the Government before the National Assembly to the Government's programme or possibly a general policy statement.

The National Assembly invokes the responsibility of the Government by a vote on a motion of censure. Such a motion is only admissible if it is signed by at least one tenth of the members of the National Assembly. The vote may not take place until forty-eight hours have elapsed after the tabling. Solely votes in favour of the motion of censure are counted, which may only be adopted by a majority of the members composing the Assembly. Except in the case stipulated by the paragraph hereunder, a deputy may not be a signatory to more than three motions of censure during one ordinary session and to more than one during one extraordinary session.

The Prime Minister may, after deliberation by the Council of Ministers, make a matter of the responsibility of the Government before the National Assembly the adoption of a government bill for a financial statute or a social security financing statute. In that event, the government bill is considered adopted unless a motion of censure, tabled within the twenty-four hours that follow, is adopted under the conditions provided for by the foregoing paragraph. The Prime Minister may furthermore resort to this procedure for one other government bill or one private member's bill per session.

The Prime Minister has the option to request from the Senate the approval of a general policy statement.

Article 50. When the National Assembly adopts a motion of censure or when it disapproves the programme or a general policy statement of the Government, the Prime Minister must tender the resignation of the Government to the President of the Republic.

Article 50-1. Before one of the chambers the Government may, on its own initiative or at the request of a parliamentary group in the sense of Article 51-1, make a statement on a specified subject that is followed by a debate and that may, if it so decides, be the object of a vote without making it a matter of its responsibility.

Article 51. The closure of an ordinary session or of extraordinary sessions is postponed by operation of law in order to allow, where applicable, the application of Article 49. For that same purpose, supplementary meetings are held by operation of law.

Article 51-1. The rules of procedure of each chamber determine the rights of parliamentary groups constituted within it. It recognizes the rights specific to opposition groups of the chamber concerned as well as to minority groups.

Article 51-2. For the exercise of the controlling and evaluation tasks defined in the first paragraph of Article 24, commissions of inquiry may be created within each chamber in order to gather information under the conditions stipulated by statute. Statute determines their rules of organization and functioning. The conditions of their establishment are determined by the rules of procedure of each chamber.

Title VI. On international treaties and agreements

Article 52. The President of the Republic negotiates and ratifies treaties [traités].
He is informed of any negotiation for the conclusion of an international agreement [accord international] not subject to ratification.

Article 53. Peace treaties, treaties on trade, treaties or agreements relating to international organization, those which affect the finances of the State, those which modify provisions of statutory nature, those which relate to the status of persons, those which entail the cession, exchange or acquisition of territory, may only be ratified or approved by statute.
They do not take effect until they have been ratified or approved.
No cession, no exchange, no acquisition of territory is valid without the consent of the population concerned.

Article 53-1. The Republic may conclude, with European States bound by commitments identical to its own in matters of asylum and the protection of human rights and fundamental freedoms, agreements determining their respective competences for the consideration of requests for asylum submitted to them.
However, even if, pursuant to these agreements, a request does not fall under its competences, the authorities of the Republic always have the right to grant asylum to any foreigner persecuted for his action in pursuit of freedom or who seeks protection by France for another reason.

Article 53-2. The Republic may recognize the jurisdiction of the International Criminal Court under the conditions provided by the treaty signed on 18 July 1998.

Article 54. If the Constitutional Council, seized by the President of the Republic, by the Prime Minister, by the president of one of the chambers or by sixty deputies or sixty senators, has declared that an international commitment contains a clause contrary to the Constitution, the authorization to ratify or approve the international commitment in question may only be given after amendment of the Constitution.

Article 55. Treaties or agreements duly ratified or approved have, upon their publication, authority superior to that of statutes, subject, with respect to each agreement or treaty, to their application by the other party.

Title VII. The Constitutional Council

Article 56. The Constitutional Council [Conseil Constitutionnel] comprises nine members whose mandate lasts nine years and is not renewable. One third of the Constitutional Council is renewed every three years. Three of the members are appointed by the President of the Republic, three by the president of the National Assembly, three by the president of the Senate. The procedure stipulated in the last paragraph of Article 13 is applicable to these appointments. The appointments made by the president of each chamber are submitted for an opinion only to the competent permanent committee of the relevant chamber.
In addition to the nine members provided for above, former Presidents of the Republic are by operation of law members of the Constitutional Council for life.
The president is appointed by the President of the Republic. He has the decisive vote in case of a tie.

Article 57. The office of a member of the Constitutional Council is incompatible with that of a minister or a member of Parliament. Other incompatibilities are established by an organic statute.

Article 58. The Constitutional Council ensures the proper conduct of the election of the President of the Republic.
It examines complaints and proclaims the result of the election.

Article 59. The Constitutional Council rules, in case of a challenge, on the proper conduct of the election of deputies and senators.

Article 60. The Constitutional Council ensures the proper conduct of referendums as provided for by Articles 11 and 89 and by Title XV. It proclaims the results thereof.

Article 61. Organic statutes, prior to their promulgation, private member's bills mentioned in Article 11 before they have been submitted to referendum, and the rules of procedure of the parliamentary chambers, before coming into force, must be submitted to the Constitutional Council which rules on their conformity with the Constitution.
For the same purpose, statutes may be referred to the Constitutional Council, before their promulgation, by the President of the Republic, the Prime Minister, the president of the National Assembly, the president of the Senate or sixty deputies or sixty senators.

In the cases provided for by the two foregoing paragraphs, the Constitutional Council must rule within a period of one month. However, at the request of the Government, in cases of urgency, this period is reduced to eight days.
In the same cases, referral to the Constitutional Council suspends the time period for promulgation.

Article 61-1. When, in the course of proceedings before a court, it is submitted that a statutory provision jeopardizes the rights and freedoms which the Constitution guarantees, the Constitutional Council may be seized on that question by reference from the Council of State or the Court of Cassation which decide within a determined period.
An organic statute determines the conditions for the application of the present Article.

Article 62. A provision declared unconstitutional on the basis of Article 61 may neither be promulgated nor implemented.
A provision declared unconstitutional on the basis of Article 61-1 is repealed from the moment of the publication of the decision of the Constitutional Council or a later date established in that decision. The Constitutional Council determines the conditions and limits within which the effects that the provision has created may be called into question.
The decisions of the Constitutional Council are not open to any appeal. They are binding on public authority and on all administrative and judicial authorities.

Article 63. An organic statute determines the organization and functioning of the Constitutional Council, the procedure followed before it and, in particular, the time limits for submitting complaints to it.

Title VIII. On the judicial authority

Article 64. The President of the Republic is the guarantor of the independence of the judicial authority.
He is assisted by the High Council of the Judiciary [Conseil Supérieur de la Magistrature].
An organic statute contains the rules governing magistrates.
Judges [magistrats du siège] are irremovable.

Article 65. The High Council of the Judiciary comprises a section competent with regard to judges [magistrats du siège] and one competent with regard to public prosecutors [magistrats du parquet].
The section competent with regard to judges is presided over by the first president of the Court of Cassation [Cour de cassation]. It comprises furthermore five judges and one public prosecutor, one member of the Council of State nominated by the Council of State [Conseil d'État], one advocate [avocat] as well as six distinguished persons who are not members of either Parliament or the judiciary or the administration. The President of the Republic, the president of the National Assembly and

the president of the Senate each appoint two distinguished persons. The procedure stipulated in the last paragraph of Article 13 is applicable to the appointment of distinguished persons. The appointments made by the president of each chamber of Parliament are submitted for an opinion only to the competent permanent committee of the relevant chamber.

The section competent with regard to public prosecutors is presided over by the procurator-general at the Court of Cassation. It comprises furthermore five public prosecutors and one judge, as well as the member of the Council of State, the advocate and the six distinguished persons mentioned in the second paragraph.

The section of the High Council of the Judiciary competent with regard to judges submits proposals for the appointments of judges at the Court of Cassation, for those of the first president of a court of appeals [cour d'appel] and for those of the president of a district court [tribunal de grande instance]. The other judges are appointed upon its assent.

The section of the High Council of the Judiciary competent with regard to public prosecutors gives its opinion on appointments that affect public prosecutors.

The section of the High Council of the Judiciary competent with regard to judges rules as a disciplinary council for judges. It then comprises besides the members envisaged in the second paragraph the judge who is a member of the section competent with regard to public prosecutors.

The section of the High Council of the Judiciary competent with regard to public prosecutors gives its opinion on those disciplinary sanctions that affect them. It then comprises besides the members envisaged in the third paragraph, the public prosecutor who is a member of the section competent with regard to judges.

The High Council of the Judiciary meets in plenary composition in order to answer requests for an opinion made by the President of the Republic in application of Article 64. It gives, in the same composition, its opinion on questions regarding the ethics of magistrates as well as on any question regarding the functioning of the justice system on which it is seized by the minister of justice. The plenary composition comprises three of the five judges mentioned in the second paragraph, three of the five public prosecutors mentioned in the third paragraph as well as the member of the Council of State, the advocate and the six distinguished persons mentioned in the second paragraph. It is presided over by the first president of the Court of Cassation who may be substituted by the procurator-general at that Court.

Except in disciplinary matters the minister of justice may participate in the meetings of the sections of the High Council of the Judiciary.

The High Council of the Judiciary may be seized by a person undergoing a trial under the conditions determined by organic statute.

An organic statute determines the conditions for the application of the present Article.

Article 66. No-one may be detained arbitrarily.

The judicial authority, guardian of individual liberty, ensures the observance of this principle under the conditions provided by statute.

Article 66-1. No-one may be sentenced to the death penalty.

Title IX. The High Court

Article 67. The President of the Republic is not liable for any acts committed in this capacity, subject to the provisions of the Articles 53-2 and 68.
He may not, during his mandate and before no French court or administrative authority, be required to testify, nor be the object of a court action, investigatory action, instruction or prosecution. Any period of prescription or foreclosure is suspended.
All actions and proceedings thus barred may be resumed or brought against him upon expiry of a period of one month after the end of his office.

Article 68. The President of the Republic may only be removed from office in case of a breach of his duties manifestly incompatible with the exercise of his mandate. The removal is proclaimed by Parliament sitting as the High Court [Haute Cour].
The proposal to convene the High Court adopted by one of the chambers of Parliament is immediately transmitted to the other, which reaches its decision within fifteen days.
The High Court is chaired by the president of the National Assembly. It rules within a period of one month, by secret ballot, on the removal from office. Its decision is of immediate effect.
The decisions taken in the application of the present Article are taken by two thirds of the members composing the chamber concerned or the High Court. Any delegation of votes is prohibited. Only the votes in favour of the proposal to convene the High Court or of the removal from office are counted.
An organic statute determines the conditions for the application of the present Article.

Title X. On the criminal liability of members of the government

Article 68-1. The members of the government are liable for acts committed in the exercise of their office and qualified as crimes [crime] or misdemeanours [délit] at the time they were committed.
They are tried by the Court of Justice of the Republic [Cour de justice de la République].
The Court of Justice of the Republic is bound by such definition of crimes and misdemeanours as well as by such determination of penalties as follows from statute.

Article 68-2. The Court of Justice of the Republic consists of fifteen judges: twelve parliamentarians elected from among their ranks and in equal number by the National Assembly and by the Senate after each general or partial election of these chambers, and three judges at the Court of Cassation, one of whom presides over the Court of Justice of the Republic.

Any person who claims to be a victim of a crime or misdemeanour committed by a member of the government in the exercise of his office may file a complaint with a petitions committee.

This committee orders either the closure of the procedure or its transmission to the procurator-general at the Court of Cassation for the seizing of the Court of Justice of the Republic.

The procurator-general at the Court of Cassation may also upon his own motion seize the Court of Justice of the Republic upon the assent of the petitions committee.

An organic statute determines the conditions for the application of the present Article.

Article 68-3. The provisions of the present Title are applicable to acts committed before its entry into force.

Title XI. The Economic, Social and Environmental Council

Article 69. The Economic, Social and Environmental Council [Conseil économique, social et environnemental], seized by the Government, gives its opinion on government bills, draft ordinances or draft decrees as well as on private member's bills which are submitted to it.

A member of the Economic, Social and Environmental Council may be appointed by it to present to the parliamentary chambers the opinion of the Council on the government or private member's bills which have been submitted to it.

The Economic, Social and Environmental Council may be seized by way of petition under the conditions determined by organic statute. After examination of the petition, it notifies the Government and Parliament of the follow-up actions that it proposes to take.

Article 70. The Economic, Social and Environmental Council may be consulted by the Government and Parliament on any problem of an economic, social or environmental nature. The Government may equally consult it on government bills for programming statutes defining the multiannual directions for public finances. Any plan or any government bill for a programming statute of an economic, social or environmental nature is submitted to it for its opinion.

Article 71. The composition of the Economic and Social and Environmental Council, the number of whose members may not exceed two hundred and thirty-three, and its rules of procedure are determined by an organic statute.

Title XI bis. The Defender of Rights

Article 71-1. The Defender of Rights guards the respect of rights and liberties by the administrations of the State, the territorial entities, public bodies, as well as by any body charged with a public service task, or with respect to which an organic statute confers competences on him.

He may be seized, under the conditions stipulated by an organic statute, by any person who considers himself harmed by the functioning of a public service or a body envisaged in the first paragraph. He may consider a matter on his own initiative.

An organic statute specifies the competences and the terms of intervention of the Defender of Rights. It determines the conditions under which he may be assisted by a collegiate body in the exercise of some of his competences.

The Defender of Rights is appointed by the President of the Republic for a non-renewable term of six years after application of the procedure stipulated in the last paragraph of Article 13. His functions are incompatible with those of a member of Government and of a member of Parliament. Other incompatibilities are determined by organic statute.

The Defender of Rights gives account of his activity to the President of the Republic and to Parliament.

Title XII. The territorial entities

Article 72. The territorial entities [collectivités territoriales] of the Republic are the municipalities [communes], the departments [départements], the regions [régions], the special-status entities and the overseas entities governed by Article 74. Any other territorial entity is created by statute, where appropriate in place of one or more entities referred to in the present paragraph.

Territorial entities are charged with taking decisions on the entirety of competences that can best be exercised at their level.

Under the conditions provided by statute, the entities administer themselves freely through elected councils and possess regulatory powers [réglementaire] for the exercise of their competences.

Under the conditions provided by organic statute, provided that the essential conditions for the exercise of a public liberty or a constitutionally guaranteed right is not affected, territorial entities or associations thereof may, where such is provided by statute or regulation, as the case may be, derogate on an experimental basis for limited purpose and duration from statutory or regulatory provisions governing the exercise of their competences.

No territorial entity may exercise tutelage over another. However, where the exercise of a competence requires the co-operation of several territorial entities, statute may authorize one of them or one of their associations to organize the modalities of their joint action.

In the territorial entities of the Republic, the representative of the State, representing each of the members of the Government, is responsible for the national interests, administrative supervision and the observance of statutes.

Article 72-1. Statute determines the conditions under which voters in each territorial entity may, by exercising the right of petition, request that a question relevant to its competence be included in the agenda of the deliberative assembly of that entity.

Under the conditions determined by organic statute, government bills for deliberation or acts relevant to the competence of a territorial entity may, on its initiative, by means of referendum, be submitted to the decision of the voters of that entity.

When it is envisaged that a territorial entity be created or provided with a special status or its organization be modified, it may be decided by statute to consult the voters registered in the concerned entities. The modification of the borders of territorial entities may equally give rise to a consultation of the voters under the conditions provided by statute.

Article 72-2. Territorial entities enjoy resources of which they may dispose freely under the conditions determined by statute.

They may receive all or a part of the revenue from taxes of any nature. Statute may authorize them to specify the basis and rate thereof within the limits it determines.

Fiscal revenue and other own resources of the territorial entities represent, for each category of entities, a decisive share of the entirety of their resources. Organic statute determines the conditions under which this rule is given effect.

Any transfer of competences between the State and the territorial entities is accompanied by an allocation of resources equivalent to what had been dedicated to the exercise of those competences. Any creation or extension of competences having as a consequence an increase in expenditures of territorial entities is accompanied by resources determined by statute.

Statute provides for equalization mechanisms designed to promote equality between territorial entities.

Article 72-3. The Republic recognizes, within the French people, the overseas populations in a common ideal of liberty, equality and fraternity.

Guadeloupe, Guiana, Martinique, Réunion, Mayotte, Saint-Barthélemy, Saint-Martin, Saint-Pierre-and-Miquelon, the Islands of Wallis and Futuna and French Polynesia are governed by Article 73 for departments and overseas regions and for territorial entities created by application of the last paragraph of Article 73, and by Article 74 for the other entities.

The status of New Caledonia is governed by Title XIII.

Statute determines the legislative regime and the special organization of the French Southern and Antarctic Territories and of Clipperton.

Article 72-4. No change, regarding the whole or a part of one of the entities mentioned in the second paragraph of Article 72-3, of one towards the other of the regimes provided for by Articles 73 and 74, takes place unless the consent of the voters of the entity or the part of the entity concerned has been obtained beforehand under the conditions provided by the following paragraph. This change of regime is decided on by organic statute.

The President of the Republic, on a proposal of the Government during sessions or on joint proposal of the two chambers, which are published in the Official Journal [Journal officiel], may decide to consult the voters of a territorial entity situated overseas on a question relating to its organization, to its competences or to its legislative regime. Where this consultation concerns a change stipulated in the foregoing paragraph and is organized on proposal of the Government, it makes a statement before each chamber, which is followed by a debate.

Article 73. In the overseas departments and regions, statutes and regulations are applicable by operation of law. They may be the object of adaptations in view of the particular characteristics and constraints of these entities.

These adaptations may be decided by the entities on matters where they exercise their competences and if they were enabled to do so, as the case may be, by statute or by regulation.

By derogation from the first paragraph and in order to take account of their specificities, entities governed by the present Article may be enabled, as the case may be by statute or by regulation, to themselves determine the rules applicable on their territory in a limited number of matters that can fall under the scope of statute or regulation.

These rules may not concern nationality, civil rights, guarantees of civil liberties, the status and capacity of persons, the organization of justice system, criminal law, criminal procedure, foreign policy, defence, public security and order, currency, credit and exchange, as well as electoral law. This enumeration may be specified and completed by organic statute.

The provisions stipulated in the two preceding paragraphs are not applicable to the department and to the region of Réunion.

The enabling provided for in the second and third paragraph is decided, upon request of the entity concerned, subject to the conditions and with the reservations provided by an organic statute. They may not be carried out where the essential conditions for the exercise of a public liberty or a constitutionally guaranteed right is at issue.

The creation by statute of an entity substituting an overseas department and region or the establishment of a single deliberative assembly for those two entities may not take place unless the consent of the voters registered in the territory of these entities has been obtained according to the procedure provided in the second paragraph of Article 72-4.

Article 74. The overseas entities governed by the present Article have a status that takes account of their particular interests within the Republic.

This status is defined by organic statute, adopted after an opinion of the deliberative assembly, which determines:
- the conditions under which statutes and regulations are applicable there;
- the competences of this entity; subject to those already exercised by it, the transfer of competences by the State may not concern the matters enumerated in the fourth paragraph of Article 73, specified and complemented, as the case may be, by organic statute;
- the rules on the organization and functioning of the institutions of the entity and the electoral regime of its deliberative assembly;
- the conditions under which its institutions are consulted on government bills and private member's bills and drafts of ordinances or decrees containing provisions

that are specific to the entity as well as to the ratification or approval of international commitments concluded in matters relevant to its competence.

The organic statute may equally determine, for those entities that are provided with autonomy, the conditions under which:
- the Council of State exercises specific judicial review over certain categories of acts of the deliberative assembly effected on the basis of competences that it exercises within the scope of statute;
- the deliberative assembly may amend a statute promulgated after the entry into force of the status of the entity, where the Constitutional Council, seized in particular by the authorities of that entity, has established that the statute has intervened in the scope of competence of that entity;
- measures justified by local needs may be taken by the entity in favour of its population, in matters of access to employment, the right of establishment for the exercise of a professional activity or the protection of land property;
- the entity may participate, under the control of the State, in the exercise of the competences it retains, respecting the guarantees granted to the entire national territory for the exercise of public liberties.

The other modalities of the organization specific to the entities subject to the present Article are determined and amended by statute after consultation of their deliberative assembly.

Article 74-1. In the overseas entities envisaged by Article 74 and in New Caledonia, the Government may, by ordinance, in the matters that remain in the competence of the State, extend, with the necessary adaptations, the provisions of statutory nature in force in Metropolitan France or adapt the provisions of statutory nature in force to the specific organization of the entity concerned, provided that the statute did not explicitly exclude, for the provisions in question, recourse to this procedure.

The ordinances are issued in the Council of Ministers after an opinion of the deliberative assembly concerned and the Council of State. They enter into force upon their publication. They become ineffective in the absence of ratification by Parliament within a period of eighteen months after that publication.

Article 75. The citizens of the Republic who do not have ordinary civil status, only envisaged in Article 34, retain their personal status as long as they have not renounced it.

Article 75-1. Regional languages belong to the heritage of France.

Title XIII. Transitional provisions regarding New Caledonia

Article 76. The population of New Caledonia is called upon to pronounce itself before the 31 December 1998 on the provisions of the agreement signed at Nouméa on 5 May 1998 and published on 27 May 1998 in the Official Journal of the French Republic.

Admitted to participate in the vote are the persons who fulfil the conditions determined in Article 2 of statute no. 88-1028 of 9 November 1988.

The measures necessary for the organization of the vote are taken by decree in consultation with the Council of State [Conseil d'Etat] after having been discussed in the council of ministers.

Article 77. After adoption of the agreement by the vote provided in Article 76, an organic statute, passed after an opinion of the deliberative assembly of New Caledonia, determines, in order to ensure the development of New Caledonia respecting the directions defined by that agreement and in accordance with the terms necessary in order to give it effect:

- the competences of the State that will be transferred definitively to the institutions of New Caledonia, the time scale and the modalities of the transfer, as well as the allocation of the expenditures resulting therefrom;
- the rules of the organization and functioning of the institutions of New Caledonia and in particular the conditions under which certain categories of acts of the deliberative assembly of New Caledonia may be submitted for review to the Constitutional Council [Conseil Constitutionnel] before publication;
- the rules relating to citizenship, to the electoral regime, to employment and to the customary civil status;
- the conditions and time limits within which the population concerned in New Caledonia will be led to pronounce themselves on the attainment of full sovereignty.

The other measures necessary for giving effect of the agreement mentioned in Article 76 are defined by statute.

For the definition of the electoral body called upon to elect the members of the deliberative assemblies of New Caledonia and its provinces, the list to which the agreement mentioned in Article 76 and in Article 188 and 189 of the organic statute no. 99-209 of 19 March 1999 relating to New Caledonia refer is the list drawn up in the course of the vote provided for in Article 76 and including the persons not admitted to participate in it.

Articles 78 to 86. (Repealed).

Title XIV. On the French-speaking World and on Association Agreements

Article 87. The Republic takes part in the development of solidarity and cooperation between the States and peoples which have the French language in common.

Title XV. On the European Union

Article 88-1. The Republic participates in the European Union, constituted by States that have freely chosen to exercise certain of their powers conjointly by virtue of the Treaty on European Union and the Treaty on the Functioning of the European Union as they result from the Treaty signed at Lisbon on 13 December 2007.

Article 88-2. Statute determines the rules regarding the European arrest warrant by application of the acts taken by the institutions of the European Union.

Article 88-3. Subject to reciprocity and in accordance with the terms laid down by the Treaty on European Union signed on 7 February 1992, the right to vote and to stand in municipal elections may be granted only to citizens of the Union residing in France. These citizens may neither exercise the office of mayor or deputy mayor, nor participate in the designation of senatorial electors and in the election of senators. An organic statute adopted in identical terms by both chambers determines the conditions under which the present Article is applied.

Article 88-4. The Government submits to the National Assembly and to the Senate, when they have been transmitted to the Council of the European Union, drafts of or proposals for acts of the European Communities and of the European Union.
In accordance with the terms set by the rules of procedure of each chamber, European resolutions may be adopted, also outside sessions where appropriate, on the drafts and proposals mentioned in the first paragraph, as well as on any document emanating from an institution of the European Union.
Within each parliamentary chamber a committee responsible for European affairs is established.

Article 88-5. Any government bill authorizing the ratification of a Treaty regarding the accession of a State to the European Union and to the European Communities is submitted to referendum by the President of the Republic.
However, by a vote on a motion adopted in identical terms by each assembly by a majority of three fifths, Parliament may authorize the adoption of the government bill in accordance with the procedure stipulated in the third paragraph of Article 89.

[*Note: This Article does not apply to accessions made following an intergovernmental conference whose convocation was decided by the European Council before 1 July 2004.*]

Article 88-6. The National Assembly or the Senate may adopt a reasoned opinion on the compliance of a draft European legislative act with the principle of subsidiarity. The opinion is addressed by the president of the chamber concerned to the presidents of the European Parliament, of the Council and of the European Commission. The Government is informed of this.
Each chamber may bring an action before the Court of Justice of the European Union against a European legislative act for a violation of the principle of subsidiarity. The action is transmitted to the Court of Justice of the European Union by the Government.
To that end, resolutions may be adopted, also outside sessions where appropriate, in accordance with the terms on initiative and debate set by the rules of procedure of each chamber. Upon request of sixty deputies or of sixty senators, the action is brought by operation of law.

Article 88-7. By adoption of a motion passed in identical terms by the National Assembly and the Senate, Parliament may oppose an amendment of the rules for the adoption of acts of the European Union in the cases envisaged, under the simplified treaty revision procedure or judicial cooperation in civil matters, by the Treaty on European Union and the Treaty on the Functioning of the European Union as they result from the Treaty signed at Lisbon on 13 December 2007.

Title XVI. On amendments

Article 89. The right of initiative for a revision of the Constitution lies concurrently with the President of the Republic, upon a proposal by the Prime Minister, and with the members of Parliament.

A government or private member's bill for a revision must be examined under the conditions of the fixed periods determined in the third paragraph of Article 42 and adopted by both chambers in identical terms. The revision is final after having been approved by referendum.

However, a government bill for a revision is not submitted to referendum where the President of the Republic decides to submit it to Parliament convened in Congress [Congrès]; in that case, the government bill for revision is not approved unless it is adopted by a majority of three fifths of the votes cast. The bureau of the Congress is that of the National Assembly.

No procedure of revision may be initiated or continued where the integrity of the territory is jeopardized.

The republican form of Government may not be the object of a revision.

Title XVII. (Repealed).

Electoral Code
[Code Electoral], as last amended in its relevant parts by Statute No. 2013-702 of 2 August 2013. Selected provisions: Book I, Title II: Chapters I and II as well as Articles L 162 and L 163 of Chapter V; Book II: Title I, Title II, Articles L 283 to L 285 of Title III, and Chapter I of Title IV[1]

Statutory part

Book I. The election of deputies, members of the departmental councils and members of the municipal councils

[*Title I is omitted.*]

Title II. Special provisions regarding the election of deputies

Chapter I. Composition of the National Assembly and the length of the mandate of the deputies

Article LO 119. The number of deputies is five hundred seventy seven.

Article LO 120. The National Assembly is re-elected in full.

Article LO 121. The powers of the National Assembly expire on the third Tuesday of June in the fifth year following its election.

Article LO 122. Save for a case of dissolution, general elections take place within sixty days prior to the expiry of the powers of the National Assembly.

Chapter II. Election procedure

Article L 123. The deputies are elected in single-vote majority voting with two rounds.

Article L 124. The vote takes place in electoral districts.

Article L 125. The electoral districts are determined in conformity with Table 1, annexed to the present Code, for the departments, Table 1bis for New Caledonia and the overseas entities governed by article 74 of the Constitution, and Table 1ter for French citizens residing outside French territory.

Article L 126. No-one is elected in the first round of the vote if he has not received:
1. the absolute majority of votes cast;

---

[1] Translation by S. Hardt and Ph. Kiiver.

2. a number of votes equal to one quarter of the number of registered voters.
In the second round, a relative majority suffices.
In case of a tie, the oldest of the candidates is elected.

[*Chapters III and IV are omitted.*]

Chapter V. Declarations of candidacies

[*Articles L 154 to L 161 are omitted.*]

Article L 162. The declarations of candidacies for the second round of the vote must be filed before 18.00 hours on the Tuesday that follows the first round.
However if, because of a case of force majeure, the counting of the votes could not be completed in the period prescribed in Article L 175, declarations are accepted until 18.00 hours on Wednesday.
Save for the provisions of Article L 163, no-one may be candidate in the second round if he did not run in the first round and if he did not receive a number of votes at least equal to 12.5 % of the number of registered voters.
In case a single candidate fulfils these conditions, the candidate who has received, after him, the largest number of votes in the first round may proceed to the second.
In case no candidate fulfils these conditions, the two candidates who have received the largest number of votes in the first round may proceed to the second.
A candidate may not present in the second round of the vote any alternate other than the one he designated in his declaration of candidacy for the first round.
The provisions of the second and third paragraph of Article L 157 and those of Article L 159 are applicable to declarations of candidacies for the second round of the vote. In that case, the administrative tribunal decides within a period of twenty-four hours.

Article L 163. Where a candidate dies after the expiry of the period prescribed for filing declarations of candidacies, his alternate becomes candidate and may designate a new alternate.
Where an alternate dies during the same period, the candidate may designate a new alternate.

[*The remainder of Book I is omitted.*]

Book II. The election of senators of the departments

Title I. Composition of the Senate and the length of the mandate of the senators

Article LO 274. The number of Senators elected within the departments is 326.

Article LO 275. Senators are elected for six years.

Article LO 276. The Senate is re-elected by half. For this purpose, the senators are divided into two classes, 1 and 2, of approximately equal importance, in accordance with Table 5 annexed to the present Code.

[*Note: Until the partial elections of 2010, Article LO 276 provides: The Senate is re-elected by thirds. For this purpose, the senators are divided into three classes, A, B and C, of approximately equal importance, in accordance with Table 5 annexed to the present Code.*]

Article LO 277. In each class, the mandate of the senators begins at the opening of the ordinary session which follows their election, at which date the mandate of the senators previously in office expires.

Article LO 278. The election of senators takes place within sixty days prior to the date of the beginning of their mandate.

Title II. Composition of the electoral college

Article L 279. The seats of the senators representing the departments are distributed in accordance with Table 6 annexed to the present Code.

Article L 280. The composition of the electoral college charged with the election of the senators ensures, in each department, representation of the different categories of territorial entities and of the variety of municipalities, taking into account the population residing in them.
The electoral college is composed of:
1. deputies and senators;
2. members of the regional council [conseillers régionaux] from the departmental section corresponding to the department and the members of the Assembly of Corsica designated under the conditions envisaged by Title III bis of the present Book;
2bis. members of the Assembly of Guyana and the Assembly of Martinique;
3. members of the departmental council [conseillers généraux];
4. delegates of the municipal councils or the substitutes of these delegates.

Article L 281. The deputies, the members of the regional council, the members of the Assembly of Corsica, the members of the Assembly of Guyana, the members of the Assembly of Martinique and the members of the departmental council [conseillers généraux] who have been appointed by the census commissions are registered in the list of senatorial electors and take part in the vote even if their election is contested. In case they are prevented by a major hindrance, they may exercise, upon written request, their right to vote by proxy. The mandatary must be a member of the senatorial electoral college and may not dispose of more than one proxy.

Article L 282. In case a member of the departmental council is a deputy, a member of the regional council or a member of the Assembly of Corsica, a replacement is designated for him, upon his proposal, by the president of the departmental council. In case a member of the regional council, a member of the Assembly of Corsica, a member of the Assembly of Guyana or a member of the Assembly of Martinique is a deputy, a replacement is designated for him, upon his proposal, by the president of the regional council, the president of the Assembly of Corsica, the president of the Assembly of Guyana or the president of the Assembly of Martinique.

Title III. Designation of delegates of municipal councils

Article L 283. The decree calling up the senatorial electors determines the day on which the delegates of the municipal councils and their substitutes must be designated. An interval of at least six weeks must separate these elections and the ones of the senators.

Article L 284. In municipalities of less than 9,000 inhabitants, the municipal councils elect from among their members:
- one delegate for municipal councils of seven and eleven members;
- three delegates for municipal councils of fifteen members;
- five delegates for municipal councils of nineteen members;
- seven delegates for municipal councils of twenty-three members;
- fifteen delegates for municipal councils of twenty-seven and twenty-nine members.

In case the municipal council is formed by application of Articles L 2113-6 and L 2113-7 of the General Code of Territorial Entities [code général des collectivités territoriales] regarding mergers of municipalities as worded prior to the enactment of statute no. 2010-1563 of 16 December 2010 on the reform of the territorial entities, the number of delegates is equal to the number to which the former municipalities would have been entitled before the merger.

Article L 285. In municipalities of 9,000 inhabitants and more, all members of the municipal council are delegates ex officio.
Furthermore, in municipalities of more than 30,000 inhabitants, the municipal councils elect additional delegates, namely 1 for every 800 inhabitants in excess of 30,000.

[*The remainder of Title III as well as Title IIIbis are omitted.*]

Title IV. Election of senators

Chapter I. Election procedure

Article L 294. In departments where two senators or less are elected, the election takes place by majority voting in two rounds.
No-one is elected senator in the first round of the vote if he has not obtained:

1. the absolute majority of votes cast;
2. a number of votes equal to one quarter of registered voters.
In the second round of the vote, a relative majority suffices. In case of a tie, the oldest of the candidates is elected.

Article L 295. In departments where three senators or more are elected, the election takes place by proportional representation following the rule of largest averages, without spreading votes over multiple lists [panachage] and without preference votes.
On each list, seats are attributed to candidates in the order of nomination.

[The remainder of the Code is omitted.]

GERMANY

Basic Law for the Federal Republic of Germany
[Grundgesetz für die Bundesrepublik Deutschland] of 23 May 1949, as last amended by federal statute of 11 July 2012 (BGBl. I p. 1478)[1]

Preamble
Conscious of its responsibility before God and man, inspired by the will to serve world peace as an equal partner in a united Europe, the German people, by virtue of its constituent power, has adopted for itself this Basic Law. Germans in the States of Baden-Württemberg, Bavaria, Berlin, Brandenburg, Bremen, Hamburg, Hesse, Mecklenburg-Western Pomerania, Lower Saxony, North Rhine-Westphalia, Rhineland-Palatinate, Saar, Saxony, Saxony-Anhalt, Schleswig-Holstein and Thuringia have achieved the unity and freedom of Germany in free self-determination. This Basic Law thus applies to the entire German people.

I. The fundamental rights

Article 1. (1) Human dignity is inviolable. To respect and protect it is the duty of all state authority.
(2) The German people therefore acknowledges inviolable and inalienable human rights as the basis of every community of people, of peace and of justice in the world.
(3) The following fundamental rights bind the legislature, the executive and the judiciary as directly applicable law.

Article 2. (1) Everyone has the right to the free development of his personality, as far as he does not infringe on the rights of others and does not violate the constitutional order or the law of morality.

---

[1] Translation by Ph. Kiiver, G. Kristoferitsch, G. Rotering and S. Hardt.

(2) Everyone has the right to life and physical integrity. The freedom of the person is inviolable. These rights may be interfered with only pursuant to a statute.

Article 3. (1) All people are equal before the law.
(2) Men and women have equal rights. The state promotes the actual implementation of equal rights for women and men and takes measures to remove existing disadvantages.
(3) No-one may be disadvantaged or preferred because of his sex, his descent, his race, his language, his homeland and origin, his faith, his religious or political views. No-one may be disadvantaged because of his disability.

Article 4. (1) The freedom of faith, of conscience, and the freedom to manifest one's religious and world-view conviction, are inviolable.
(2) The undisturbed exercise of religion is ensured.
(3) No-one may be forced against his conscience into armed military service. Details are regulated by a federal statute.

Article 5. (1) Everyone has the right to freely express and disseminate his opinion in speech, writing and picture and to inform himself without interference from generally accessible sources. The freedom of the press and the freedom of reporting through radio and film are ensured. Censorship does not take place.
(2) These rights find their limits in the regulations of general statutes, in statutory provisions for the protection of the youth and in the right to personal honour.
(3) Art and science, research and teaching are free. The freedom of teaching does not release from the loyalty to the constitution.

Article 6. (1) Marriage and family are placed under the special protection of the state order.
(2) The care and upbringing of children are the natural right of the parents and are an obligation that is primarily theirs. The community of the state watches over their performance.
(3) Children may be separated from the family pursuant to a statute against the will of their custodians only when the custodians fail or when the children are in danger of becoming victims of neglect for other reasons.
(4) Every mother is entitled to the protection and care of the community.
(5) Legislation is to provide children born outside wedlock with conditions for their physical and mental development and their position in society equal to those of children born within wedlock.

Article 7. (1) The entire school system is placed under the supervision of the state.
(2) Custodians have the right to decide over the participation of their child in religion classes.
(3) Religion classes are a regular course at public schools with the exception of non-denominational schools. Without prejudice to the state right of supervision, religious classes are taught in accordance with the principles of the religious communities. No teacher may be obliged against his will to teach religion classes.

(4) The right to establish private schools is ensured. Private schools as a substitute for public schools require the approval of the state and are subject to State legislation. Approval is to be granted when private schools are not inferior to state schools in their teaching aims and facilities as well as the scientific training of their teaching staff, and when a segregation of pupils according to the economic standing of the parents is not promoted. Approval is to be denied when the economic and legal position of the teaching staff is insufficiently secured.
(5) A private primary-cum-secondary school is only to be allowed if the curriculum administration recognizes a special educational interest or, upon custodians' request, if it is to be established as a community school, a denominational school or as a school based on a particular world view and a public primary-cum-secondary school of that kind is lacking in the municipality.
(6) Nursery schools remain abolished.

Article 8. (1) All Germans have the right to assemble peacefully and unarmed without notification or permission.
(2) Regarding gatherings outdoors, this right may be limited by or pursuant to a statute.

Article 9. (1) All Germans have the right to form clubs and societies.
(2) Associations whose purposes or activities run counter to criminal law or which are aimed against the constitutional order or the idea of understanding between nations are prohibited.
(3) The right to form associations for the promotion of working and economic conditions is ensured for everyone and for all professions. Agreements that limit or seek to hinder this right are void, measures taken with a view thereto are illegal. Measures in the sense of Articles 12a, 35 (2) and (3), Article 87a (4) and Article 91 may not be directed against industrial dispute action that is taken for the protection and promotion of working and economic conditions by associations in the meaning of the first sentence.

Article 10. (1) The privacy of correspondence as well as the privacy of mail and telecommunications are inviolable.
(2) Limitations may be ordered only pursuant to a statute. If the limitation serves the protection of the liberal-democratic fundamental order or of the integrity or security of the Federation or a State, then statute may provide that it not be notified to those affected and that recourse to the courts be replaced by review by organs and auxiliary organs appointed by Parliament.

Article 11. (1) All Germans enjoy freedom of movement on the entire territory of the Federation.
(2) This right may be limited only by or pursuant to a statute and only for those cases where sufficient means to support life are lacking and where this would result in a special burden on the community or where it is necessary for the aversion of a danger to the integrity or the liberal democratic fundamental order of the Federa-

tion or a State, for the countering of an epidemic threat, natural disasters or very serious accidents, for the protection of the youth from neglect or for the prevention of criminal acts.

Article 12. (1) All Germans have the right to freely choose their profession, place of work and of their training. The exercise of a profession may be regulated by or pursuant to a statute.
(2) No-one may be forced to perform a particular work, except within the framework of a regular general public service obligation that is the same for everyone.
(3) Forced labour is permissible only in the context of a court-ordered deprivation of freedom.

Article 12a. (1) Men from the age of eighteen onwards can be obliged to serve in the armed forces, the Federal Border Guard [Bundesgrenzschutz] or in a civil defence organization.
(2) He who refuses armed military service on conscientious grounds may be obliged to serve in an alternative service. The length of the alternative service may not exceed the length of the military service. Details are regulated by a statute which may not compromise the freedom of conscientious decision and which must also provide for an alternative service option which is not connected with the units of the armed forces and the Federal Border Guard.
(3) Persons liable to conscription who have not been drafted in accordance with sub-paragraphs 1 or 2 may in a state of defence, by or pursuant to a statute, be committed to an employment for civilian services for defence purposes including the protection of the civilian population; commitment to public employment is only permissible for the exercise of police tasks or such sovereign tasks of public administration that can be fulfilled only within a public employment. Employments in the meaning of the first sentence may be established with the armed forces, in the context of their supply, as well as in the public administration; commitment to employment in the context of the supply of the civilian population is permissible only to secure its basic needs or to maintain its safety.
(4) If in a state of defence the demand for civilian services in the civilian medical and health system as well as in the stationary military hospital system cannot be met on a voluntary basis, women from the age of eighteen until the age of fifty-five may be drafted to such services by or pursuant to a statute. They may in no event be drafted to armed service.
(5) For the time period before the state of defence, obligations under sub-paragraph 3 may only be established within the guidelines of Article 80a (1). For the preparation to services according to sub-paragraph 3 for which special knowledge or skills are required, by or pursuant to a statute the participation in training courses may be made mandatory. In that respect, the first sentence does not apply.
(6) If in a state of defence the demand for workers in the contexts stipulated in sub-paragraph 3, second sentence, cannot be met on a voluntary basis, the freedom of Germans to give up a profession or a place of work may be limited, in order to meet this demand, by or pursuant to a statute. Prior to the beginning of a state of defence, sub-paragraph 5, first sentence, applies mutatis mutandis.

Article 13. (1) The home is inviolable.
(2) Searches may be ordered only by a judge or, in case of an imminent threat, also by other organs provided for by statutes, and may be conducted only in the form stipulated there.
(3) When certain facts support the suspicion that someone has committed a certain very serious crime defined individually by statute, then, for the prosecution of this act, on the basis of a court order, technical means for the acoustic surveillance of homes in which the suspect is presumably staying may be used, if the investigation of the case by other means would be disproportionately burdensome or futile. The measure is to be of a limited duration. The order is to be given by a body staffed with three judges. In case of an imminent threat, it may also be given by a single judge.
(4) To avert acute threats to public safety, especially a threat to the public or to life, technical means for the surveillance of homes may be used only on the basis of a court order. In case of an imminent threat, the measure may also be ordered by another instance stipulated by statute; a court decision must afterwards be obtained without delay.
(5) If technical means are exclusively meant for the protection of persons operating in a home, the measure may be ordered by an instance stipulated by statute. Any other use of the information thus obtained is permissible only for the purpose of criminal prosecution or the aversion of dangers and only if the lawfulness of the measure has been established by a court; in case of an imminent threat, a court decision must afterwards be obtained without delay.
(6) The Federal Government informs the Bundestag annually about the use that has been made of technical means under sub-paragraph 3, under sub-paragraph 4 within the competence of the Federation, and under sub-paragraph 5 in as far as it requires judicial review. A body elected by the Bundestag exercises parliamentary control on the basis of this report. The States ensure an equivalent parliamentary control.
(7) Interferences and limitations may otherwise be effected only for the aversion of a threat to the public or to the life of individual persons, pursuant to a statute also for the prevention of acute threats to public safety and order, especially to address a shortage of housing space, to combat epidemic threats or to protect endangered adolescents.

Article 14. (1) Property and the right of inheritance are ensured. The content and limits thereof are defined by statutes.
(2) Property entails obligations. Its use should also serve the public good.
(3) An expropriation is only permissible for the public good. It may be effected only by or pursuant to a statute which regulates the kind and extent of compensation. The compensation is to be established by justly weighing the interests of the community and of those involved. Recourse to the ordinary courts is open in case of a dispute regarding the amount of the compensation.

Article 15. Land, natural resources and means of production may, for the purpose of socialization, by a statute which regulates the kind and extent of compensation, be transferred into public ownership or into other forms of collective concern. As regards the compensation, Article 14 (3), third and fourth sentence, applies mutatis mutandis.

Article 16. (1) German citizenship may not be withdrawn. A loss of citizenship may occur only pursuant to a statute and, if against the will of the person affected, only when the person affected does not become stateless as a result.
(2) No German may be extradited to a foreign state. By statute a different regime may be established concerning extraditions to a member state of the European Union or an international tribunal, as long as principles of the rule of law are secured.

Article 16a. (1) Those politically persecuted enjoy the right to asylum.
(2) He who arrives from a member state of the European Communities or from another third country where the application of the Convention relating to the status of refugees and the Convention for the protection of human rights and fundamental freedoms is ensured, cannot rely on sub-paragraph 1. The states outside the European Communities to which the conditions of the first sentence apply are designated by a statute which requires the consent of the Bundesrat. In cases stipulated by the first sentence, measures for the termination of a stay may be taken irrespectively of any court actions filed against them.
(3) By a statute which requires the consent of the Bundesrat, states may be designated where, based on the state of the law, the application of the law and the general political circumstances, it appears certain that neither political persecution nor inhuman or degrading punishment or treatment takes place. It is presumed that an alien from such a state is not being persecuted as long as he does not provide facts which support the conclusion that he is being politically persecuted contrary to this presumption.
(4) The execution of measures for the termination of a stay are, in the cases of sub-paragraph 3 and in other cases that are manifestly ill-founded or are presumed manifestly ill-founded, suspended by a court only when serious doubts exist as to the lawfulness of the measure; the scope of review may be limited and belated submissions be disregarded. Details are to be regulated by statute.
(5) Sub-paragraphs 1 to 4 do not bar any international treaties of member states of the European Communities among themselves and with third countries which, while respecting the obligations under the Convention relating to the status of refugees and the Convention for the protection of human rights and fundamental freedoms, the application of which must be ensured in the contracting states, provide for rules on jurisdiction for the review of applications for asylum, including the mutual recognition of decisions regarding asylum.

Article 17. Everyone has the right, individually or together with others in a group, to address in writing the competent authorities and parliament with petitions or complaints.

Article 17a. (1) Statutes regarding military and alternative service may provide that for members of the armed forces and the alternative service, for the duration of the military or alternative service, the fundamental right to freely express and disseminate one's opinion in speech, writing and picture (Article 5 (1), first sentence, first clause), the fundamental right of freedom of assembly (Article 8) and the right of petition (Article 17) in as far as it grants the right to submit petitions or complaints together with others in a group, be limited.
(2) Statutes which serve the purpose of defence, including the protection of the civilian population, may provide that the fundamental rights of free movement (Article 11) and the inviolability of the home (Article 13) be limited.

Article 18. He who abuses the freedom of expression, in particular the freedom of the press (Article 5 (1)), the freedom of teaching (Article 5 (3)), the freedom of assembly (Article 8), the freedom of association (Article 9), the privacy of the correspondence, the mail and telecommunications (Article 10), property (Article 14) or the right to asylum (Article 16a) in order to fight against the liberal democratic fundamental order, forfeits these fundamental rights. The forfeiture and its scope are established by the Federal Constitutional Court [Bundesverfassungsgericht].

Article 19. (1) In as far as a fundamental right may be limited by or pursuant to a statute in accordance with this Basic Law, such statute must be of a general nature and may not merely apply to an individual case. In addition, the statute must state the fundamental right and the Article concerned.
(2) In no event may a fundamental right be compromised in its essence.
(3) The fundamental rights also cover domestic legal persons, in as far as they are applicable in the light of their nature.
(4) If someone's rights are violated by public authority, he has recourse to the courts. In as far as no other jurisdiction applies, recourse may be had to the ordinary courts. Article 10 (2), second sentence, remains unaffected by this.

II. The Federation and the States

Article 20. (1) The Federal Republic of Germany is a democratic and social federal state.
(2) All state authority derives from the people. It is exercised by the people through elections and votes and through specific organs of the legislature, of executive power and the judiciary.
(3) The legislature is bound by the constitutional order, the executive power and the judiciary by law and justice.
(4) All Germans have the right to resist any person seeking to abolish this order, if no other remedy is available.

Article 20a. The state protects, also under its responsibility for future generations, the natural foundations of life and the animals, within the framework of the constitutional order through legislation and within the guidelines of law and justice through executive power and the judiciary.

Article 21. (1) Political parties contribute to the political will-formation of the people. Their establishment is free. Their internal order must correspond to democratic principles. They must render account about the origin and use of their means as well as about their assets in public.
(2) Political parties which, based on their aims or the conduct of their followers, are committed to jeopardizing or eliminating the liberal democratic fundamental order or to threatening the integrity of the Federal Republic of Germany, are unconstitutional. The Federal Constitutional Court [Bundesverfassungsgericht] rules on the question of unconstitutionality.
(3) Details are regulated by federal statutes.

Article 22. (1) The capital of the Federal Republic of Germany is Berlin. The representation of the state as a whole in the capital is a matter for the Federation. Details are regulated by statute.
(2) The federal flag is black-red-gold.

Article 23. (1) With a view to achieving a united Europe, the Federal Republic of Germany participates in the development of the European Union which is com mitted to democratic, rule-of-law, social, and federal principles and to the principle of subsidiarity, and which guarantees a level of protection of fundamental rights essentially comparable to that afforded by this Basic Law. To this end the Federation may, by a statute with the consent of the Bundesrat, transfer sovereign powers. For the establishment of the European Union, as well as for changes to its treaty foundations and comparable regulations that amend or supplement this Basic Law in its content, or that make such amendments or supplements possible, Article 79 (2) and (3) applies.
(1a) The Bundestag and the Bundesrat have the right to bring an action before the Court of Justice of the European Union if a legislative act of the European Union infringes upon the principle of subsidiarity. The Bundestag is obliged to do so on application by a quarter of its members. A statute which requires the consent of the Bundesrat may, with respect to the exercise of the rights accorded to the Bundestag and the Bundesrat in the treaty framework of the European Union, make deviations from the first sentence of Article 42 (2), first sentence, and Article 52 (3), first sentence.
(2) The Bundestag and, through the Bundesrat, the States, participate in matters concerning the European Union. The Federal Government must inform the Bundestag and the Bundesrat comprehensively and at the earliest possible time.
(3) The Federal Government provides the Bundestag with an opportunity to state its opinion prior to its participation in legislative acts of the European Union. The Federal Government takes into account the statements of opinion of the Bundestag during negotiations. Details are regulated by a statute.

(4) The Bundesrat is to be included in the will-formation of the Federation in as far as it would have had to participate in an equivalent domestic measure or in as far as the States would have been competent domestically.

(5) In as far as, in an area of exclusive competence of the Federation, interests of the States are affected, or in as far as the Federation has otherwise legislative competence, the Federal Government takes into account the statements of opinion of the Bundesrat. If primarily legislative competences of the States, the organization of their authorities or their administrative procedures are affected, the opinion of the Bundesrat must to that extent be given greatest consideration during the will-formation of the Federation; the responsibility of the Federation for the state as a whole must in that context be upheld. In matters that may result in an increase in spending or a decrease in revenue for the Federation, the consent of the Federal Government is required.

(6) If primarily exclusive legislative competences of the States in the areas of schooling, culture or broadcasting are affected, the exercise of the rights that the Federal Republic of Germany has as a member state of the European Union is transferred from the Federation to a representative of the States appointed by the Bundesrat. The exercise of these rights is carried out with the participation of and in coordination with the Federal Government; the responsibility of the Federation for the state as a whole must in that context be upheld.

(7) Details regarding sub-paragraphs 4 to 6 are regulated by a statute that requires the consent of the Bundesrat.

Article 24. (1) The Federation may, by statute, transfer sovereign powers to international organizations.

(1a) In as far as the States are competent for the exercise of state power and the fulfilment of state tasks, they may, with the consent of the Federal Government, transfer sovereign powers to cross-border neighbourhood institutions.

(2) The Federation may, for the preservation of peace, enter into a system of mutual collective security; it will in that context agree to limitations of its sovereign powers which bring about and secure a peaceful and permanent order in Europe and between the nations of the world.

(3) For the settlement of international disputes, the Federation will accede to agreements regarding general, comprehensive and mandatory international arbitration.

Article 25. The general rules of international law are an integral part of federal law. They take precedence over statutes and directly create rights and obligations for the inhabitants of the territory of the Federation.

Article 26. (1) Acts that are capable of and are committed with the intent to disturb the peaceful coexistence of nations, in particular prepare the conduct of a war of aggression, are unconstitutional. They are to be made punishable offences.

(2) Weapons designed for warfare may be produced, transported and brought into circulation only with the consent of the Federal Government. Details are regulated by a federal statute.

Article 27. All German merchant vessels form a uniform merchant fleet.

Article 28. (1) The constitutional order in the States must comply with the principles of a republican, democratic and social state based on the rule of law in the meaning of this Basic Law. In the States, rural counties [Kreise] and municipalities [Gemeinden], the people must have a representative body that is formed in general, direct, free, equal and secret-ballot elections. At elections within rural counties and municipalities, persons with the citizenship of a member state of the European Community, within the guidelines of the law of the European Community, also have the right to vote and may be elected. In municipalities, a municipal assembly may take the place of an elected body.
(2) Municipalities must have the secured right to regulate all affairs of the local community, within the framework of statutes, on their own responsibility. Also associations of municipalities [Gemeindeverbände] have, within the framework of their statutory function, within the guidelines of statutes, the right to self-government. The securing of self-government also includes the foundations of financial autonomy; part of these foundations is a source of revenue related to economic strength to which municipalities with the right to set tax rates are entitled.
(3) The Federation ensures that the constitutional order of the States complies with fundamental rights and the provisions of sub-paragraphs 1 and 2.

Article 29. (1) The territory of the Federation may be restructured so as to ensure that the States, in the light of their size and capacity, are able to effectively fulfil the tasks vested in them. Account is to be taken of regional attachment, historical and cultural connections, economic opportunity, as well as the requirements of regional planning and zoning.
(2) Measures for the restructuring of the territory of the Federation are effected by a federal statute which requires approval in a referendum [Volksentscheid]. The affected States are to be heard.
(3) The referendum takes place in those States from the territory or from parts of the territory of which a new or a redrawn State is to be formed (affected States). The object of the referendum is the question whether the affected States should continue to exist as before or whether the new or redrawn State should be formed. A referendum in favour of a new or redrawn State is established when majorities vote in favour of the change both within its future territory and within the territories or parts of territories of an affected State whose State affiliation is to be changed. It is not established when a majority within the territory of one of the affected States rejects the change; such rejection is however ineffective if in a part of a territory whose affiliation with the affected State is to be changed, a two-thirds majority votes in favour of the change, except when within the territory of the affected State as a whole a two-thirds majority rejects the change.
(4) If within a contiguous, separated residential and economic area whose parts lie in several States and which has at least one million inhabitants, one-tenth of the population entitled to vote for the Bundestag there demands by popular initiative [Volksbegehren] that for this area a single State affiliation be created, then within two years a federal statute is either to determine whether the State affiliation will be

changed in accordance with sub-paragraph 2 or that a consultative referendum [Volksbefragung] will be held in the affected States.

(5) The consultative referendum is aimed at establishing whether a change of State affiliation to be proposed by the statute finds approval. The statute may subject different, yet not more than two proposals to the consultative referendum. If a majority votes in favour of a proposed change of State affiliation, then within two years a federal statute is to determine whether the State affiliation will be changed in accordance with sub-paragraph 2. If a proposal subjected to a consultative referendum receives an approval corresponding with the provisions of sub-paragraph 3, third and fourth sentence, then within two years after the consultative referendum a federal statute regarding the creation of the proposed State is to be adopted, which does no longer require approval by referendum.

(6) A majority in a referendum and in a consultative referendum is the majority of the votes cast, if that includes at least one quarter of the population entitled to vote for the Bundestag. As for the rest, details regarding the referendum, the popular initiative and the consultative referendum are regulated by a federal statute; this statute may also provide that popular initiatives may not be repeated within a time period of five years.

(7) Further changes to the territorial shape of the States may be effected by inter-State agreements [Staatsverträge] between the affected States or by a federal statute with the consent of the Bundesrat, if the territory whose State affiliation is to be changed has no more than 50,000 inhabitants. Details are regulated by a federal statute which requires the consent of the Bundesrat and the approval of the majority of the members of the Bundestag. It must provide for a hearing of the affected municipalities and rural counties.

(8) The States may regulate a restructuring of their territory or parts of their territory, in deviation from the provisions of sub-paragraphs 2 to 7, by inter-State agreement. The affected municipalities and rural counties are to be heard. The inter-State agreement requires approval by referendum in each participating State. If the inter-State agreement concerns parts of the territories of States, the approval may be confined to referendums in these parts of the territories; the fifth sentence, second clause, does not apply. In a referendum the majority of votes cast decides if it includes at least one quarter of the population entitled to vote for the Bundestag; details are regulated by a statute. The inter-State agreement requires the consent of the Bundestag.

Article 30. The exercise of state power and the fulfilment of state tasks is a matter for the States, in as far as this Basic Law does not stipulate or permit otherwise.

Article 31. Federal law prevails over State law.

Article 32. (1) The conduct of relations with foreign states is a matter for the Federation.
(2) Before the conclusion of a treaty which affects the special circumstances of a State, that State is to be heard.

(3) In as far as the States have legislative competence, they may conclude treaties with foreign states with the consent of the Federal Government.

Article 33. (1) Every German has the same citizenship rights and obligations in all States.
(2) Every German has, in view of his aptitude, ability and professional performance, equal access to every public office.
(3) The enjoyment of civil and political rights, the admission to public offices as well as the rights acquired in public service are independent of religious conviction. No-one may be subject to disadvantage due to his adherence or non-adherence to a conviction or world view.
(4) The exercise of sovereign powers as a permanent task is, as a rule, to be transferred to members of the public service who are in a public-law relation of service and loyalty.
(5) The law on the public service is to be regulated and developed further, taking into account the traditional principles of the professional civil service.

Article 34. If someone violates his official duties with respect to a third person in the exercise of a public office entrusted to him, then liability lies in principle with the state or with the entity in the service of which he is. In case of intent or gross negligence, individual liability for indemnity is reserved. For the right to damages and indemnity, recourse to the ordinary courts may not be excluded.

Article 35. (1) All authorities of the Federation and the States provide to each other legal and inter-administrative assistance.
(2) In order to maintain or restore public safety or order, a State may in cases of special significance request forces and facilities of the Federal Border Guard to support its police, if the police could, without such support, not fulfil a task at all or only with great difficulty. For relief in case of a natural disaster or a very serious accident, a State may request police forces of other States, forces and facilities of other administrations as well as the Federal Border Guard and the armed forces.
(3) If the natural disaster or the accident threatens the territory of more than one State, the Federal Government may, in as far as that is necessary for effective relief, give the State governments the order to make police forces available to other States, and use units of the Federal Border Guard and the armed forces to support the police forces. Measures of the Federal Government under the first sentence must at any time be lifted upon request of the Bundesrat, otherwise without delay after the removal of the threat.

Article 36. (1) In the supreme federal authorities, civil servants from all States must be employed in appropriate proportions. Persons employed in the other federal authorities should, as a rule, be drawn from the State in which they serve.
(2) Statutes regarding the military must also take into account the division of the Federation into States and their special regional attachments.

Article 37. (1) If a State does not fulfil its federal duties according to the Basic Law or another federal statute, the Federal Government may, with the consent of the Bundesrat, take the necessary measures to compel that State to fulfil its duties by way of federal enforcement [Bundeszwang].
(2) For the execution of federal enforcement, the Federal Government or its representative has the right to give instructions to all States and their authorities.

III. The Bundestag

Article 38. (1) The members of the German Bundestag are elected in general, direct, free, equal and secret-ballot elections. They are the representatives of the whole people, not bound by orders or instructions, and responsible only to their conscience.
(2) He who has attained the age of eighteen years has the right to vote; he who has reached the age at which majority begins, has the right to be elected.
(3) Details are regulated by a federal statute.

Article 39. (1) The Bundestag is elected, subject to the following provisions, for four years. Its term ends with the convention of a new Bundestag. New elections take place at the earliest forty-six, at the latest forty-eight months after the beginning of a term. In the case of a dissolution of the Bundestag, new elections take place within sixty days.
(2) The Bundestag convenes, at the latest, on the thirtieth day after elections.
(3) The Bundestag determines the end and the beginning of its sessions. The president of the Bundestag may convene it earlier. He is obliged to do so if one-third of the members, the Federal President or the Federal Chancellor so demand.

Article 40. (1) The Bundestag elects its president, his deputy and the secretaries. It adopts its rules of procedure.
(2) The president exercises proprietary and police powers in the Bundestag building. Without his permission, no search or seizure may take place on the premises of the Bundestag.

Article 41. (1) Review of elections is a matter for the Bundestag. It also decides whether a member of the Bundestag has lost his membership.
(2) Complaints against the decision of the Bundestag are admissible before the Federal Constitutional Court.
(3) Details are regulated by a federal statute.

Article 42. (1) The Bundestag deliberates in public. Upon the request of one-tenth of its members or upon request of the Federal Government, the public may be excluded by a two-thirds majority. The decision on the request takes place in a non-public session.

(2) A decision of the Bundestag requires a majority of the votes cast, in as far as this Basic Law does not provide otherwise. For the elections to be carried out by the Bundestag, the rules of procedure may allow for exceptions.
(3) Truthful reports about the public sessions of the Bundestag and its committees do not give rise to any liability.

Article 43. (1) The Bundestag and its committees may demand the presence of any member of the Federal Government.
(2) The members of the Bundesrat and the Federal Government as well as their representatives have access to all sessions of the Bundestag and its committees. They have the right to be heard at all times.

Article 44. (1) The Bundestag has the right and, upon request of one quarter of its members the obligation, to establish an investigative committee [Untersuchungs ausschuss] which gathers the necessary evidence in public deliberation. The public may be excluded.
(2) The rules regarding criminal procedure are applicable mutatis mutandis to the gathering of evidence. The privacy of the correspondence, mail and telecommunications remains unaffected.
(3) Courts and administrative authorities are obliged to provide legal and inter-administrative assistance.
(4) The decisions of investigative committees are outside the scope of judicial assessment. In the consideration and qualification of the facts subject to the investigation, the courts are free.

Article 45. The Bundestag establishes a committee for the affairs of the European Union. It may authorize it to exercise the rights of the Bundestag under Article 23 with respect to the Federal Government. It may also authorize it to exercise the rights that have been accorded to the Bundestag in the treaty framework of the European Union.

Article 45a. (1) The Bundestag establishes a committee for foreign affairs and a committee for defence.
(2) The committee for defence also has the rights of an investigative committee. Upon the request of one quarter of its members it has the obligation to make a matter the subject of an investigation.
(3) Article 44 (1) does not apply to the area of defence.

Article 45b. For the protection of fundamental rights and as an auxiliary organ of the Bundestag in the exercise of parliamentary control, a commissioner for the armed forces [Wehrbeauftragter] is appointed. Details are regulated by a federal statute.

Article 45c. (1) The Bundestag establishes a petitions committee which has as its task the consideration of petitions and complaints addressed to the Bundestag under Article 17.
(2) The competences of the committee for the consideration of complaints are regulated by a federal statute.

Article 45d. (1) The Bundestag establishes a body to control the intelligence activities of the Federation.
(2) Details are regulated by a federal statute.

Article 46. (1) A member of the Bundestag may at no time be prosecuted by judicial or disciplinary means or be in any other way held liable outside the Bundestag because of his voting or because of a statement which he made in the Bundestag or in one of its committees. This does not apply to defamatory insults.
(2) A member of the Bundestag may be held liable or arrested because of a punishable act only with the permission of the Bundestag, unless he is arrested as he committed the act or on the following day.
(3) Permission of the Bundestag is furthermore required for any other limitation of the personal freedom of a member of the Bundestag or for the commencement of a procedure against a member of the Bundestag under Article 18.
(4) Any criminal procedure and any procedure under Article 18 against a member of the Bundestag, any detention and any other limitation of his personal freedom must be suspended upon demand of the Bundestag.

Article 47. The members of the Bundestag have the right to refuse to testify regarding persons who have confided information to them in their capacity as members of the Bundestag or to whom they have in that capacity confided information, as well as regarding the information itself. In as far as this right to refuse to testify applies, the seizure of written documents is not permissible.

Article 48. (1) He who runs as a candidate for a seat in the Bundestag has a right to the leave necessary for the preparation of his election.
(2) No-one may be hindered from assuming and exercising the office of a member of the Bundestag. A dismissal or discharge from employment on this ground is not permissible.
(3) The members of the Bundestag have the right to an appropriate allowance that secures their independence. They have the right to the free use of all state-run means of transport. Details are regulated by a federal statute.

Article 49. (Repealed).

IV. The Bundesrat

Article 50. Through the Bundesrat, the States participate in the legislation and administration of the Federation and in matters concerning the European Union.

Article 51. (1) The Bundesrat consists of members of the State governments, which appoint and recall them. They may be represented by other members of their governments.
(2) Each State has at least three votes; States with more than two million inhabitants have four, States with more than six million inhabitants five, States with more than seven million inhabitants six votes.
(3) Each State may send as many members as it has votes. The votes of each State may be cast only as a unit and only by members present or their alternates.

Article 52. (1) The Bundesrat elects its president for one year.
(2) The president convenes the Bundesrat. He must convene it if the representatives of at least two States or the Federal Government so demand.
(3) The Bundesrat takes its decisions with at least a majority of its votes. It adopts its rules of procedure. It deliberates in public. The public may be excluded.
(3a) For matters concerning the European Union, the Bundesrat may establish a European affairs chamber whose decisions are considered decisions of the Bundesrat; the number of votes of the States to be cast as a unit is determined by Article 51 (2).
(4) In the committees of the Bundesrat, other members or representatives of the governments of the States may be members.

Article 53. The members of the Federal Government have the right and, upon demand, the duty to participate in the deliberations of the Bundesrat and its committees. They have the right to be heard at all times. The Bundesrat is to be kept informed by the Federal Government about the conduct of affairs.

IVa. The Joint Committee

Article 53a. (1) Two-thirds of the members of the Joint Committee [Gemeinsamer Ausschuss] comprise members of the Bundestag and one-third members of the Bundesrat. The members of the Bundestag are appointed by the Bundestag according to the relative strength of the political party groups; they may not be members of the Federal Government. Each State is represented by a member of the Bundesrat appointed by it; these members are not bound by any instructions. The establishment of the Joint Committee and its procedures are regulated by rules of procedure which are to be adopted by the Bundestag and which require the consent of the Bundesrat.
(2) The Federal Government must inform the Joint Committee about its planning for the state of defence. The rights of the Bundestag and its committees under Article 43 (1) are not affected.

V. The Federal President

Article 54. (1) The Federal President is elected without debate by the Federal Convention [Bundesversammlung].

Any German may be elected who is entitled to vote for the Bundestag and who has attained the age of forty.
(2) The term of office of the Federal President is five years. A subsequent re-election is permissible only once.
(3) The Federal Convention consists of the members of the Bundestag and an equal number of members who are elected by the parliaments of the States on the basis of proportional representation.
(4) The Federal Convention convenes, at the latest, thirty days before the expiry of the term of office of the Federal President, and in case of an early termination thirty days after that moment at the latest. It is convened by the president of the Bundestag.
(5) After the expiry of a term, the period under sub-paragraph 4, first sentence, begins with the first convention of the Bundestag.
(6) He who has received the votes of a majority of the members of the Federal Convention is elected. If after two ballots such majority is not obtained by any candidate, then he who receives the most votes in a further ballot is elected.
(7) Details are regulated by a federal statute.

Article 55. (1) The Federal President may not be a member of the Federal Government or of a legislative body of the Federation or of a State.
(2) The Federal President may not exercise any other remunerated office, he may pursue no trade or profession and may not be a member of either the board or the supervisory board of a profit-oriented company.

Article 56. The Federal President, when assuming office, takes the following oath before the assembled members of the Bundestag and the Bundesrat:
"I swear that I shall dedicate my strength to the well-being of the German people, promote its welfare, protect it from harm, uphold and defend the Basic Law and the legislation of the Federation, fulfil my duties conscientiously, and do justice to all. So help me God."
The oath may also be taken without the religious assertion.

Article 57. The powers of the Federal President, in case he is prevented from exercising his functions or in case of an early termination of his term, are exercised by the president of the Bundesrat.

Article 58. Instructions and orders of the Federal President require for their validity the countersignature by the Federal Chancellor or the competent federal minister. This does not apply to the appointment and dismissal of the Federal Chancellor, the dissolution of the Bundestag under Article 63 and the request under Article 69 (3).

Article 59. (1) The Federal President represents the Federation under international law. He concludes, in the name of the Federation, treaties with foreign states. He accredits and receives envoys.

(2) Treaties which regulate the political relations of the Federation, or which refer to objects of federal legislation, require the consent or participation of the organs competent for such federal legislation in the form of a federal statute. For administrative agreements, the regulations regarding the federal administration apply mutatis mutandis.

Article 59a. (Repealed).

Article 60. (1) The Federal President appoints and dismisses federal judges, federal civil servants, officers and non-commissioned officers, as far as statutory regulations do not provide otherwise.
(2) He exercises, in individual cases, the right of pardon for the Federation.
(3) He may transfer these competences to other authorities.
(4) Sub-paragraphs 2 to 4 of Article 46 apply to the Federal President mutatis mutandis.

Article 61. (1) The Bundestag or the Bundesrat may impeach the Federal President for an intentional violation of the Basic Law or another federal statute before the Federal Constitutional Court. The motion to impeach must be tabled by at least a quarter of the members of the Bundestag or a quarter of the votes of the Bundesrat. The decision to impeach requires a majority of two-thirds of the members of the Bundestag or two-thirds of the votes of the Bundesrat. The prosecution is conducted by a representative of the impeaching organ.
(2) If the Federal Constitutional Court establishes that the Federal President is guilty of having committed an intentional violation of the Basic Law or another federal statute, it may declare that he is removed from office. By interim order after impeachment it may rule that he is prevented from exercising his functions.

VI. The Federal Government

Article 62. The Federal Government consists of the Federal Chancellor [Bundeskanzler] and the federal ministers.

Article 63. (1) The Federal Chancellor is elected, on the proposal of the Federal President, by the Bundestag without debate.
(2) He who receives the votes of a majority of the members of the Bundestag is elected. The person elected is to be appointed by the Federal President.
(3) If the nominee is not elected, the Bundestag may within fourteen days after the ballot, by the votes of more than half of its members, elect a Federal Chancellor.
(4) If no election is successful within this period, a new ballot takes place without delay, in which he who receives the most votes is elected. If the person elected receives the votes of a majority of the members of the Bundestag, the Federal President must appoint him within seven days after the election. If the person elected does not receive such a majority, then within seven days the Federal President must either appoint him or dissolve the Bundestag.

Article 64. (1) The federal ministers are appointed and dismissed by the Federal President on the proposal of the Federal Chancellor.
(2) The Federal Chancellor and the federal ministers, when assuming office, take the oath as stipulated in Article 56 before the Bundestag.
Article 65. The Federal Chancellor determines the guidelines of policy and bears responsibility for that. Within these guidelines, each federal minister directs his portfolio autonomously and on his own responsibility. The Federal Government rules in case of disagreements between federal ministers. The Federal Chancellor directs its affairs according to rules of procedure as adopted by the Federal Government and approved by the Federal President.

Article 65a. (1) The federal minister of defence has the command over the armed forces.
(2) (Repealed).

Article 66. The Federal Chancellor and the federal ministers may not exercise any other remunerated office, they may pursue no trade or profession and may not be a member of either the board or, without consent of the Bundestag, the supervisory board of a profit-oriented company.

Article 67. (1) The Bundestag may express its lack of confidence in the Federal Chancellor only by electing a successor by the vote of a majority of its members and by requesting the Federal President to dismiss the Federal Chancellor. The Federal President must comply with the request and appoint the person elected.
(2) Forty-eight hours must pass between the motion and the election.

Article 68. (1) If a motion of the Federal Chancellor for a vote of confidence is not supported by the majority of the members of the Bundestag, the Federal President may, on the proposal of the Federal Chancellor, dissolve the Bundestag within twenty-one days. The right of dissolution lapses as soon as the Bundestag elects another Federal Chancellor by the vote of a majority of its members.
(2) Forty-eight hours must pass between the motion and the vote.

Article 69. (1) The Federal Chancellor appoints a federal minister as his deputy.
(2) The office of the Federal Chancellor ends in any event with the convention of a new Bundestag, the office of a federal minister ends also with any other termination of the office of the Federal Chancellor.
(3) On the request of the Federal President, the Federal Chancellor is obliged, and on the request of the Federal Chancellor or the Federal President a federal minister is obliged to continue the affairs until the appointment of a successor.

VII. The legislation of the Federation

Article 70. (1) The States have the right to legislate in as far as this Basic Law does not confer legislative power on the Federation.

(2) The delimitation of competences between the Federation and the States is guided by the provisions of this Basic Law regarding exclusive and concurrent legislation.

Article 71. In the area of exclusive legislative power of the Federation, the States have power to legislate only when and in as far as they are expressly authorized to do so by a federal statute.

Article 72. (1) In the area of concurrent legislative power, the States have power to legislate so long as and to the extent that the Federation has not exercised its legislative power through a statute.
(2) The Federation has legislative power in the areas of Article 74 (1) no. 4, 7, 11, 13, 15, 19a, 20, 22, 25 and 26 when and to the extent that the bringing about of equivalent living standards throughout the territory of the Federation or the upholding of legal or economic unity in the interest of the state as a whole require a federal statutory regulation.
(3) If the Federation has made use of its legislative competence, the States may by statute adopt regulations that deviate therefrom regarding:
1. hunting (except the law on hunting permits);
2. nature conservation and landscape management (except the general principles of nature conservation, the law on the protection of species or maritime nature conservation);
3. the distribution of land;
4. regional planning;
5. water resources (except regulations on substances and facilities);
6. admissions to higher education and higher education diplomas.
Federal statutes in these areas enter into force at the earliest six months after their publication, in as far as nothing is provided otherwise with the consent of the Bundesrat. In the areas of the first sentence, in the relation between federal law and State law the later statute prevails.
(4) A federal statute may determine that a federal statutory regulation a need for which in the sense of sub-paragraph 2 no longer exists, may be replaced by State law.

Article 73. (1) The Federation has exclusive legislative power regarding:
1. foreign relations as well as defence including the protection of the civilian population;
2. citizenship in the Federation;
3. free movement, the passport regime, population registers and identity documents, immigration, emigration and extradition;
4. currency, the money and coinage regime, measures and weights as well as the determination of the time;
5. the unity of the customs and trade area, trade and navigation agreements, the free movement of goods and the movement of goods and capital with foreign states including customs and border protection;
5a. the protection of German cultural assets from transfers abroad;
6. air traffic;

6a. rail traffic which falls entirely or predominantly under the ownership of the Federation (the railways of the Federation), the construction, maintenance and operation of tracks of the railways of the Federation as well as the levying of charges for the use of these tracks;
7. post and telecommunications;
8. legal relations of persons in the service of the Federation and of directly federal entities of public law;
9. intellectual property, copyright and publishing law;
9a. the protection from the dangers of international terrorism by the Federal Criminal Investigations Police Office [Bundeskriminalpolizeiamt] in cases where a danger transcending State borders is at hand, where the jurisdiction of a State police authority is not apparent or where a supreme State authority requests a takeover of jurisdiction;
10. the cooperation between the Federation and the States
a. regarding criminal police investigation,
b. for the protection of the liberal democratic fundamental order, the integrity and security of the Federation or a State (domestic intelligence [Verfassungsschutz]) and
c. for the protection against attempts within the territory of the Federation which jeopardize, through the use of force or preparatory acts with such aim, the external interests of the Federal Republic of Germany,
as well as the establishment of a Federal Criminal Investigations Police Office and the international fight against crime;
11. statistics for federal purposes;
12. the law on weapons and explosives;
13. care for those disabled in war and surviving dependants of war dead, and support for former prisoners of war;
14. the production and use of nuclear energy for peaceful purposes, the establishment and operation of facilities serving these purposes, the protection against dangers arising from the release of nuclear energy or from ionizing radiation, and the disposal of radioactive material.
(2) Statutes under sub-paragraph 1 no. 9a require the consent of the Bundesrat.

Article 74. (1) Concurrent legislative power extends to the following areas:
1. private law, criminal law, the court system, judicial procedure (except the law on the execution of detentions pending criminal investigation), the advocacy, the notary and legal advice system;
2. the civil status registry;
3. the law on associations;
4. the law on the sojourn and establishment of aliens;
5. (repealed);
6. the affairs of refugees and expellees;
7. public welfare (except the law on homes);
8. (repealed);
9. war damages and reparations;
10. war graves and the graves of other victims of war and victims of tyranny;

11. commercial law (mining, industry, energy, crafts, trade, commerce, banking and stock exchange, private insurance) except the law on the closing times for shops, on bars and restaurants, on gambling halls, on acting performance by persons, fairs, exhibitions and markets;
12. labour law including the organization of enterprises, work safety and job agency services, as well as social security including unemployment insurance;
13. the regulation of education allowances and the promotion of scientific research;
14. the law on expropriation in as far as it is relevant in the areas of Articles 73 and 74;
15. the transfer of land, natural resources and means of production into public ownership or other forms of collective concern;
16. the prevention of abuses of economically powerful positions;
17. the promotion of agricultural and forestry production (except the law on rearrangements of terrain), the securing of food supply, the import and export of agricultural and forestry products, high-seas and coastal fisheries and coastal protection;
18. the transfer of urban real estate, land law (except the law on contributions for land development) and the law on housing allowances, the law on old debt relief, the law on homebuilding premiums, the law on homebuilding for miners and miner settlement law;
19. measures against human and animal diseases that are dangerous to the public or communicable, the admission to medical and other healing professions and the healing services, as well as the law on the pharmacy system, medicines, medical products, cures, narcotics and poisons;
19a. the securing of the economic viability of hospitals and the regulation of hospital charges;
20. the law on food including the animals used for the production thereof, the law on recreational consumables, on commodities for use and on feed, as well as the safety in the trade in agricultural and forestry seeds and seedlings, the protection of plants against diseases and pests as well as animal protection;
21. high-seas and coastal shipping as well as naval signalling, inland navigation, meteorological services, shipping routes and inland waterways serving general traffic;
22. road traffic, motor transport, the construction and maintenance of country roads for long-distance traffic, as well as the levying and distribution of fees or charges for the use of public roads by vehicle;
23. railways, which are not railways of the Federation, with the exception of mountain railways;
24. waste management, air pollution control and noise abatement (except protection from behaviour-related noise);
25. state liability;
26. the medically assisted creation of human life, the analysis and artificial modification of genetic information as well as regulations concerning transplantation of organs, tissues and cells;

27. the rights and obligations deriving from the status of civil servants of States, municipalities and other public-law entities as well as judges in the States except careers, salary and support;
28. hunting;
29. nature conservation and landscape management;
30. the distribution of land;
31. regional planning;
32. water resources;
33. admissions to higher education and higher education diplomas.
(2) Statutes under sub-paragraph 1 no. 25 and 27 require the consent of the Bundesrat.

Articles 74a and 75. (Repealed).

Article 76. (1) Bills are introduced in the Bundestag by the Federal Government, from the floor of the Bundestag, or by the Bundesrat.
(2) Bills of the Federal Government must first be transmitted to the Bundesrat. The Bundesrat is entitled to give a reaction to such bills within six weeks. If it demands for important reasons, especially with regard to the size of a bill, an extension of the period, then the period is nine weeks. The Federal Government may transmit a bill, which it has by way of exception, when transmitting it to the Bundesrat, qualified as particularly urgent, to the Bundestag after three weeks or, if the Bundesrat has made a demand pursuant to the third sentence, after six weeks, even when it has not yet received the reaction of the Bundesrat; it must in that case transmit the reaction of the Bundesrat to the Bundestag without delay. In the case of bills for an amendment of this Basic Law and for the transfer of sovereign powers pursuant to Article 23 or Article 24, the period for a reaction is nine weeks; the fourth sentence does not apply.
(3) Bills of the Bundesrat must be transmitted to the Bundestag by the Federal Government within six weeks. The Federal Government, when transmitting them, is to give a statement of its opinion. If it demands for important reasons, especially with regard to the size of a bill, an extension of the period, the period is nine weeks. If the Bundesrat has by way of exception qualified a bill as particularly urgent, the period is three weeks or, if the Federal Government has made a demand pursuant to the third sentence, six weeks. In the case of bills for an amendment of this Basic Law and for the transfer of sovereign powers pursuant to Article 23 or Article 24, the period is nine weeks; the fourth sentence does not apply. The Bundestag must deliberate and decide on the bills within a reasonable time.
Article 77. (1) Federal statutes are adopted by the Bundestag. They must, after their adoption, be transmitted to the Bundesrat by the president of the Bundestag without delay.
(2) The Bundesrat may, within three weeks after receiving an adopted bill, demand that a committee for the joint consideration of bills, composed of members of the Bundestag and of the Bundesrat, be convened. The composition and procedure of this committee is regulated by rules of procedure which are adopted by the Bundes-

tag and which require the consent of the Bundesrat. The members of the Bundesrat sent to this committee are not bound by instructions. If a statute requires the consent of the Bundesrat, then also the Bundestag and the Federal Government may demand a convention. If the committee proposes an amendment to the adopted bill, the Bundestag must decide again.

(2a) In as far as a statute requires the consent of the Bundesrat, the Bundesrat, if a demand under sub-paragraph 2, first sentence, is not made or the conciliation procedure is concluded without any proposals for an amendment to the adopted bill, must decide on its consent within a reasonable time.

(3) In as far as a statute does not require the consent of the Bundesrat, the Bundesrat, once the procedure under sub-paragraph 2 is completed, may within two weeks object to a statute adopted by the Bundestag. The period for objection starts, in the case under sub-paragraph 2, last sentence, with the receipt of the new decision adopted by the Bundestag, and in all other cases with the receipt of the statement of the chairman of the committee stipulated under sub-paragraph 2 that the procedure before the committee has been concluded.

(4) If the objection is adopted by the majority of the votes of the Bundesrat, it may be rejected by a decision of the majority of the members of the Bundestag. If the Bundesrat has adopted the objection by a majority of at least two-thirds of its votes, then its rejection by the Bundestag requires a two-thirds majority, including at least a majority of the members of the Bundestag.

Article 78. A statute adopted by the Bundestag is successfully completed if the Bundesrat consents to it, or does not make a demand pursuant to Article 77 (2), or does not enter an objection within the period stipulated in Article 77 (3) or withdraws such objection, or if the objection is overridden by the Bundestag.

Article 79. (1) The Basic Law may be amended only by a statute which expressly amends or supplements its text. In the case of international treaties which have as their object a peace settlement, the preparation of a peace settlement or the phasing out of an occupation regime, or which are intended to serve the defence of the Federal Republic, a clarification that the provisions of the Basic Law do not preclude the conclusion and entry into force of such treaties requires only a supplement to the text of the Basic Law which is confined to such clarification.

(2) Any such statute requires the approval by two-thirds of the members of the Bundestag and two-thirds of the votes of the Bundesrat.

(3) Any amendment to this Basic Law affecting the division of the Federation into States, the participation of the States in principle in the legislative process, or the principles laid down in Articles 1 and 20, is inadmissible.

Article 80. (1) By statute, the Federal Government, a federal minister or the State governments may be authorized to adopt ordinances [Rechtsverordnungen]. In that case, the content, purpose and scope of the given authorization must be determined in the statute. The legal basis must be stated in the ordinance. If by statute it is provided that an authorization may be delegated further, then such authorization of a delegation requires an ordinance.

(2) The consent of the Bundesrat is required, save for federal statutory regulations providing otherwise, for ordinances of the Federal Government or a federal minister regarding the principles and charges for the use of the facilities of the post and telecommunications system, regarding the principles of the levying of charges for the use of the facilities of the railways of the Federation, regarding the construction and operation of railways, as well as ordinances based on federal statutes which require the consent of the Bundesrat or which are executed by the States on behalf of the Federation or as their own affairs.

(3) The Bundesrat may transmit to the Federal Government proposals for the adoption of ordinances which require its consent.

(4) In as far as State governments are authorized to adopt ordinances by federal statute or pursuant to federal statutes, the States are also competent to regulate by statute.

Article 80a. (1) If this Basic Law or a federal statute regarding defence including the protection of the civilian population provides that regulations may be applied only within the guidelines of this Article, then such application except in a state of defence is only permissible when the Bundestag has declared the beginning of a state of tension [Spannungsfall] or when it has approved such application explicitly. The declaration of a state of tension and the special approval in the cases of Article 12a (5), first sentence, and (6), second sentence, require a majority of two-thirds of votes cast.

(2) Measures pursuant to regulations under sub-paragraph 1 must be lifted when the Bundestag so demands.

(3) By deviation from sub-paragraph 1, the application of such regulations is permissible also on the basis and within the guidelines of a decision that is taken by an international body in the framework of an alliance treaty with the consent of the Federal Government. Measures under this sub-paragraph must be lifted when the Bundestag by the majority of its members so demands.

Article 81. (1) If in the case of Article 68 the Bundestag is not dissolved, the Federal President may, upon request of the Federal Government with the consent of the Bundesrat, declare a legislative emergency [Gesetzgebungsnotstand] for a bill if the Bundestag rejects it although the Federal Government has qualified it as urgent. The same applies when a bill has been rejected although the Federal Chancellor had linked it to a motion under Article 68.

(2) If the Bundestag rejects the bill after the declaration of a legislative emergency again or if it adopts it in a version qualified as unacceptable by the Federal Government, then the statute is deemed adopted if the Bundesrat consents to it. The same applies when the bill has not been adopted by the Bundestag within four weeks after the new introduction.

(3) During the term of office of a Federal Chancellor, also any other bill rejected by the Bundestag may be adopted within a period of six months following the first declaration of a legislative emergency under sub-paragraphs 1 and 2. After the

period has lapsed, during the term of office of that same Federal Chancellor another declaration of a legislative emergency is not permissible.

(4) The Basic Law may be neither amended nor wholly or partly suspended or rendered inapplicable by a statute that has been adopted under sub-paragraph 2.

Article 82. (1) Statutes completed in accordance with the provisions of this Basic Law are, after counter-signature, certified by the Federal President and published in the Federal Law Gazette [Bundesgesetzblatt]. Ordinances are certified by the organ which adopts them and are, save for other statutory regulations, published in the Federal Law Gazette.

(2) All statutes and all ordinances are to determine the day of entry into force. If such a provision is lacking, they enter into force on the fourteenth day after the end of the day when the Federal Law Gazette has been published.

VIII. The execution of federal statutes and the federal administration

Article 83. The States execute federal statutes as their own affairs in as far as this Basic Law does not otherwise provide or permit.

Article 84. (1) Where the States execute federal statutes as their own affairs, they regulate the establishment of authorities and the administrative procedure. Where federal statutes provide otherwise, the States may make adopt regulations in deviation therefrom. Where a State has adopted a deviating regulation pursuant to the second sentence, subsequent federal regulations regarding the establishment of authorities and the administrative procedure relating to this enter into force in that State at the earliest six months after their publication, in as far as nothing is provided otherwise with the consent of the Bundesrat. Article 72 (3) third sentence applies mutatis mutandis. In exceptional cases the Federation may, because of a special need for uniform federal regulation, regulate the administrative procedure without a possibility of deviation for the States. Such statutes require the consent of the Bundesrat. A federal statute may not delegate tasks to municipalities and associations of municipalities.

(2) The Federal Government may, with the consent of the Bundesrat, issue general administrative regulations.

(3) The Federal Government exercises supervision to ensure that the States execute federal statutes in accordance with applicable law. The Federal Government may, for this purpose, send agents to the highest State authorities, with their consent or, if such consent is refused, with the consent of the Bundesrat, also to subordinate authorities.

(4) Should shortcomings which the Federal Government has established in the execution of federal statutes in the States not be corrected, the Bundesrat decides, at the request of the Federal Government or the State concerned, whether the State has violated the law. The decision of the Bundesrat may be challenged before the Federal Constitutional Court.

(5) The Federal Government may, by federal statute which requires the consent of the Bundesrat, be granted authorization, for the execution of federal statutes, to

issue individual instructions in particular cases. They are, unless the Federal Government considers the matter urgent, to be addressed to the highest States authorities.

Article 85. (1) Where the States execute federal statutes on behalf of the Federation, the establishment of the authorities remains the concern of the States, unless federal statutes with the consent of the Bundesrat provide otherwise. A federal statute may not delegate tasks to municipalities and associations of municipalities.
(2) The Federal Government may, with the consent of the Bundesrat, issue general administrative regulations. It may regulate the uniform training of civil servants and employees. The heads of intermediate authorities are to be appointed with its approval.
(3) The State authorities are subordinate to the instructions of the competent highest federal authorities. The instructions are, unless the Federal Government considers the matter urgent, to be addressed to the highest State authorities. Execution of the instructions is to be ensured by the highest State authorities.
(4) Federal supervision extends to the lawfulness and expediency of execution. The Federal Government may, for this purpose, require reporting and submission of files and send agents to all authorities.

Article 86. Where the Federation executes statutes by direct federal administration or by directly federal entities or institutions of public law, the Federal Government issues, to the extent that a statute does not provide details, the general administrative regulations. It regulates, unless statute provides otherwise, the establishment of the authorities.

Article 87. (1) The Foreign Service [Auswärtiger Dienst], the Federal Revenue Administration [Bundesfinanzverwaltung] and, pursuant to Article 89, the administration of the federal waterways and navigation are managed by direct federal administration with a dedicated administrative substructure. By federal statute federal border guard authorities [Bundesgrenzschutzbehörden], and central offices for police information and communications, for the criminal police and for the collection of documents for the purposes of domestic intelligence [Verfassungsschutz] and of protection against endeavours on federal territory which, through the use of force or preparatory acts thereto endanger the foreign interests of the Federal Republic of Germany, may be established.
(2) Social insurance institutions whose competence extends beyond the territory of one State are managed as directly federal entities of public law. Social insurance institutions whose competence extends beyond the territory of one State but not more than three States are managed in deviation from the first sentence as directly State entities of public law if the supervising State is determined by the States involved.
(3) In addition, for matters on which the Federation is competent to legislate, independent higher federal authorities as well as new directly federal entities and institutions of public law may be established by federal statute. Where new tasks

arise for the Federation in matters on which it has the power to legislate, then in cases of urgent need federal authorities at the intermediate and lower levels may be established with the consent of the Bundesrat and of the majority of the members of the Bundestag.

Article 87a. (1) The Federation establishes armed forces for the purpose of defence. Their numerical strength and the general outline of their organization must follow from the budget.
(2) Except for defence, the armed forces may only be deployed to the extent explicitly permitted by this Basic Law.
(3) The armed forces have, in a state of defence and in a state of tension [Spannungsfall], the competence to protect civilian objects and to perform tasks of traffic control to the extent that this is required for the accomplishment of their defence mission. Furthermore, during a state of defence or a state of tension the armed forces may also be assigned to protect civilian objects so as to support police measures; in such case the armed forces cooperate with the competent authorities.
(4) In order to avert an imminent danger to the existence or liberal democratic fundamental order of the Federation or of a State, the Federal Government may, if the conditions of Article 91 (2) are fulfilled and the police forces as well as the Federal Border Guard [Bundesgrenzschutz] are not sufficient, deploy the armed forces to support the police and the Federal Border Guard in protecting civilian objects and in fighting organized and militarily armed insurgents. The deployment of the armed forces is to be discontinued if the Bundestag or the Bundesrat so demands.

Article 87b. (1) The Federal Armed Forces Administration [Bundeswehrverwaltung] is managed by direct federal administration with a dedicated administrative substructure. It performs tasks of personnel management and tasks to cover the immediate material requirements of the armed forces. Tasks related to the maintenance of injured persons or construction work may only be delegated to the Federal Armed Forces Administration by federal statute which requires the consent of the Bundesrat. The consent of the Bundesrat is furthermore required for statutes to the extent that they authorize the Federal Armed Forces Administration to interfere with the rights of third parties; this does not apply to statutes in the area of personnel management.
(2) In addition, federal statutes concerning defence, including recruitment for military service and the protection of the civilian population may, with the consent of the Bundesrat, provide that they be executed, wholly or in part, by direct federal administration with a dedicated administrative substructure or by the States on behalf of the Federation. Where such statutes are executed by the States on behalf of the Federation, they may, with the consent of the Bundesrat, provide that the powers appertaining to the Federation and the competent supreme federal authorities pursuant to Article 85 are delegated wholly or in part to higher federal authorities; in such case it may be provided that these authorities do not require the consent of the Bundesrat in issuing general administrative regulations pursuant to Article 85 (2) first sentence.

Article 87c. Statutes that are enacted pursuant to Article 73 (1) no. 14, may, with the consent of the Bundesrat, provide that they be executed by the States on behalf of the Federation.

Article 87d. (1) The air traffic administration is managed by federal administration. Tasks related to air traffic control may also be executed by foreign air traffic organizations that are authorized pursuant to European Community law. Details are regulated by a federal statute.
(2) A federal statute requiring the consent of the Bundesrat may delegate tasks relating to air traffic administration to the States as commissioned administration [Auftragsverwaltung].

Article 87e. (1) The railway transport administration for railways of the Federation is managed by direct federal administration. By federal statute tasks relating to the railway transport administration may be delegated to the States as their own affairs.
(2) The Federation discharges tasks relating to the railway transport administration extending beyond the area of the railways of the Federation that are delegated to it by federal statute.
(3) Railways of the Federation are managed as commercial enterprises established under private law. These are owned by the Federation, to the extent that the activities of the commercial enterprise comprise the construction, maintenance and the operation of railroads. The transfer of federal shares in these commercial enterprises under to the second sentence is effected pursuant to a statute; the majority of the shares remains with the Federation. Details are regulated by a federal statute.
(4) The Federation ensures that account be taken of the benefit of the general public, especially the transportation needs, in developing and maintaining the federal railroad network of the railways of the Federation as well as in their transportation services on that railroad network, to the extent that they do not concern local passenger rail services. Details are regulated by a federal statute.
(5) Statutes enacted pursuant to sub-paragraphs 1 to 4 require the consent of the Bundesrat. The consent of the Bundesrat is furthermore required for statutes which regulate the dissolution, merger and splitting-up of railway enterprises of the Federation, the transfer of railway tracks of the railways of the Federation to third parties as well as the abandonment of railroad tracks of railways of the Federation or which affect local passenger rail services.

Article 87f. (1) Within the guidelines of a federal statute requiring the consent of the Bundesrat, the Federation ensures area-wide adequate and sufficient services in the area of post and telecommunications.
(2) Services within the meaning of sub-paragraph 1 are provided as private commercial activities by the enterprises that emerged from the special asset German Federal Post Office [Deutsche Bundespost] and by other private providers. Sovereign tasks in the area of post and telecommunications are performed by direct federal administration.

(3) Without prejudice to sub-paragraph 2 second sentence, the Federation, in the form of a directly federal institution of public law, performs particular tasks with respect to the enterprises that emerged from the special asset German Federal Post Office within the guidelines of a federal statute.

Article 88. The Federation establishes a currency bank and bank of issue as the Federal Bank [Bundesbank]. Its tasks and powers may, within the framework of the European Union, be transferred to the European Central Bank, which is independent and committed to the primary goal of securing price stability.

Article 89. (1) The Federation is the owner of the former Reich waterways.
(2) The Federation manages the federal waterways through its own authorities. It performs the state tasks of inland navigation extending beyond the area of a single State and the tasks of maritime navigation which are assigned to it by statute. It may assign the management of federal waterways, to the extent that they lie within the territory of one State, upon request to that State as commissioned administration. If a waterway touches the territory of several States, the Federation may commission the State which is designated by the States concerned.
(3) In the administration, development and new construction of waterways, the requirements of land and water management are to be observed in agreement with the States.

Article 90. (1) The Federation is the owner of the former Reich motorways [Reichsautobahnen] and Reich roads.
(2) The States or the self-governing entities competent under State law manage the federal motorways [Bundesautobahnen] and other federal roads for long-distance traffic on behalf of the Federation.
(3) Upon the request by a State, the Federation may place federal motorways and other federal roads for long-distance traffic, to the extent that they lie within the territory of that State, under direct federal administration.

Article 91. (1) In order to avert an imminent danger to the existence or the liberal democratic fundamental order of the Federation or of a State, a State may request the services of the police forces of other States as well as forces and institutions of other administrations and of the Federal Border Guard [Bundesgrenzschutz].
(2) If the State where such danger is imminent is not itself prepared or able to combat the danger, the Federal Government may place the police in that State and police forces of other States under its own authority and deploy units of the Federal Border Guard. The order is to be lifted after the removal of the danger and, otherwise, at any time upon the demand of the Bundesrat. Where the danger extends to the territory of more than one State, the Federal Government may, to the extent that this is necessary for the effective combating, issue instructions to the State governments; the first and second sentence remain unaffected.

VIIIa. Joint tasks

Article 91a. (1) The Federation participates in the fulfilment of the tasks of the States in the following areas, if these tasks are important for the whole and the participation of the Federation is necessary for the improvement of living standards (joint tasks):
1. improvement of regional economic structure,
2. improvement of agricultural structure and coastal protection.

(2) By federal statute with the consent of the Bundesrat, joint tasks as well as the details of coordination are determined.

(3) The Federation bears in the cases of sub-paragraph 1 no. 1 half of the costs in each State. In the cases of sub-paragraph 1 no. 2, the Federation bears at least half; the contribution must be fixed uniformly for all States. Details are regulated by statute. The making available of funds remains a matter for the adoption of the budgets of the Federation and the States.

Article 91b. (1) The Federation and the States may, on the basis of agreements in cases of importance that transcends regions, cooperate in the promotion of:
1. establishments and projects of scientific research outside the universities;
2. projects of science and research at universities;
3. research facilities at universities including large machines.

Agreements under the first sentence, no. 2, require the consent of all States.

(2) The Federation and the States may cooperate on the basis of agreements for the assessment of the effectiveness of the educational system in international comparison and on reports and recommendations in that matter.

(3) The allocation of the financial burden is regulated in the agreement.

Article 91c. (1) The Federation and the States may cooperate in the planning, establishment and operation of the information systems needed for the fulfilment of their tasks.

(2) The Federation and the States may on the basis of agreements establish the standards and security requirements necessary for the communication between their information systems. Agreements concerning the principles of the cooperation pursuant to the first sentence may provide for individual tasks, circumscribed with regard to their content and extent, that details enter into force for the Federation and the States with the consent of a qualified majority to be determined by the agreement. They require the consent of the Bundestag and the parliaments of the participating States; the right to terminate these agreements may not be excluded. The agreements also regulate the bearing of burdens.

(3) The States may furthermore agree on the joint operation of information systems and the establishment of dedicated institutions.

(4) The Federation establishes a connecting network in order to connect the information systems of the Federation and of the States. The details regarding the establishment and the operation of the connecting network are regulated by federal statute which requires the consent of the Bundesrat.

Article 91d. The Federation and the States may, in order to determine and promote the performance of their administrations, conduct comparative studies and publish the results.

Article 91e. (1) In the execution of federal statutes in the area of basic social security for jobseekers, the Federation and the States or the municipalities and associations of municipalities competent under State law cooperate, as a rule, in joint institutions.
(2) The Federation may allow that a limited number of municipalities and associations of municipalities, on their request and with the consent of the supreme State authority, exercises the tasks under sub-paragraph 1 alone. The necessary expenditure including administrative costs are borne by the Federation, to the extent that in an execution of statutes pursuant to sub-paragraph 1 the tasks are to be exercised by the Federation.
(3) Details are regulated by a federal statute which requires the consent of the Bundesrat.

IX. The judiciary

Article 92. Judicial power is vested in the judges; it is exercised by the Federal Constitutional Court, by the federal courts provided for in this Basic Law, and by the courts of the States.

Article 93. (1) The Federal Constitutional Court [Bundesverfassungsgericht] rules:
1. on the interpretation of this Basic Law in the event of disputes concerning the extent of the rights and duties of a supreme federal body or of other parties vested with rights of their own by this Basic Law or by the rules of procedure of a supreme federal body;
2. in the event of disagreements or doubts regarding the formal or substantive compatibility of federal law or State law with this Basic Law, or the compatibility of State law with other federal law, on application of the Federal Government, a State government or one-quarter of the members of the Bundestag;
2a. in the event of disagreements whether a statute complies with the conditions under Article 72 (2) on application of the Bundesrat, a State government or the parliament of a State;
3. in the event of disagreements regarding the rights and duties of the Federation and the States, especially as regards the execution of federal law by the States and the performance of federal supervision;
4. in other public-law disputes between the Federation and the States, between different States, or within one State, in as far as another recourse is not available;
4a. on constitutional complaints, which may be filed by any person with the allegation that one of his fundamental rights or one of his rights contained in Article 20 (4), 33, 38, 101, 103 and 104 has been violated by public authority;
4b. on constitutional complaints of municipalities or associations of municipalities based on a violation of the right to self-government pursuant to Article 28 by a

statute, or by State legislation yet only in as far as no complaint may be filed with the State constitutional court;
4c. on objections of associations to their non-recognition as a party for elections of the Bundestag;
5. in the other cases provided by this Basic Law.
(2) The Federal Constitutional Court furthermore rules on the application of the Bundesrat, a State government or the parliament of a State whether in the case of Article 72 (4) the need for a federal statutory regulation under Article 72 (2) no longer exists or whether in the cases of Article 125a (2), first sentence, federal law could no longer be adopted. The finding that the need has ceased to exist or that federal law could no longer be adopted replaces a federal statute under Article 72 (4) or Article 125a (2), second sentence. An application under the first sentence is admissible only when a bill under Article 72 (4) or Article 125a (2), second sentence, has been rejected in the Bundestag or is not deliberated and decided upon within one year or when such bill has been rejected in the Bundesrat.
(3) The Federal Constitutional Court furthermore becomes active in the other cases assigned by federal statute.

Article 94. (1) The Federal Constitutional Court is composed of federal judges and other members. Half of the members of the Federal Constitutional Court are elected by the Bundestag and half by the Bundesrat. They may not be members of the Bundestag, the Bundesrat, the Federal Government or equivalent bodies of a State.
(2) A federal statute regulates its organization and its procedures and determines in which cases its decisions have statutory force. It may make the prior exhaustion of judicial remedies a precondition for constitutional complaints and stipulate a special admissibility procedure.

Article 95. (1) For the areas of general, administrative, tax, labour and social-security jurisdiction, the Federation establishes as supreme courts the Federal Supreme Court [Bundesgerichtshof], the Federal Administrative Court, the Federal Tax Court, the Federal Labour Court and the Federal Social-Security Court.
(2) The appointment of judges at these courts is decided by the federal minister competent for the respective subject-matter together with a judicial nomination committee [Richterwahlausschuss] which is composed of the ministers from the States competent for the respective subject-matter and an equal number of members who are elected by the Bundestag.
(3) For the upholding of the unity of jurisprudence, a Joint Chamber of the courts stipulated in sub-paragraph 1 must be established. Details are regulated by a federal statute.

Article 96. (1) The Federation may establish a federal court for intellectual property law.
(2) The Federation may establish courts of military criminal justice for the armed forces as federal courts. They may exercise criminal law jurisdiction only in a state of defence as well as over members of the armed forces who are deployed abroad or

are serving on board of warships. Details are regulated by a federal statute. These courts fall within the competence of the Federal minister of justice. Their salaried judges must possess the qualifications to be a judge.

(3) The supreme court for the courts stipulated in sub-paragraphs 1 and 2 is the Federal Supreme Court.

(4) The Federation may, for persons in a public-law service relation to it, establish federal courts to decide in disciplinary and complaint procedures.

(5) For criminal procedures in the following areas, a federal statute with the consent of the Bundesrat may provide that State courts are to exercise the jurisdiction of the Federation:

1. genocide;
2. crimes against humanity under international criminal law;
3. war crimes;
4. other acts that are capable of and are committed with the intent to disturb the peaceful coexistence of nations (Article 26 (1));
5. protection of the state.

Article 97. (1) Judges are independent and are subject only to the law.

(2) Judges who are salaried and appointed permanently may be dismissed or suspended in their function permanently or temporarily or be transferred to another post or made to retire before the expiry of their term against their will only by virtue of a judicial decision and only for reasons and in the form provided by statutes. Legislation may determine age limits upon the reaching of which judges appointed for life retire. In the context of changes to the organization of courts or their districts, judges may be transferred to another court or removed from office, yet only while preserving their full salary.

Article 98. (1) The legal position of federal judges is to be regulated by a special federal statute.

(2) If a federal judge violates, in the exercise of his office or outside, the principles of the Basic Law or the constitutional order of a State, then the Federal Constitutional Court may order by a two-thirds majority upon request of the Bundestag that the judge be transferred to a different post or be made to retire. In case of an intentional violation, dismissal may be ordered.

(3) The legal position of judges in the States is to be regulated by special State statutes, in as far as Article 74 (1) no. 27 does not provide otherwise.

(4) The States may provide that the State minister of justice decides together with a judicial nomination committee over the appointment of judges in the States.

(5) The States may, as regards State judges, provide for a regulation corresponding to sub-paragraph 2. State constitutional law in force remains unaffected. The Federal Constitutional Court may decide over the prosecution of a judge.

Article 99. By State statute, the Federal Constitutional Court may be assigned the jurisdiction to decide in constitutional disputes within one State, and the supreme courts stipulated in Article 95 (1) may be assigned last-instance jurisdiction to decide in cases where the application of State law is of the issue.

Article 100. (1) If a court concludes that a statute on the validity of which its decision depends is unconstitutional, then the proceedings are to be stayed, and, where a violation of the constitution of a State is of the issue, a decision is to be obtained from the State court which is competent for constitutional disputes, or, when a violation of this Basic Law is of the issue, a decision from the Federal Constitutional Court is to be obtained. The same applies where a violation of this Basic Law by State law or an incompatibility between State statute and a federal statute is of the issue.
(2) If in a judicial dispute it is doubtful whether a rule of international law is part of federal law and whether it directly creates rights and obligations for individuals (Article 25), then the court must obtain a decision from the Federal Constitutional Court.
(3) If the constitutional court of a State wishes to deviate from a decision of the Federal Constitutional Court or the constitutional court of another State in the interpretation of the Basic Law, then the constitutional court must obtain a decision from the Federal Constitutional Court.

Article 101. (1) Extraordinary tribunals are inadmissible. No-one may be deprived of his right to a lawful judge.
(2) Courts for special subject-areas may be established only by statute.

Article 102. The death penalty is abolished.

Article 103. (1) Before a court, everyone has the right to a hearing in accordance with the law.
(2) An act may be punished only when the liability to punishment was determined by statute before the act was committed.
(3) No-one may be punished several times on the basis of general criminal statutes for the same act.

Article 104. (1) The freedom of a person may be limited only pursuant to a formal statute and only in accordance with the form prescribed therein. Detained persons may not be abused either psychologically or physically.
(2) The permissibility and continuation of a deprivation of freedom is decided only by a judge. In all cases of a deprivation of freedom that are not based on a court order, a judicial decision must be obtained without delay. The police may, based on their own powers, detain no-one any longer than until the end of the day following the arrest. Details must be regulated statutorily.
(3) Everyone provisionally detained based on the suspicion of a criminal act must, at the latest on the day following the arrest, be brought before a judge who must inform him of the reasons for the arrest, question him, and give him an opportunity to object. The judge must without delay either issue a written arrest warrant stating the reasons, or order a release.

(4) A relative [Angehöriger] of the detainee or a person of his trust must be notified without delay of any judicial decision regarding the order or continuation of a deprivation of freedom.

X. The finances system

Article 104a. (1) The Federation and the States bear the costs resulting from the exercise of their tasks separately to the extent that this Basic Law does not provide otherwise.
(2) Where the States act on behalf of the Federation, the Federation bears the costs resulting therefrom.
(3) Federal statutes that confer pecuniary benefits and are executed by the States may provide that the pecuniary benefits are borne wholly or in part by the Federation. Where the statute provides that the Federation bears half of the costs or more, it is executed on behalf of the Federation.
(4) Federal statutes that establish obligations for the States to provide pecuniary benefits, benefits in kind with pecuniary value, or comparable services with respect to third parties and that are executed by the States as their own affairs or pursuant to sub-paragraph 3, second sentence, on behalf of the Federation, require the consent of the Bundesrat, if the costs resulting therefrom are to be borne by the States.
(5) The Federation and the States bear the administrative costs arising for their administrative authorities and are liable to each other for ensuring a proper administration. Details are regulated by a federal statute which requires the consent of the Bundesrat.
(6) The Federation and the States bear the burdens of a violation of supranational or international-law obligations of Germany according to the domestic distribution of responsibilities and tasks. In cases of financial corrections of the European Union affecting several States, the Federation and the States bear these burdens at a ratio of 15 to 85. In such case the collectivity of the States bears 35 percent of the total burdens in mutual solidarity pursuant to a general key; 50 percent are borne by the States that caused the burdens, proportionate to the amount of the funds received. Details are regulated by a federal statute which requires the consent of the Bundesrat.

Article 104b. (1) The Federation may, to the extent that this Basic Law confers legislative competences upon it, grant financial aids to the States for particularly significant investments of the States and municipalities (associations of municipalities) that are required to
1. avert a disturbance of the macro-economic equilibrium or to
2. equalize diverging economic strengths in the federal territory or to
3. stimulate economic growth.
In deviation from the first sentence, the Federation may, in cases of natural disasters or exceptional emergencies that are beyond the state's control and substantially compromise the state financial situation, grant financial aids even without legislative competences.

(2) Details, particularly the kinds of investments to be supported, are regulated by federal statute which requires the consent of the Bundesrat, or pursuant to the Federal Budget Act [Bundeshaushaltsgesetz] by administrative agreement. The funds are to be granted for a limited time period and to be reviewed at regular intervals with respect to their use. The financial aids are to be administered with annual sums decreasing over time.
(3) The Bundestag, the Federal Government and the Bundesrat are, upon request, to be informed about the execution of the measures and the improvements achieved.

Article 105. (1) The Federation has exclusive legislative power regarding customs duties and fiscal monopolies.
(2) The Federation has concurrent legislative power regarding other taxes where it is entitled, wholly or in part, to the revenue generated by these taxes, or where the conditions of Article 72 (2) are met.
(2a) The States have competence to legislate regarding local consumption and expenditure taxes for as long as and to the extent that they are not equivalent to taxes regulated by federal statute. They have competence to determine the tax rate of the real estate acquisition tax.
(3) Federal statutes regarding taxes whose revenue flows wholly or in part to the States or the municipalities (associations of municipalities) require the consent of the Bundesrat.

Article 106. (1) The Federation is entitled to the yield of fiscal monopolies and to the revenue from the following taxes:
1. customs duties;
2. consumption taxes, to the extent that they are not due to the States pursuant to sub-paragraph 2 or jointly to the Federation and the States pursuant to sub-paragraph 3 or to the municipalities pursuant to sub-paragraph 6;
3. the road freight transportation tax, the motor vehicle tax and other traffic taxes related to motorized transportation;
4. capital transactions taxes, the insurance tax and the exchange tax;
5. one-time levies on property and compensation levies raised for the implementation of the equalization of burdens;
6. the supplementary levy on the income tax and corporation tax;
7. levies within the framework of the European Communities.
(2) The States are entitled to the revenue from the following taxes:
1. the property tax;
2. the inheritance tax;
3. the traffic taxes to the extent that they are not due to the Federation pursuant to sub-paragraph 1 or jointly to the Federation and the States pursuant to sub-paragraph 3;
4. the beer tax;
5. the levies of casinos.
(3) The revenue from the income tax, the corporation tax and the turnover tax is due to the Federation and the States jointly (joint taxes) to the extent that pursuant to

sub-paragraph 5 the revenue from the income tax and pursuant to sub-paragraph 5a the revenue from the turnover tax is not allocated with the municipalities. The revenue from the income tax and the corporation tax is shared equally between the Federation and the States. The respective shares of the Federation and the States in the revenue from the turnover tax are determined by a federal statute that requires the consent of the Bundesrat. This determination is to be based on the following principles:

1. Within the framework of current revenues, the Federation and the States have an equal claim to recover their necessary expenditures. The extent of these expenditures is to be determined with regard to multi-annual financial planning.

2. The coverage requirements of the Federation and the States are to be coordinated in such way that a fair balance is achieved, an excessive burden on the taxpayers is avoided, and uniformity of living standards throughout the federal territory is maintained.

In addition, in the determination of the respective shares of the Federation and the States in the revenue from the turnover tax, losses in tax revenue incurred by the States from 1 January 1996 because of the consideration of children in income tax law are also to be taken into account. Details are regulated by the federal statute enacted pursuant to the third sentence.

(4) The respective shares of the Federation and the States in the turnover tax is to be determined anew when the ratio between revenue and expenditure of the Federation and the States develops in a substantially different manner; losses of revenue that are additionally taken into account under sub-paragraph 3, fifth sentence, in determining the respective shares in the turnover tax remain disregarded in that context. Where additional tasks are assigned to or revenue is withdrawn from the States by federal statute, then the additional burden may be compensated by federal grants pursuant to a federal statute which requires the consent of the Bundesrat, if it is limited to a short time period. In the statute, the principles for calculating these grants and for their distribution among the States are to be established.

(5) The municipalities receive a share in the revenue of the income tax that is to be passed on by the States to their municipalities on the basis of the income tax payments of their inhabitants. Details are regulated by a federal statute which requires the consent of the Bundesrat. It may provide that municipalities may establish rate factors [Hebesatz] for the municipalities' share.

(5a) The municipalities receive a share in the revenue of the turnover tax from 1 January 1998. It is passed on by the States on the basis of a geographical and economic key. Details are regulated by a federal statute requiring the consent of the Bundesrat.

(6) The revenue from the real property tax and the trade tax is due to the municipalities; revenue from local consumption and expenditure taxes is due to the municipalities or, in accordance with State legislation, to the associations of municipalities. Municipalities are to be granted the right to establish rate factors for the real property tax and the trade tax within the framework of the statutes. Where there are no municipalities in a State, revenue from the real property tax and the trade tax as well as revenue from local consumption and expenditure taxes is due to the State. The Federation and the States may, by virtue of an apportionment, share

in the revenue from the trade tax. Details regarding the apportionment are regulated by a federal statute which requires the consent of the Bundesrat. In accordance with State legislation, the real property tax and the trade tax as well as the municipalities' share of the revenue from the income tax and turnover tax may be taken as a calculation basis for determining apportionments.

(7) From the State' share of the total revenue from joint taxes, a percentage to be determined by State legislation flows to the municipalities and associations of municipalities collectively. For the rest, State legislation determines whether and to what extent revenues from State taxes are due to municipalities (associations of municipalities).

(8) Where the Federation arranges for special facilities in individual States or municipalities (associations of municipalities) which directly result in an increase of expenditure or a loss of revenue (special burdens) for these States or municipalities (associations of municipalities), the Federation grants the necessary compensation where and to the extent that States or municipalities (associations of municipalities) cannot reasonably be expected to bear the special burdens. Compensations from third parties and financial benefits arising for the States or municipalities (associations of municipalities) from the facilities are to be taken into account in granting the compensation.

(9) Revenues and expenditures of municipalities (associations of municipalities) are considered to be States revenues and expenditures for the purposes of this Article.

Article 106a. The States are entitled, from 1 January 1996, to a sum from the tax revenue of the Federation for local public transport. Details are regulated by a federal statute which requires the consent of the Bundesrat. The sum pursuant to the first sentence is not taken into account in the assessment of financial strength pursuant to Article 107 (2).

Article 106b. The States are entitled from 1 July 2009 to a sum from the tax revenue of the Federation in consequence of the transfer of the motor vehicle tax to the Federation. Details are regulated by a federal statute which requires the consent of the Bundesrat.

Article 107. (1) The revenue from State taxes and the States' share of revenue from the income tax and the corporation tax belongs to the individual States to the extent that the taxes are collected by tax authorities within their territories (local revenue). A federal statute which requires the consent of the Bundesrat is to make more detailed provisions for the corporation tax and the wage tax regarding the delimitation as well as the manner and scope of the disaggregation of the local revenue. The statute may also make provision for the delimitation and disaggregation of local revenue from other taxes. The States' share of revenue from the turnover tax belongs to the individual States in accordance with their population numbers; for a part, but not for more than a quarter of that States' share, a federal statute which requires the consent of the Bundesrat may provide for supplementary shares for those States whose revenue per capita from State taxes, from the income tax and the corporation tax and pursuant to Article 106b is below the average of the States; for the real estate acquisition tax, the tax capacity is to be taken into account.

(2) It is to be ensured by statute that the diverging financial strengths of the States is appropriately equalized; at this the financial strength and financial requirements of municipalities (associations of municipalities) are to be taken into account. The conditions governing equalization claims of States entitled to equalization payments as well equalization duties of States obliged to provide equalization payments as well as the criteria for determining the amounts of equalization payments are to be specified in the statute. It may also provide that the Federation provides grants from its own funds to financially weak States in order to complement the coverage of their general financial requirements (supplementary grants).

Article 108. (1) Customs duties, fiscal monopolies, consumption taxes regulated by federal legislation including the import turnover tax, as well as the motor vehicle tax and other traffic taxes related to motorized transportation from 1 July 2009 onwards and charges within the framework of the European Communities are administered by federal tax authorities. The organization of these authorities is regulated by a federal statute. Where intermediate authorities are established, their heads are appointed in consultation with the State governments.

(2) The remaining taxes are administered by State tax authorities. The organization of these authorities and the uniform training of their civil servants may be regulated by a federal statute which requires the consent of the Bundesrat. Where intermediate authorities are established, their heads are appointed in agreement with the Federal Government.

(3) Where State tax authorities administer taxes which flow wholly or in part to the Federation, they act on behalf of the Federation. Article 85 (3) and (4) applies with the proviso that the Federal Government is substituted by the Minister of Finance.

(4) A federal statute which requires the consent of the Bundesrat may provide for a collaboration in the administration of taxes between federal and State tax authorities as well as in the case of taxes under sub-paragraph 1 for administration by State tax authorities or in the case of other taxes for their administration by federal tax authorities if and to the extent that the execution of tax laws will thereby be substantially facilitated or improved. For the taxes flowing exclusively to the municipalities (associations of municipalities), the administration that State tax authorities are entitled to may be delegated by the States to the municipalities (associations of municipalities) wholly or in part.

(5) The procedures to be applied by federal tax authorities are regulated by a federal statute. The procedures to be applied by State tax authorities, or, as provided by the second sentence of sub-paragraph 4, by municipalities (associations of municipalities) may be regulated by a federal statute which requires the consent of the Bundesrat.

(6) Financial jurisdiction is uniformly regulated by a federal statute.

(7) The Federal Government may issue general administrative rules, which require the consent of the Bundesrat to the extent that the administration is incumbent upon State tax authorities or municipalities (associations of municipalities).

Article 109. (1) The Federation and the States are autonomous and independent from one another in their budget management.
(2) The Federation and the States jointly fulfil the responsibilities of the Federal Republic of Germany arising from legal acts of the European Community on the basis of Article 104 of the Treaty establishing the European Community for compliance with budgetary discipline and, within this framework, take due account of the requirements of the macro-economic equilibrium.
(3) The budgets of the Federation and the States are in principle to be balanced without revenue from credits. The Federation and the States may provide regulations regarding the consideration that is symmetrical for the upturn and downturn of the effects of an economic development that is deviating from the normal situation as well as an exception for natural disasters or exceptional emergencies that are beyond the state's control and that substantially compromise the state financial situation. For the exception, a corresponding redemption regulation is to be provided. Further details for the budget of the Federation are regulated by Article 115 with the proviso that the first sentence is complied with if the revenue from credits does not exceed 0.35 percent in proportion to the nominal gross domestic product. Details for the budgets of the States are regulated by them within the framework of their constitutional competences with the proviso that the first sentence is only complied with if no revenue from credits is admitted.
(4) By federal statute which requires the consent of the Bundesrat, common principles applying to the budgetary law, to budget management in line with cyclical economic requirements and to multi-annual financial planning may be established for the Federation and the States.
(5) Sanctions imposed by the European Community in relation to the provisions of Article 104 of the Treaty establishing the European Community for compliance with budgetary discipline are borne by the Federation and the States in a ratio of 65 to 35. The collectivity of the States bears 35 percent of the burdens allocated with the States in mutual solidarity and in proportion to their population; 65 percent of the burdens allocated with to the States is borne by the States in accordance with their share of causation. Details are regulated by a federal statute which requires the consent of the Bundesrat.

Article 109a. In order to avoid budgetary emergencies, a federal statute which requires the consent of the Bundesrat regulates
1. the continuous supervision of the budget management of the Federation and the States by a common panel (stability council [Stabilitätsrat]),
2. the requirements and the procedures for determining an imminent budgetary emergency,
3. the principles for establishing and executing restructuring programmes to avoid budgetary emergencies.
The decisions of the stability council and the underlying documentation of the deliberations are to be published.

Article 110. (1) All revenues and expenditures of the Federation are to be included in the budget; for federal enterprises and special assets only allocations or withdrawals need to be included. The budget is to be balanced for revenues and expenditures.
(2) The budget is established for one or more fiscal years divided by years, in a budget statute before the beginning of the first fiscal year. Parts of the budget may apply to different periods of time, divided by fiscal years.
(3) Bills pursuant to the first sentence of sub-paragraph 2 as well as bills to amend the budget statute and the budget are to be submitted to the Bundesrat simultaneously with their transmission to the Bundestag; the Bundesrat is entitled to give a reaction on the bills within six weeks or, in the case of amendment bills, within three weeks.
(4) The budget statute may only contain provisions relating to revenues and expenditures of the Federation and to the period for which the budget statute is enacted. The budget statute may prescribe that its provisions expire only upon publication of the next budget statute or, in the event of an authorization pursuant to Article 115, at a later date.

Article 111. (1) If, by the end of a fiscal year, the budget for the following year has not been established by a statute, the Federal Government is authorized, until its entry into force, to make all expenditures that are necessary
a. to maintain statutory institutions and to carry out statutory measures,
b. to fulfil the legal obligations of the Federation,
c. to continue constructions, acquisitions and other services, or to continue to grant benefits for these purposes, to the extent that amounts have already been approved in the budget of a previous year.
(2) To the extent that revenues not based upon specific statutes from taxes, charges or other sources or the operational capital reserves do not cover the expenditures referred to in sub-paragraph 1, the Federal Government may mobilize the funds necessary for sustaining operational management up to a maximum of one quarter of the total amount of the previous budget by way of a credit.

Article 112. Expenditures in excess of or outside the budgetary planning require the consent of the Minister of Finance. It may only be granted in the case of an unforeseen and irrefutable necessity. Details may be regulated by a federal statute.

Article 113. (1) Statutes which increase the expenditures of the budget proposed by the Federal Government or which comprise or will bring about in the future new expenditures require the consent of the Federal Government. The same applies to statutes that comprise or will bring about in the future decreases in revenue. The Federal Government may demand that the Bundestag suspend its decision-making on these statutes. In such case the Federal Government is to transmit a statement to the Bundestag within six weeks.
(2) The Federal Government may, within four weeks after the Bundestag has adopted this statute, demand that it make a decision again.

(3) Where the statute has become effective pursuant to Article 78, the Federal Government may withhold its consent only within six weeks and only after having initiated the procedure provided for in the third and fourth sentence of sub-paragraph 1 or in sub-paragraph 2. Upon the expiry of that period, consent is deemed to have been given.

Article 114. (1) The Minister of Finance is to render annually to the Bundestag and to the Bundesrat an account of all revenues and expenditures as well as of assets and debts during the following fiscal year, for the relief of the Federal Government.
(2) The Federal Court of Audit [Bundesrechnungshof] whose members enjoy judicial independence audits the account as well as the economic efficiency and regularity of the budget and operational management. It is to report annually directly to the Bundestag and to the Bundesrat in addition to the Federal Government. In all other respects, the competences of the Federal Court of Audit are regulated by federal statute.

Article 115. (1) The raising of credit and the assumption of co-signing of obligations, of guaranties or of other commitments which may lead to expenditures in future fiscal years require authorization to a quantified or quantifiable amount by a federal statute.
(2) Revenues and expenditures are in principle to be balanced without revenues from credits. This principle is complied with if the revenues from credits do not exceed 0.35 percent in proportion to the nominal gross domestic product. In addition, for an economic development that is deviating from the normal situation, the effects on the budget are to be considered symmetrically for the upturn and the downturn. Deviations in the effective raising of credit from the credit maximum permissible pursuant to the first through third sentences are registered on a control account; burdens that exceed the threshold of 1.5 percent in proportion to the nominal gross domestic product are to be reduced in line with the economic development. Details, especially the correction of revenues and expenditures for financial transactions and the procedure for calculating the maximum limit of the annual net borrowing taking into account the economic developments on the basis of a procedure for economic development correction as well as the control and the offsetting of deviations in the effective raising of credit from the maximum limit, are regulated by a federal statute. In the case of natural disasters or exceptional emergencies that are beyond the state's control and that substantially compromise the state financial situation, these maximum credit limits may be exceeded on the basis of a decision of the majority of the members of the Bundestag. The decision is to be connected with a redemption plan. The redemption of the credits raised pursuant to the sixth sentence is to take place within an adequate timeframe.

Xa. State of defence

Article 115a. (1) The finding that the territory of the Federation is being attacked by force of arms or that there is an imminent threat of such an attack (state of defence)

is pronounced by the Bundestag with the consent of the Bundesrat. The finding is pronounced on request of the Federal Government and requires a majority of two-thirds of votes cast, including at least the majority of the members of the Bundestag.
(2) If the situation imperatively requires immediate action and insurmountable impediments prevent the timely convention of the Bundestag or if it does not have capacity to take decisions, then the Joint Committee pronounces the finding with a majority of two-thirds of votes cast, including a majority if its members.
(3) The finding is published by the Federal President in accordance with Article 82 in the Federal Law Gazette. If this cannot be done in time, the publication takes place in another manner; it must later be effected in the Federal Law Gazette as soon as the circumstances permit.
(4) If the territory of the Federation is being attacked by force of arms and the competent federal organs are incapable of immediately pronouncing a finding under sub-paragraph 1, first sentence, such finding is deemed pronounced and published as from the time when the attack started. The Federal President specifies that time as soon as the circumstances permit.
(5) If the finding of a state of defence has been published and the territory of the Federation is being attacked by force of arms, the Federal President may, with the consent of the Bundestag, make declarations under international law regarding the existence of a state of defence. Under the conditions of sub-paragraph 2, the position of the Bundestag is assumed by the Joint Committee.

Article 115b. With the publication of the state of defence, the command over the armed forces passes to the Federal Chancellor.

Article 115c. (1) The Federation has the right of concurrent legislation for the state of defence also in the matters that fall within the legislative power of the States. These statutes require the consent of the Bundesrat.
(2) To the extent that the circumstances during the state of defence so require, for the state of defence a statute may
1. in case of expropriations in deviation from Article 14 (3) second sentence, regulate the compensation provisionally,
2. regarding deprivations of freedom, provide for a time limit deviating from Article 104 (2) third sentence and (3) first sentence, at most however one of four days, for the case that a judge could not act within the time limit applied in normal times.
(3) To the extent that it is necessary for the aversion of a present or immediately threatening attack, for the state of defence by federal statute with the consent of the Bundesrat the administration and the finances system of the Federation and the States may be regulated in deviation from the sections VIII, VIIIa and X, in which case the viability of the States, municipalities and associations of municipalities, especially in a financial perspective, is to be respected.
(4) Federal statutes in the sense of sub-paragraph 1 and 2 no. 1 may for the purpose of the preparation of their execution already be applied before the beginning of the state of defence.

Article 115d. (1) Regarding legislation of the Federation in a state of defence, the provisions of sub-paragraphs 2 and 3 apply in deviation from Article 76 (2), Article 77 (1) second sentence and (2) to (4), Article 78 and Article 82 (1).
(2) Bills of the Federal Government which it has qualified as urgent are to be transmitted to the Bundesrat at the same time as their submission to the Bundestag. The Bundestag and the Bundesrat immediately deliberate on these bills jointly. In as far as the consent of the Bundesrat is required for a statute, the majority of its votes are required for the adoption of the statute. Details are regulated by rules of procedure which are adopted by the Bundestag and which require the consent of the Bundesrat.
(3) For the publication of statutes, Article 115a (3) second sentence applies mutatis mutandis.

Article 115e. (1) If the Joint Committee declares in a state of defence with a majority of two thirds of the votes cast, at least with the majority of its members, that an insurmountable impediments prevent the timely convention of the Bundestag or that it does not have capacity to take decisions, the Joint Committee has the position of Bundestag and Bundesrat and exercises their rights unitarily.
(2) By statute of the Joint Committee the Basic Law may neither be amended nor wholly or partly suspended or rendered inapplicable. The Joint Committee is not entitled to adopt statutes under Article 23 (1) second sentence, Article 24 (1) or Article 29.

Article 115f. (1) The Federal Government may, in a state of defence, in as far as the circumstances so require,
1. use the Federal Border Guard throughout the entire territory of the Federation;
2. give orders, besides to the federal administration, also to the State governments and, if it considers it to be urgent, to the State authorities and transfer this power to members of the State governments to be determined by it.
(2) The Bundestag, the Bundesrat and the Joint Committee are to be informed of the measures taken under sub-paragraph 1 immediately.

Article 115g. The constitutional position and the fulfilment of the constitutional tasks of the Federal Constitutional Court and its judges may not be jeopardized. The statute regarding the Federal Constitutional Court may be amended by a statute of the Joint Committee only to the extent that this is also in the opinion of the Federal Constitutional Court required in order to maintain the capacity of the Court to function. Until the adoption of such a statute the Federal Constitutional Court may take the measures necessary for maintaining the capacity of the Court to function. The Federal Constitutional Court takes decisions under the second and third sentence by majority of the judges present.

Article 115h. (1) Electoral terms of the Bundestag or the parliaments of the States expiring during a state of defence end six months after the termination of the state of defence. The term of the Federal President expiring during a state of defence as

well as the exercise of his powers in case of early termination of his term by the president of the Bundesrat end nine months after the termination of the state of defence. The term of a member of the Federal Constitutional Court expiring during a state of defence ends six months after the termination of the state of defence.
(2) Where a new election of a Federal Chancellor by the Joint Committee becomes necessary, it elects a new Federal Chancellor by a majority of its members; the Federal President submits a proposal to the Joint Committee. The Joint Committee may express its lack of confidence in the Federal Chancellor only by electing a successor by the vote of two-thirds of its members.
(3) For the duration of the state of defence, a dissolution of the Bundestag is excluded.

Article 115i. (1) If the competent federal organs are incapable of taking the measures necessary for the aversion of the danger and the situation imperatively requires an immediate autonomous action in certain parts of the territory of the Federation, the State governments or authorities or representatives appointed by them are authorized to take measures in the sense of Article 115f (1) in matters within their competence.
(2) Measures under sub-paragraph 1 may at any time be repealed by the Federal Government, in relation to State authorities and subordinated federal authorities also by the prime ministers of the States.

Article 115k. (1) For the duration of their applicability, statutes under Articles 115c, 115e and 115g and ordinances that are adopted pursuant such statutes render conflicting law inapplicable. This does not apply to earlier law that has been adopted pursuant to Articles 115c, 115e and 115g.
(2) Statutes that the Joint Committee has adopted and ordinances that were adopted pursuant to such statutes expire at the latest six months after the termination of the state of defence.
(3) Statutes that contain rules deviating from Articles 91a, 91b, 104a, 106 and 107 apply at the latest until the end of the second fiscal year following the termination of the state of defence. They may, after the termination of the state of defence, be amended by federal statute with the consent of the Bundesrat, in order to lead over to the regime under sections VIIIa and X.

Article 115l. (1) The Bundestag may at any time with the consent of the Bundesrat repeal statutes of the Joint Committee. The Bundesrat may demand that the Bundestag decide on this matter. Other measures taken for the aversion of the danger by the Joint Committee or the Federal Government are to be lifted when the Bundestag and the Bundesrat so decide.
(2) The Bundestag may at any time with the consent of the Bundesrat, by a decision which is to be published by the Federal President, declare the state of defence terminated. The Bundesrat may demand that the Bundestag decide on this matter. The state of defence is to be declared terminated immediately when the conditions for its declaration are no longer present.
(3) The conclusion of peace is decided by federal statute.

XI. Transitional and final provisions

Article 116. (1) German within the meaning of this Basic Law is, subject to other statutory provisions, he who has the German citizenship or who, as a refugee or expellee of German ethnicity or as his spouse or descendant found admittance to the territory of the German Reich as it existed on 31 December 1937.
(2) Former German citizens, who, between 30 January 1933 and 8 May 1945, had their citizenship revoked for political, racial or religious reasons, and their descendants, are, on application, to be renaturalized. They are considered as not denaturalized if they, after 8 May 1945, took up residence in Germany and have not expressed a contrary intention.

Article 117. (1) Law contrary to Article 3 (2) remains in force until its adaptation to that provision of the Basic Law, but not for longer than until 31 March 1953.
(2) Statutes which limit the right to freedom of movement due to the current shortage of living space remain in force until their repeal by federal statute.

Article 118. The reorganization in the territories comprising the States of Baden, Württemberg-Baden and Württemberg-Hohenzollern may be effected, in derogation from the provisions of Article 29, by agreement between the States concerned. If no agreement is reached, the reorganization will be regulated by federal statute which must provide for a consultative referendum.

Article 118a. The reorganization in the territory comprising the States of Berlin and Brandenburg may be effected, in derogation from the provisions of Article 29, by agreement, with the participation of their eligible voters, between the States concerned.

Article 119. In matters relating to refugees and expellees, in particular as regards their distribution among the States, the federal government, until the adoption of a settlement by federal statute, may, with the consent of the Bundesrat, issue ordinances having the force of statute. For special cases, the federal government may be authorized to issue individual instructions. These instructions are, unless in case of an imminent danger, to be addressed to the highest States authorities.

Article 120. (1) The Federation bears the expenses for occupation costs and other internal and external burdens resulting from the war, in accordance with the more detailed federal statutes. To the extent that these burdens resulting from the war have been regulated by federal statutes by 1 October 1969, the Federation and the States bear such expenses in the proportion established by such federal statutes. To the extent that expenditures for burdens resulting from the war which neither have been nor are regulated by federal statutes have been assumed by 1 October 1965 by the States, municipalities (associations of municipalities) or other agencies performing functions of the States or municipalities, the Federation is not obliged to assume expenditures of this nature even after that date. The Federation bears the supplementary contributions towards the expenses of social security, including unemployment insurance and unemployment assistance. The distribution of burdens resulting from the war between the Federation and the States regulated by this sub-paragraph does not affect the statutory regulation of compensation claims for effects of the war.

(2) Revenues pass to the Federation at the same time as it takes over the expenditures.

Article 120a. (1) The statutes concerning the implementation of the equalization of burdens may, with the consent of the Bundesrat, stipulate that in the field of equalization payments they will be executed partly by the Federation and partly by the States on behalf of the Federation and that the powers appertaining to the federal government and the competent highest federal authorities pursuant to Article 85 are delegated to the Federal Equalization of Burdens Office [Bundesausgleichsamt]. The Federal Equalization of Burdens Office does not require the consent of the Bundesrat in the exercise of these competences; its instructions are, except in cases of urgency, to be directed to the highest States authorities (State equalization of burdens offices).

(2) Article 87 (3), second sentence, remains unaffected.

Article 121. A majority of the members of the Bundestag and the Federal Convention within the meaning of this Basic Law is the majority of their statutory number.

Article 122. (1) From the convention of the Bundestag onwards, statutes are exclusively enacted by the legislative bodies recognized by this Basic Law.

(2) Legislative bodies and entities participating in the legislative process in an advisory capacity whose competence expires pursuant to sub-paragraph 1 are dissolved from that moment.

Article 123. (1) Law predating the convention of the Bundestag remains in force to the extent that it does not conflict with the Basic Law.

(2) Treaties concluded by the German Reich, which pursuant to this Basic Law concern matters falling within the competence of State legislation, if under general principles of law they are and continue to be valid, remain in force, subject to all rights and objections of the parties, until new treaties are concluded by the authorities competent pursuant to this Basic Law or until their termination is otherwise effected by virtue of provisions contained in them.

Article 124. Law concerning matters falling within the exclusive legislative competence of the Federation becomes federal law within its scope of application.

Article 125. Law concerning matters falling within concurrent legislative powers of the Federation becomes federal law within its scope of application,
1. insofar as it applies uniformly within one or more occupation zones,
2. insofar as it is law by which after 8 May 1945 former Reich law has been amended.

Article 125a. (1) Law which has been enacted as federal law, but due to the amendment of Article 74 (1), the insertion of Article 84 (1) seventh sentence, Article 85 (1) second sentence or Article 105 (2a) second sentence or due to the repeal of Articles 74a, 75 or 98 (3) second sentence could no longer be enacted as federal law remains in force as federal law. It may be replaced by State law.
(2) Law which has been enacted pursuant to Article 72 (2) in the version applicable until 15 November 1994, but which due to the amendment of Article 72 (2) could no longer be enacted as federal law, remains in force as federal law. By federal statute it may be stipulated that it may be replaced by State law.
(3) Law which has been enacted as State law but due to the amendment of Article 73 could no longer be enacted as State law remains in force as State law. It may be replaced by federal law.

Article 125b. (1) Law which has been enacted pursuant to Article 75 in the version applicable until 1 September 2006 and which also after this date could be enacted as federal law, remains in force. Competences and obligations of the States to legislate remain in place in that respect. With respect to the areas mentioned in Article 72 (3) first sentence, the States may adopt regulations in deviation from this law; in the areas of Article 72 (3) first sentence, nos. 2, 5 and 6 however only when and to the extent that the Federation has exercised its legislative powers after 1 September 2006, in the cases of numbers 2 and 5 from 1 January 2010 at the latest, in the case of number 6 from 1 August 2008 at the latest.
(2) The States may adopt regulations in deviation from federal legal provisions that have been enacted pursuant to Article 84 (1) in the version applicable until 1 September 2006, they may adopt regulations in deviation from regulations regarding administrative procedure until 31 December 2008 however only if after 1 September 2006 regulations regarding administrative procedure have been amended in the relevant federal statute.

Article 125c. (1) Law which has been enacted pursuant to Article 91a (2) in conjunction with sub-paragraph 1 no. 1 in the version applicable until 1 September 2006 remains in force until 31 December 2006.
(2) The legal provisions in the areas of municipal traffic financing and promotion of social housing created pursuant to Article 104a (4) in the version applicable until 1 September 2006 remain in force until 31 December 2006. The legal provisions created for special programmes pursuant to § 6 (1) of the Municipal Traffic Financing Act [Gemeindeverkehrsfinanzierungsgesetz] in the area of municipal traffic financing as well as the other legal provisions created pursuant to Article 104a (4) in the version applicable until 1 September 2006 remain in force until 31 December 2019, unless a prior date is or will be set for expiry.

Article 126. Disagreements about the continuance of law as federal law are resolved by the Federal Constitutional Court.

Article 127. The federal government may, with the consent of the governments of the States concerned, within one year after the promulgation of this Basic Law, enact law of the Bizone administration [Vereinigtes Wirtschaftsgebiet], to the extent that it remains in force as federal law under Article 124 or 125, in the States of Baden, Greater Berlin, Rhineland-Palatinate and Württemberg-Hohenzollern.

Article 128. To the extent that law remaining in force provides for powers to issue instructions within the meaning of Article 84 (5), they remain in force until statutory regulation provides otherwise.

Article 129. (1) To the extent that legal provisions that remain in force as federal law contain an authorization to enact ordinances or general administrative regulations or to issue administrative acts, it passes to the authorities henceforth competent in the subject matter. In cases of doubt, the federal government decides in agreement with the Bundesrat; the decision is to be published.
(2) To the extent that legal provisions that remain in force as State law contain such an authorization, it is exercised by the authorities competent under State law.
(3) To the extent that legal provisions within the meaning of sub-paragraphs 1 and 2 authorize their amendment or supplementation or the enactment of legal provisions in the place of statutes, such authorization is expired.
(4) The provisions of sub-paragraphs 1 and 2 apply mutatis mutandis where legal provisions refer to provisions no longer in force or to institutions no longer existent.

Article 130. (1) Administrative bodies and other institutions serving the public administration or the administration of justice that are not based on State law or agreements between States as well as the administration of the South West German Railways and the administrative board for postal and telecommunications services for the French occupation zone are subordinate to the federal government. The latter regulates with the consent of the Bundesrat their transfer, dissolution or liquidation.
(2) The supreme disciplinary superior of the members of these administrations and institutions is the competent federal minister.
(3) Institutions and entities under public law not directly subordinate to a State and not based on agreements between the States are under the supervision of the competent supreme federal authority.

Article 131. The legal relationships of persons including refugees and expellees who on 8 May 1945 were employed in the public service, who have left it for reasons related to other than to civil servant or labour agreement law and who have not yet been employed or not in a position corresponding to their former one, are to be regulated by federal statute. The same applies mutatis mutandis to persons including refugees and expellees who on 8 May 1945 were entitled to support and who for reasons related to other than to civil servant or labour agreement law no longer receive support or equivalent support. Until the entry into force of the federal statute, no legal entitlements may be claimed save for other regulations under State law.

Article 132. (1) Civil servants and judges who, on the moment of the entry into force of this Basic Law, are appointed for life, may within six months after the first convention of the Bundestag be retired, suspended or transferred to an office with a lower salary if they lack the personal or professional aptitude required for their office. This provision applies mutatis mutandis to employees with a non-terminable employment. In the case of employees whose employment can be terminated, periods of notice exceeding those set by labour agreement may be terminated within the same time period.
(2) This provision does not apply to members of the public service who are not affected by the provisions regarding the "Liberation from National Socialism and Militarism" or who are recognized victims of National Socialism, unless an important personal ground obtains.
(3) Those affected may have recourse to the courts pursuant to Article 19 (4).
(4) Details are regulated by an ordinance of the federal government which requires the consent of the Bundesrat.

Article 133. The Federation succeeds to the rights and obligations of the Bizone administration [Vereinigtes Wirtschaftsgebiet].

Article 134. (1) The assets of the Reich in principle become federal assets.
(2) To the extent that they were, pursuant to their originally intended use, to be used principally for administrative tasks which pursuant to this Basic Law are not administrative tasks of the Federation, they are to be transferred free of charge to the authorities now competent and, to the extent that they, pursuant to their current and not merely temporary use, serve for administrative tasks that pursuant to this Basic Law are now to be performed by the States, they are to be transferred to the States. The Federation may also transfer other assets to the States.
(3) Assets that were placed at the disposal of the Reich free of charge by States and municipalities (associations of municipalities) become assets of the States and municipalities (associations of municipalities) again, to the extent that the Federation does not require them for its own administrative tasks.
(4) Details are regulated by a federal statute which requires the consent of the Bundesrat.

Article 135. (1) If after 8 May 1945 and before the entry into force of this Basic Law the affiliation of a territory to a State has changed, then the State to which the territory now belongs is entitled to the assets of the State to which it previously belonged that are located in that territory.
(2) The assets of no longer existing States and other entities and institutions under public law, to the extent that, pursuant to their originally intended use, they were to be used principally for administrative tasks or, pursuant to their current and not merely temporary use, serve principally administrative tasks, pass to the State or entity or institution under public law that now performs these tasks.

(3) Land property of no longer existing States including appurtenances pass to the State within which it is located to the extent that it is not already included among the assets within the meaning of sub-paragraph 1.
(4) To the extent that an overriding interest of the Federation or the particular interest of a territory so requires, arrangements deviating from the provisions of sub-paragraphs 1 to 3 of this Article may be adopted by federal statute.
(5) In all other respects, the succession and disposition of assets, to the extent that it has not been resolved by 1 January 1952 by agreement between the States or entities or institutions under public law concerned, is regulated by a federal statute which requires the consent of the Bundesrat.
(6) Holdings of the former State of Prussia in private-law enterprises pass to the Federation. Details are regulated by a federal statute which may also deviate from this provision.
(7) To the extent that assets which would fall to a State or entity or institution under public law pursuant to sub-paragraphs 1 to 3 had been used by the beneficiary by a State statute, pursuant to a State statute or in any other manner at the entry into force of this Basic Law, the transfer of assets is considered to have taken place before the use.

Article 135a. (1) By federal legislation reserved pursuant to Article 134 (4) and Article 135 (5) it may be provided that the following do not have to be fulfilled or do not have to be fulfilled in full:
1. liabilities of the Reich as well as liabilities of the former State of Prussia and other no longer existing entities and institutions under public law,
2. liabilities of the Federation or other entities or institutions under public law which are related to the passing of assets pursuant to Article 89, 90, 134 and 135 and liabilities of these legal bodies that are based on measures taken by the legal bodies designated under sub-paragraph 1,
3. liabilities of the States and municipalities (associations of municipalities) which have arisen from measures which these legal bodies have taken before 1 August 1945 in order to implement orders of the occupying powers or to remedy a state of emergency resulting from the war within the framework of the administrative tasks incumbent upon or delegated by the Reich.
(2) Sub-paragraph 1 applies mutatis mutandis to liabilities of the German Democratic Republic or its legal bodies as well as to liabilities of the Federation or other entities or institutions under public law which are related to the passing of assets of the German Democratic Republic to the Federation, States and municipalities, and to liabilities arising from measures of the German Democratic Republic or its legal bodies.

Article 136. (1) The Bundesrat convenes for the first time on the day of the first convention of the Bundestag.
(2) Until the election of the first Federal President, his competences are exercised by the president of the Bundesrat. He does not have the right to dissolve the Bundestag.

Article 137. (1) The right of civil servants, employees in the public service, professional soldiers, temporary volunteer soldiers and judges to run in elections in the Federation, in the States and the municipalities may be restricted by statute.
(2) The electoral law to be adopted by the Parliamentary Council [Parlamentarischer Rat] applies to the election of the first Bundestag, the first Federal Convention and the first Federal President of the Federal Republic.
(3) The competence of the Federal Constitutional Court pursuant to Article 42 (2) is, until its establishment, exercised by the German High Court for the Bizone [Deutsches Obergericht für das Vereinigte Wirtschaftsgebiet] which decides in accordance with its own rules of procedure.

Article 138. Changes to the constitutions of the profession of notary public as it now exists in the States of Baden, Bavaria, Württemberg-Baden and Württemberg-Hohenzollern require the consent of the governments of these States.

Article 139. The legal provisions enacted for the "Liberation of the German People from National Socialism and Militarism" [Befreiung des deutschen Volkes vom Nationalsozialismus und Militarismus] are not affected by the provisions of this Basic Law.

Article 140. The provisions of Articles 136, 137, 138, 139 and 141 of the German Constitution of 11 August 1919 are part of this Basic Law.

Article 141. Article 7 (3) first sentence does not apply in any State where State law providing otherwise was in force on 1 January 1949.

Article 142. Notwithstanding the provision of Article 31, provisions of State constitutions remain in force to the extent that they guarantee fundamental rights in conformity with Articles 1 to 18 of this Basic Law.

Article 142a. (Repealed).

Article 143. (1) Law in the territory specified in Article 3 of the Unification Treaty [Einigungsvertrag] may deviate from the provisions of this Basic Law at the latest until 31 December 1992, to the extent and so long as, due to the differing circumstances, a complete adaptation to the order of the Basic Law cannot be achieved yet. Deviations may not violate Article 19 (2) and must be compatible with the principles stipulated in Article 79 (3).
(2) Deviations from Titles II, VIII, VIIIa, IX, X and XI are permissible at the latest until 31 December 1995.
(3) Notwithstanding sub-paragraphs 1 and 2, Article 41 of the Unification Treaty and provisions for its implementation remain in force to the extent that they provide that interference with property in the territory specified in Article 3 of that Treaty cannot be reversed.

Article 143a. (1) The Federation has exclusive legislative competence in all matters arising from the transformation of the federal railways administered by the Federation into commercial enterprises. Article 87e (5) applies mutatis mutandis. Civil servants of the federal railways may be assigned by statute, without prejudice to their legal status or the responsibility of the employer, to provide services for railways of the Federation organized under private law.
(2) The Federation executes statutes enacted pursuant to sub-paragraph 1.
(3) The performance of the tasks relating to local public railway transport of the former federal railways is the responsibility of the Federation until 31 December 1995. The same applies to the corresponding tasks of the Rail Transport Administration [Eisenbahnverkehrsverwaltung]. Details are regulated by a federal statute that requires the consent of the Bundesrat.

Article 143b. (1) The special assets of the German Federal Post Office [Deutsche Bundespost] is transformed into private-law enterprises pursuant to a federal statute. The Federation has exclusive legislative competence in all matters arising therefrom.
(2) The exclusive rights of the Federation existing before the transformation may be conferred by a federal statute for a transitional period on the enterprises that succeed the postal service of the German Federal Post Office [Deutsche Bundespost Postdienst] and the telecommunications service of the German Federal Post Office [Deutsche Bundespost Telekom]. The majority interest in the enterprise that succeeds the postal service of the German Federal Post Office may be surrendered by the Federation at the earliest five years after the entry into force of the statute. To do so requires a federal statute with the consent of the Bundesrat.
(3) The federal civil servants employed by the German Federal Post Office are employed by the private enterprises without prejudice to their legal status and the responsibility of their employer. The enterprises exercise employer's authority. Details are regulated by a federal statute.

Article 143c. (1) The States are entitled from 1 January 2007 until 31 December 2019 to receive amounts out of the federal budget annually for the discontinuation of the Federation's share in financing due to the abolition of the joint tasks of upgrading and constructing universities including university hospitals and educational guidance and due to the abolition of financial aid for the improvement of the traffic situation of the municipalities and for social housing subsidies. Until 31 December 2013, these amounts are calculated on the basis of the average financing shares of the Federation in the 2000 to 2008 frame of reference.
(2) The amounts are, until 31 December 2013, distributed among the States as follows:
1. as annual fixed amounts whose height is calculated on the basis of the average share of each State over the time period of 2000 to 2003;
2. for a specific purpose of the responsibilities under the previous mixed financing.
(3) The Federation and the States review until the end of 2013 to what extent the financing means the States have been assigned under sub-paragraph 1 are still suitable and necessary for the performance of the States' tasks. From 1 January 2014

onwards, the purpose-bound appropriation designated in sub-paragraph 2 (2) of the financing means assigned pursuant to sub-paragraph 1 will lapse; the investment-related appropriation of the median volume remains valid. The agreements from the Second Solidarity Agreement [Solidarpakt II] remain unaffected.
(4) Details are regulated by a federal statute that requires the consent of the Bundesrat.

Article 143d. (1) Articles 109 and 115 in the version applicable until 31 July 2009 are to be applied for the last time to the 2010 fiscal year. Articles 109 and 115 in the version applicable as from 1 August 2009 are to be applied for the first time to the 2011 fiscal year; credit authorizations existing on 31 December 2010 for special assets [Sondervermögen] already established remain unaffected. The States may, in the period from 1 January 2011 to 31 December 2019, deviate from the target of Article 109 (3) in accordance with the applicable provisions of State law. The States' budgets are to be shaped in such way that in the 2020 fiscal year the target under Article 109 (3) fifth sentence is met. The Federation may, in the time period from 1 January 2011 to 31 December 2015 deviate from the target of Article 115 (2) second sentence. The reduction of the existing deficit shall begin in the 2011 fiscal year. The annual budgets are to be shaped in such way that in the 2016 fiscal year the target under Article 115 (2) second sentence is met; details are regulated by a federal statute.
(2) As an aid for compliance with the target under Article 109 (3) from 1 January 2020 onwards, the States of Berlin, Bremen, Saarland, Saxony-Anhalt and Schleswig-Holstein may be granted a total of 800 million euros in consolidation aids per year out of the federal budget for the time period of 2011 to 2019. Thereof, 300 million euros are allotted to Bremen, 260 million euros to Saarland, and 80 million euros each to Berlin, Saxony-Anhalt and Schleswig-Holstein. The aids are provided on the basis of an administrative agreement pursuant to a federal statute with the consent of the Bundesrat. The granting of aids presupposes a complete clearing of the financing deficits by the end of 2020. Details, in particular the annual stages of reduction of the financing deficit, the supervision of the reduction of the financing deficits by the Stability Council [Stabilitätsrat] as well as consequences in case of non-compliance with the stages of reduction are regulated by a federal statute with the consent of the Bundesrat and an administrative agreement. A simultaneous granting of consolidation aids and stabilization aids due to an extreme budgetary emergency is excluded.
(3) The financing burden resulting from the granting of consolidation aids is distributed in equal parts between the Federation and the States, in the case of the latter from their share of the turnover tax. Details are regulated by a federal statute with the consent of the Bundesrat.

Article 144. (1) This Basic Law requires ratification by the representative assemblies in two thirds of the States in which it is to apply initially.
(2) To the extent that the application of this Basic Law is subject to restrictions in one of the States listed in Article 23 or in a part of these States, that State or that part of

the State has the right to send representatives to the Bundestag pursuant to Article 38 and to the Bundesrat pursuant to Article 50.

Article 145. (1) The Parliamentary Council [Parlamentarischer Rat], with the participation of the representatives of Greater Berlin, declares the adoption of this Basic Law in public session, promulgates and publishes it.
(2) This Basic Law enters into force at the end of the day on which it is published.
(3) It is to be published in the Federal Law Gazette [Bundesgesetzblatt].

Article 146. This Basic Law, which since the completion of the unity and freedom of Germany applies to the entire German people, shall cease to apply on the day on which a constitution enters into force which has been freely adopted by the German people.

Federal Elections Act
[Bundeswahlgesetz] of 7 may 1956, as last amended by federal statute of 3 May 2013 (BGBl. I p. 1084). Selected provisions: Chapter 1 (§§ 1 to 7)[1]

§ 1. (1) The German Bundestag is composed, subject to the deviations resulting from this Act, of 598 members. They are elected in general, direct, free, equal and secret-ballot elections by the Germans entitled to vote, according to the principle of proportional representation in combination with person-based voting.
(2) 299 of the members of the Bundestag are elected upon electoral district candidacies within electoral districts and the remaining members upon State candidacies (State lists).

§ 2. (1) The electoral territory is the territory of the Federal Republic of Germany.
(2) The division of the electoral territory into electoral districts is based on the Annex to this Act.
(3) Each electoral district is, for the purposes of polling, divided into polling districts.

§ 3. (1) The following principles must be observed in the division of the electoral territory into electoral districts:
1. State borders must be respected.
2. The number of electoral districts in the individual States must correspond as far as possible to their share of the population. It is established with the same calculation method which is applied to the distribution of seats to the State lists in accordance with § 6 (2), second to seventh sentence.
3. The population size of an electoral district should not deviate from the average population size of electoral districts by more than 15 per cent, above or below; if the deviation is more than 25 per cent, a re-delimitation of the district must take place.
4. An electoral district is to form a contiguous area.
5. The borders of municipalities, rural counties and autonomous cities are to be respected as far as possible.
During the calculation of population numbers, aliens (§ 2 (1) Sojourn Act [Aufenthaltsgesetz]) are not taken into account.
(2) The Federal President appoints a permanent electoral district commission. It consists of the president of the Federal Statistics Office [Statistisches Bundesamt], one judge at the Federal Administrative Court [Bundesverwaltungsgericht] and five other members.
(3) The electoral district commission has the task of reporting on changes of population numbers in the electoral territory and to submit whether and which changes in the division of electoral districts it considers necessary in view thereof. It may submit in its report proposals for changes also for other reasons. Regarding its proposals for changes in the division of electoral districts it must respect the principles stipulated in sub-paragraph 1; if following the calculation under sub-

---

[1] Translation by S. Hardt.

paragraph 1 no. 2, several possible affiliations with electoral districts may result, it draws up proposals on that matter.

(4) The report of the electoral district commission must be submitted to the Federal Ministry of Internal Affairs within fifteen months following the beginning of the term of the German Bundestag. The Federal Ministry of Internal Affairs transmits it without delay to the German Bundestag and publishes it in the Federal Gazette [Bundesanzeiger]. Upon request of the Federal Ministry of Internal Affairs, the electoral district committee must submit a supplementary report; for this case, the second sentence applies mutatis mutandis.

(5) If State borders are being redrawn in accordance with statutory provisions regarding the procedure on further changes to the territorial shape of the States under Article 29 (7) of the Basic Law, then the borders of the affected electoral districts also change accordingly. If in the receiving State two or more electoral districts are affected or if an exclave of a State is created, then the electoral district affiliation of the new part of the State is determined by the electoral district affiliation of the municipality, municipal district or autonomous area to which it has been attached. Changes to State borders which are carried out after the end of the thirty-second month following the beginning of the term have an effect on the division of electoral districts only in the following term.

§ 4. Each voter has two votes, a first vote for the election of a member of the Bundestag from the electoral district, and a second vote for the election of a State list.

§ 5. In each electoral district, one member of the Bundestag is elected. The candidate who receives the most votes is elected. In case of a tie, a lot to be drawn by the district returning officer [Kreiswahlleiter] decides.

§ 6. (1) For the distribution of seats to be filled from State lists, the second votes cast for each State list are added. The second votes of those voters who have cast their first votes for a candidate who was successful in his electoral district and who has been put forward in accordance with § 20 (3) or by a political party which is not eligible for the allocation of seats pursuant to sub-paragraph 3 or for which no State list was admitted in the respective State are not taken into account. The number of successful electoral district candidates stipulated in the second sentence is subtracted from the total number of members of the Bundestag (§ 1 (1)).

(2) In a first distribution, the total number of seats (§ 1 (1)) is initially allocated, pursuant to the calculation method described in the second to seventh sentence, to the States according to their share of the population (§ 3 (1)) and in each State the number of seats remaining there pursuant to sub-paragraph 1, third sentence, is subsequently allocated to the State lists on the basis of the second votes to be taken into account. Each State list receives as many seats as result from the division of the sum of the second votes it received by an allocation divisor. Decimals under 0.5 are rounded down to the whole number below, those over 0.5 are rounded up to the whole number above. Decimals which are equal to 0.5 are rounded off either upwards or downwards so as to maintain the total number of seats to be

distributed; if this results in several possible allocations of seats, the lot, to be drawn by the federal returning officer [Bundeswahlleiter], decides. The allocation divisor must be determined in such a way that, in total, as many seats are allocated to State lists as there are seats available. For that purpose, first the total number of second votes of all State lists to be taken into account is divided by the total number of seats remaining pursuant to sub-paragraph 1, third sentence. If, after this, more seats are allocated to the State lists than there are seats available, then the distribution divisor must be raised so that the number of available seats is obtained in the calculation; if too few seats are allocated to the State lists, the distribution divisor is to be lowered accordingly.

(3) In the allocation of the seats to the State lists, only parties which have received at least five per cent of the valid second votes cast in the electoral territory or which have won a seat in at least three electoral districts are taken into account. The first sentence does not apply to lists submitted by parties of national minorities.

(4) From the number of seats thus determined for each State list the number of seats won by the party in the electoral districts of the state (§ 5) is subtracted. Seats won in the electoral districts remain in the hands of a party, even if their number exceeds that determined pursuant to sub-paragraphs 2 and 3.

(5) The number of seats remaining pursuant to sub-paragraph 1, third sentence, is raised until every party receives at least as many seats in the second distribution pursuant to sub-paragraph 6, first sentence, as have been allocated to it in the first distribution pursuant to sub-paragraphs 2 and 3 in addition to the seats won in electoral districts which cannot be subtracted, pursuant to sub-paragraph 4, first sentence, from the number of seats determined for the State list. The total number of seats (§ 1 (1)) increases by the difference.

(6) The seats to be allocated pursuant to sub-paragraph 5, first sentence, are in any event distributed nationwide, according to the number of second votes to be taken into account, among the parties to be taken into account pursuant to sub-paragraph 3, using the calculation method described in sub-paragraph 2, second to seventh sentence. Within the parties, the seats are distributed, according to the number of second votes to be taken into account, to the State lists, using the calculation method described in sub-paragraph 2, second to seventh sentence; each State list is allocated at least the number of seats won by the party in the electoral districts of the State. From the number of seats determined for each State list the number of seats won by the party in the electoral districts of the State (§ 5) is subtracted. The remaining seats are filled from the State list in the order specified therein. Candidates who have been elected in an electoral district are not considered on the state list. If a State list is allocated more seats than candidates are nominated, these seats remain vacant.

(7) If, in the distribution pursuant to sub-paragraphs 2 to 6, a party which has received more than half of the second votes cast for all parties to be taken into account does not receive more than half of the seats, it is allocated additional seats until it holds one seat more than half of the seats. Within the party, the seats are distributed pursuant to sub-paragraph 6, second to sixth sentence. In such a case, the total number of seats (§ 1 (1)) determined pursuant to sub-paragraph 5 increases by the difference.

§ 7. (Repealed).

[The remaining Chapters of the Act are omitted.]

THE NETHERLANDS

Charter for the Kingdom of the Netherlands
[Statuut voor het Koninkrijk der Nederlanden] of 28 October 1954, as last amended by Kingdom Statute of 7 September 2010 (Stb. 333)[1]

Preamble
The Netherlands, Aruba, Curacao and Saint Martin,
noting that the Netherlands, Suriname and the Netherlands Antilles in 1954 have declared by free will to accept a new legal order in the Kingdom of the Netherlands, in which they conduct their own interests autonomously and pursue their common interests on a basis of equality and accord each other assistance, and have resolved in mutual consultation to adopt the Charter for the Kingdom;
noting that the connection with Surinam under the Charter has come to an end as per 25 November 1975 by virtue of an amendment of the Charter by Kingdom Statute of 22 November 1975, Stb. 617, PbNA 233;
noting that Aruba has declared by free will to accept this legal order as a country as per 1 January 1986 for a period of ten years and as per 1 January 1996 for an indefinite period;
considering that Curacao and Saint Martin have both declared by free will to accept this legal order as countries;
have resolved in mutual consultation to adopt the Charter for the Kingdom as follows.

§ 1. General provisions

Article 1. (1) The Kingdom comprises the countries of the Netherlands, Aruba, Curacao and Saint Martin.
(2) Bonaire, Saint Eustatius and Saba each form part of the state order of the Netherlands. For these islands regulations may be adopted and other specific measures may be taken on account of the economic and social circumstances, the

---

[1] Translation by Ph. Kiiver.

large distance from the European part of the Netherlands, their island character, small territory and population size, geographical circumstances, the climate and other factors by which these islands significantly differ from the European part of the Netherlands.

Article 1a. The crown of the Kingdom is held by inheritance by Her Majesty Queen Juliana, Princess of Orange-Nassau, and, by succession, by her lawful successors.

Article 2. (1) The King heads the government of the Kingdom and of each of the countries. He is inviolable, the ministers are responsible.
(2) The King is represented in Aruba, Curacao and Saint Martin by the Governor [Gouverneur]. The competences, duties and responsibility of the Governor as representative of the government of the Kingdom are regulated by Kingdom Statute [rijkswet] or, where applicable, by Kingdom Ordinance [algemene maatregel van rijksbestuur].
(3) Kingdom Statute regulates that which relates to the appointment and the dismissal of the Governor. The appointment and the dismissal are effected by the King as head of the Kingdom.

Article 3. (1) Notwithstanding what is provided elsewhere in the Charter, matters for the Kingdom are:
a. the maintenance of the independence and the defence of the Kingdom;
b. foreign relations;
c. Dutch citizenship;
d. the regulation of chivalric orders as well as the flag and the coat of arms of the Kingdom;
e. the regulation of the nationality of vessels and the laying down of conditions regarding the safety and navigation of seagoing vessels which fly the flag of the Kingdom, except sailing vessels;
f. oversight over the general rules regarding the admission and expulsion of Dutch citizens;
g. the laying down of general conditions for the admission and expulsion of aliens;
h. extradition.
(2) Other matters may in mutual consultation be declared to be matters for the Kingdom. In that context, Article 55 applies mutatis mutandis.

Article 4. (1) Royal authority is exercised in matters for the Kingdom by the King as head of the Kingdom.
(2) Legislative authority is exercised in matters for the Kingdom by the legislator of the Kingdom. In cases of bills for Kingdom Statutes, consideration takes place with due regard to Articles 15 to 21.

Article 5. (1) The monarchy and the succession to the throne, the organs of the Kingdom referred to in the Charter, the exercise of royal and legislative authority in matters for the Kingdom are regulated, in as far as that is not provided for by the Charter, by the Constitution [Grondwet] for the Kingdom.

(2) The Constitution respects the provisions of the Charter.
(3) To a proposal for an amendment of the Constitution containing provisions regarding matters for the Kingdom, as well as to bills stating that there is reason to consider such a proposal, Articles 15 to 20 apply.

§ 2. The conduct of matters for the Kingdom

Article 6. (1) The matters for the Kingdom are conducted in cooperation between the Netherlands, Aruba, Curacao and Saint Martin in accordance with the following provisions.
(2) During the conduct of these matters, organs of the countries are involved where possible.
Article 7. The council of ministers of the Kingdom is composed of the ministers appointed by the King and the Minister Plenipotentiary [Gevolmachtigde Minister] appointed by the government of Aruba, Curacao and Saint Martin, respectively.

Article 8. (1) The Ministers Plenipotentiary act on behalf of the governments of their country, which appoint and dismiss them. They must be Dutch citizens.
(2) The government of the country involved determines who replaces the Minister Plenipotentiary in case of his being hindered or absent. That which is provided in this Charter regarding the Minister Plenipotentiary applies mutatis mutandis with respect to his substitute.

Article 9. (1) The Minister Plenipotentiary, before assuming his office, takes an oath or makes a promise of allegiance to the King and the Charter before the Governor. The formula for the oath or promise is established by Kingdom Ordinance.
(2) When in the Netherlands, the Minister Plenipotentiary takes the oath or makes the promise before the King.

Article 10. (1) The Minister Plenipotentiary participates in the deliberations in the meetings of the council of ministers and of the permanent bodies and special commissions of the council regarding matters for the Kingdom which affect the country in question.
(2) The governments of Aruba, Curacao and Saint Martin each have the right – if a certain subject-matter calls for such action – to also let a minister with an advisory vote participate next to the Minister Plenipotentiary in the deliberations stipulated in the preceding paragraph.
Article 11. (1) Proposals for an amendment of the Constitution containing provisions regarding matters for the Kingdom affect Aruba, Curacao and Saint Martin.
(2) As regards defence, it is assumed that the defence of the territory of Aruba, Curacao or Saint Martin, as well as agreements or understandings regarding an area that belongs to their sphere of interests, affect Aruba, Curacao and Saint Martin, respectively.
(3) As regards foreign affairs, it is assumed that foreign affairs where the interests of Aruba, Curacao or Saint Martin are involved, or where the conduct thereof can have

serious consequences for these interests, affect Aruba, Curacao and Saint Martin, respectively.
(4) The determination of the contribution to the costs referred to in Article 35 affects Aruba, Curacao and Saint Martin, respectively.
(5) Proposals for naturalization are only considered to affect Aruba, Curacao and Saint Martin if persons are concerned who reside in the country in question.
(6) The governments of Aruba, Curacao and Saint Martin may state which matters for the Kingdom other than those stipulated in the first to fourth paragraph affect their country.

Article 12. (1) If the Minister Plenipotentiary of Aruba, Curacao or Saint Martin, indicating his reasons based on which he expects serious detriment to his country, has declared that his country should not be bound by a proposed instrument containing generally binding regulations, such instrument may not be adopted in a way that it applies in the country in question, unless this would be incompatible with the ties of the country within the Kingdom.
(2) If the Minister Plenipotentiary of Aruba, Curacao or Saint Martin has serious objections to the initial opinion of the council of ministers regarding the requirement of binding nature as stipulated in the first paragraph, or regarding any other matter in the consideration of which he has participated, then upon his request deliberations are continued, if necessary with due regard to a time limit to be determined by the council of ministers.
(3) The deliberations referred to above are conducted between the prime-minister, two ministers, the Minister Plenipotentiary and a minister or special plenipotentiary to be nominated by the government involved.
(4) If several Ministers Plenipotentiary wish to participate in continued deliberations, then these deliberations are conducted between these Ministers Plenipotentiary, an equal number of ministers and the prime-minister. The second paragraph of Article 10 applies mutatis mutandis.
(5) The council of ministers decides in accordance with the result of the continued deliberations. If the opportunity for continued deliberations has not been seized within the specified time limit, then the council of ministers takes its decision.

Article 12a. By Kingdom Statute provisions are adopted for the treatment of such disputes as stipulated by Kingdom Statute between the Kingdom and the countries.

Article 13. (1) There is a Council of State of the Kingdom [Raad van State van het Koninkrijk].
(2) If the government of Aruba, Curacao or Saint Martin makes known such wish, the King appoints a member to the Council of State for Aruba, Curacao and Saint Martin, respectively, whose appointment is effected in agreement with the government of the country involved. His dismissal is effected after consultation with that government.
(3) The members of the Council of State for Aruba, Curacao and Saint Martin participate in the activities of the Council of State in case the Council or a division of the Council is heard regarding bills for Kingdom Statutes and Kingdom Ordinances

which shall apply in Aruba, Curacao and Saint Martin, respectively, or regarding other matters which, in accordance with Article 11, affect Aruba, Curacao and Saint Martin, respectively.
(4) By Kingdom Ordinance, regulations may be adopted with respect to the mentioned members of the Council of State that deviate from the provisions of the Council of State Act [Wet op de Raad van State].

Article 14. (1) Regulations regarding matters for the Kingdom – in as far as the relevant matter is not regulated in the Constitution and save for international regulations and that which is provided in the third paragraph – are established by Kingdom Statute [rijkswet] or, in cases where that is applicable, by Kingdom Ordinance [algemene maatregel van rijksbestuur]. The Kingdom Statute or the Kingdom Ordinance may charge other organs with, or leave to other organs, the establishment of more detailed regulations. The charging of or leaving to the countries is effected with respect to the legislator or the government of the countries.
(2) If the regulation is not reserved for Kingdom Statute, it may be effected by Kingdom Ordinance.
(3) Regulations regarding matters for the Kingdom which do not apply in Aruba, Curacao or Saint Martin are established by statute [wet] or ordinance [algemene maatregel van bestuur].
(4) The naturalization of persons resident in Aruba, Curacao or Saint Martin is effected by or pursuant to Kingdom Statute.

Article 15. (1) The King transmits a bill for a Kingdom Statute, simultaneously with its introduction in the States-General, to the representative bodies of Aruba, Curacao and Saint Martin.
(2) In case of a proposal for a bill for a Kingdom Statute emanating from the States-General, the transmission of the bill by the Second Chamber [Tweede Kamer] is effected immediately after it has been introduced in the Chamber.
(3) The Minister Plenipotentiary of Aruba, Curacao or Saint Martin has the right to propose to the Second Chamber to make a proposal for a bill for a Kingdom Statute.

Article 16. The representative body of the country where the regulation shall apply has the right to scrutinize it before the public consideration of the bill in the Second Chamber and, if necessary within a time period determined for that purpose, to issue a written report on it.

Article 17. (1) The Minister Plenipotentiary of the country where the regulation shall apply is offered the opportunity to attend the oral consideration of the bill for a Kingdom Statute in the Chambers of the States-General and to provide such information to the Chambers as he considers appropriate.
(2) The representative body of the country where the regulation shall apply may decide, for the consideration of a specific matter in the States-General, to delegate one or more special delegates who also have the right to attend the oral consideration and to provide information in that context.

(3) The Ministers Plenipotentiary and the special delegates are not liable to judicial prosecution for that which they have said in the meeting of the Chambers of the States-General or which they have submitted to them in writing.
(4) The Ministers Plenipotentiary and the special delegates have the right, during the consideration in the Second Chamber, to propose amendments to the bill.

Article 18. (1) The Minister Plenipotentiary of the country where the regulation shall apply is given the opportunity, before the final vote on a bill for a Kingdom Statute in the Chambers of the States-General, to give a statement regarding that bill. If the Minister Plenipotentiary declares his opposition to the bill, he may also request the Chamber to postpone the vote until the following meeting. If the Second Chamber, after the Minister Plenipotentiary has declared his opposition to the bill, adopts it with a majority smaller than three-fifths of the number of votes cast, the consideration is suspended and further deliberations regarding the bill take place in the council of ministers.
(2) If special delegates are attending the meeting of the Chambers, the right stipulated in the first paragraph also applies to the delegate nominated by the representative body for that purpose.

Article 19. Articles 17 and 18 apply mutatis mutandis to the consideration in the joint session of the States-General.

Article 20. By Kingdom Statute, further regulations may be established regarding that which is provided in Articles 15 to 19.

Article 21. If, after concluded deliberations with the Ministers Plenipotentiary of Aruba, Curacao and Saint Martin, in case of war or in other special cases where action must be taken swiftly, it is impossible in the opinion of the King to wait for the result of the scrutiny stipulated in Article 16, the provision of that Article may be deviated from.

Article 22. (1) The government of the Kingdom ensures the publication of Kingdom Statutes and Kingdom Ordinances. It is effected where the regulation shall apply in the official journal. The governments of the countries provide the necessary assistance in that context.
(2) They enter into force on the moment to be stipulated by or pursuant to these regulations.
(3) The enactment formula of Kingdom Statutes and of Kingdom Ordinances states that the provisions of the Charter for the Kingdom have been respected.

Article 23. (1) The jurisdiction of the Supreme Court of the Netherlands [Hoge Raad der Nederlanden] as regards disputes in Aruba, Curacao and Saint Martin, as well as on Bonaire, Saint Eustatius and Saba, is regulated by Kingdom Statute.

(2) If the government of Aruba, Curacao or Saint Martin so requests, by that Kingdom Statute the possibility is opened for a member, an extraordinary member or an advisory member to be added to the Court.

Article 24. (1) Agreements with foreign states and with international organizations which affect Aruba, Curacao or Saint Martin are submitted, simultaneously with the submission to the States-General, to the representative body of Aruba, Curacao and Saint Martin, respectively.
(2) In case the agreement is submitted to the States-General for tacit approval, the Minister Plenipotentiary may, within the period set for the Chambers of the States-General for that purpose, express the wish that the agreement be submitted to explicit approval by the States-General.
(3) The preceding paragraphs apply mutatis mutandis with respect to the termination of international agreements, the first paragraph applies with the provision that the intention of termination is notified to the representative body of Aruba, Curacao and Saint Martin, respectively.

Article 25. (1) The King does not commit Aruba, Curacao or Saint Martin to international economic and financial agreements if the government of the country, indicating the reasons based on which it expects serious detriment from the commitment to the country, has declared that the country should not be committed.
(2) The King does not terminate international economic and financial agreements as regards Aruba, Curacao or Saint Martin if the government of the country, indicating the reasons based on which it expects serious detriment from the termination to the country, has declared that for the country a termination should not take place. Termination may nevertheless be effected if it is incompatible with the provisions of the agreement that the country be excluded from the termination.

Article 26. If the government of Aruba, Curacao or Saint Martin expresses the wish that an international economic or financial agreement should be concluded which is to apply exclusively to the country involved, the government of the Kingdom shall cooperate with a view to such an agreement unless this would be incompatible with the ties of the country within the Kingdom.

Article 27. (1) Aruba, Curacao and Saint Martin are involved as early as possible in the preparation of agreements with foreign states which affect them in accordance with Article 11. They are also involved in the execution of agreements which affect them thus and which are binding upon them.
(2) The Netherlands, Aruba, Curacao and Saint Martin adopt a mutual provision on the cooperation between the countries regarding the adoption of regulations or other measures which are necessary for the execution of agreements with foreign states.
(3) If the interests of the Kingdom are affected by the continued absence of regulations or other measures which are necessary for the execution of an agreement with foreign states in one of the countries, whereas the agreement can be approved for

that country only when the regulations or other measures are ready, a Kingdom Ordinance, or if necessary a Kingdom Statute may provide in which manner that agreement shall be executed.
(4) If the regulations or other measures for the execution of the agreement in question are adopted by the country, the Kingdom Ordinance or the Kingdom Statute will be repealed.

Article 28. On the basis of international agreements concluded by the Kingdom, Aruba, Curacao and Saint Martin may, if such wish exists, join international organizations as members.

Article 29. (1) The acquisition or guarantee of a credit outside the Kingdom in the name of or at the expense of one of the countries takes place in agreement with the government of the Kingdom.
(2) The council of ministers agrees with the acquisition or guarantee of such credit unless this would be contrary to the interests of the Kingdom.

Article 30. (1) Aruba, Curacao and Saint Martin provide the armed forces that are present in their territory with help and assistance which they require in the fulfillment of their task.
(2) By country statute, rules are established to ensure that the armed forces of the Kingdom in Aruba, Curacao and Saint Martin can fulfill their task.

Article 31. (1) Persons who are resident in Aruba, Curacao and Saint Martin may be obliged to serve in the armed forces or in civilian service only by country statute.
(2) It is reserved to the Regulation of State [Staatsregeling] to determine that servicemen serving in the armed forces may be deployed abroad without their consent only pursuant to country statute.

Article 32. In the armed forces for the defence of Aruba, Curacao and Saint Martin as far as possible persons shall be included who are resident in these countries.

Article 33. (1) For the purposes of defence, the confiscation of property and use of goods, the limitation of property and usage rights, the requisition of services and quartering is effected only under observance of general rules to be laid down by Kingdom Statute which also contain provisions regarding compensation.
(2) In that Kingdom Statute, further regulation is assigned where possible to country institutions.

Article 34. (1) The King may, for the maintenance of external or internal security, in case of war or threat of war or where a threat to or disruption of internal order and peace can lead to a substantial infringement on the interests of the Kingdom, declare each part of the territory in state of war or in state of siege.
(2) By or pursuant to Kingdom Statute the manner is determined in which such declaration is effected and the consequences are regulated.

(3) In this regulation is may be provided that and in which manner competences of bodies of civilian authority regarding public order and policing pass wholly or partly to other bodies of civilian authority or to military authority and that the civilian authorities in that latter case are subordinate to military authorities. Regarding the passing of competences, consultation with the government of the affected country takes place where possible. In that regulation it may be deviated from provisions regarding the freedom of the press, the right of association and assembly as well as the inviolability of the home and the respect for correspondence.
(4) For the territory declared in state of siege, in case of war in a manner determined by Kingdom Statute, military penal law and military penal jurisdiction may be wholly or partly declared applicable to everyone.

Article 35. (1) Aruba, Curacao and Saint Martin share, in accordance with their economic strength, the costs connected to the maintenance of the independence and defence of the Kingdom as well as the costs connected to the maintenance of other affairs of the Kingdom to the extent that this benefits Aruba, Curacao and Saint Martin respectively.
(2) The share for Aruba, Curacao and Saint Martin, respectively, stipulated in the first paragraph, is determined by the council of ministers for one fiscal year or for several consecutive fiscal years. Article 12 applies mutatis mutandis, with the exception that decisions are taken by unanimity.
(3) Where the determination stipulated in the second paragraph does not take place in time, pending that, for the duration of at most one fiscal year, the share determined in accordance with that paragraph for the previous fiscal year applies.
(4) The preceding paragraphs do not apply to measures for which special arrangements have been established.

§ 3. Mutual assistance, consultation and cooperation

Article 36. The Netherlands, Aruba, Curacao and Saint Martin provide to each other aid and assistance.

Article 36a. (Repealed).

Article 37. (1) The Netherlands, Aruba, Curacao and Saint Martin shall conduct as much consultation as possible regarding all matters where the interests of two or more of the countries are affected. For that purpose, special representatives may be appointed and common institutions may be established.
(2) As matters in the meaning of this Article are considered, among other things:
a. the promotion of cultural and social ties between the countries;
b. the promotion of effective economic, financial and monetary relations between the countries;
c. questions regarding the coinage and monetary system, banking and foreign-currency policy;

d. the promotion of economic resilience through mutual aid and assistance by the countries;
e. the exercise of professions and businesses by Dutch citizens in the countries;
f. matters regarding aviation, including the policy on unregulated air transportation;
g. matters regarding shipping;
h. cooperation in the field of telegraphy, telephony and radio communications.

Article 38. (1) The Netherlands, Aruba, Curacao and Saint Martin may establish regulations between each other.
(2) In mutual consultation it may be provided that such regulations and the change thereof are established by Kingdom Statute or Kingdom Ordinance.
(3) Regarding matters of private law and criminal law of an inter-regional or international nature, regulations may be established by Kingdom Statute if agreement over such regulations exists between the governments of the countries involved.
(4) The matter of the relocation of the seat of legal persons is regulated by Kingdom Statute. On this regulation, agreement between the governments of the countries is required.

Article 38a. The countries may, through mutual regulations, adopt provisions for the treatment of disputes between them. The second paragraph of Article 38 applies.

Article 39. (1) Private and commercial law, civil procedure, criminal law, criminal procedure, copyright law, industrial property, the office of the notary, as well as provisions regarding measures and weights are regulated as far as possible in an equivalent manner in the Netherlands, Aruba, Curacao and Saint Martin.
(2) A proposal for a far-reaching change in the existing legislation on this matter is not introduced in the representative body – or taken into consideration by the representative body – before the governments in the other countries have been given the opportunity to express their views in that matter.

Article 40. Judgments given by the judge in the Netherlands, Aruba, Curacao or Saint Martin, and orders issued by him, as well as engrossments of authentic acts issued there, may be executed in the entire Kingdom with due regard to the legal provisions of the country where the execution takes place.

§ 4. The constitutional system of the countries

Article 41. (1) The Netherlands, Aruba, Curacao and Saint Martin conduct their own affairs autonomously.
(2) The matters for the Kingdom are among the subjects of concern for the countries.

Article 42. (1) In the Kingdom, the constitutional system of the Netherlands is regulated in the Constitution [Grondwet], the one of Aruba, Curacao and Saint Martin in the Regulation of State [Staatsregeling] of Aruba, of Curacao and of Saint Martin.

(2) The Regulations of State of Aruba, of Curacao and of Saint Martin are established by country statute [landsverordening]. Each proposal for an amendment of the Regulation of State indicates clearly the proposed amendment. The representative body may not adopt the bill for such a country statute unless by two-thirds of votes cast.

Article 43. (1) Each of the countries ensures the realization of the fundamental human rights and freedoms, legal certainty and proper administration.
(2) The guarantee of these rights, freedoms, legal certainty and proper administration is a matter for the Kingdom.

Article 44. (1) A country statute for an amendment of the Regulation of State regarding:
a. the Articles relating to the fundamental human rights and freedoms;
b. the provisions relating to the competences of the Governor;
c. the Articles relating to the competences of the representative bodies of the countries;
d. the Articles relating to the judiciary,
is transmitted to the government of the Kingdom. It does not enter into force until after the government of the Kingdom has expressed its consent herein.
(2) A bill for a country statute regarding the preceding provisions is not presented to the representative body, nor taken into consideration by that body by way of a private member's initiative, until the opinion of the government of the Kingdom is obtained.

Article 45. Amendments to the Constitution [Grondwet] regarding:
a. the Articles relating to the fundamental human rights and freedoms;
b. the provisions relating to the competences of the government;
c. the Articles relating to the competences of the representative body;
d. the Articles relating to the judiciary,
are – notwithstanding the provisions of Article 5 – considered to affect Aruba, Curacao and Saint Martin in the meaning of Article 10.

Article 46. (1) The representative bodies are elected by the residents of the country involved who are Dutch citizens, who have reached an age to be determined by the countries, which may not be higher than 25 years. Each voter only casts one vote. The elections are free and secret. If a necessity thereto appears, the countries may establish restrictions. Every Dutch citizen may run in elections, with the provision that the countries may establish a requirement of residence and an age limit.
(2) The countries may confer the right to elect representative bodies to Dutch citizens who are not residents of the country involved, as well as the right to elect representative bodies and the right to run in elections to residents of the country involved who are not Dutch citizens, in any case provided that in that context at least the requirements for residents who are also Dutch citizens are observed.

Article 47. (1) The ministers and the members of the representative body in the countries, before assuming their office, take an oath or make a promise of allegiance to the King and the Charter.
(2) The ministers and the members of the representative body in Aruba, Curacao and Saint Martin take the oath or make the promise before the representative of the King.

Article 48. The countries respect the provisions of the Charter in their legislation and administration.

Article 49. By Kingdom Statute, regulations may be established regarding the binding effect of legislative measures which are incompatible with the Charter, an international regulation, a Kingdom Statute or a Kingdom Ordinance.

Article 50. (1) Legislative and administrative measures in Aruba, Curacao and Saint Martin which are incompatible with the Charter, an international regulation, a Kingdom Statute or a Kingdom Ordinance, or with interests the promotion or safeguarding of which is a matter for the Kingdom, may be suspended or annulled by the King as the head of the Kingdom by way of reasoned decree. The proposal for an annulment is issued by the council of ministers.
(2) For the Netherlands, this matter is regulated, where necessary, in the Constitution.

Article 51. (1) If an organ in Aruba, Curacao or Saint Martin does not, or does insufficiently perform what it must perform pursuant to the Charter, an international regulation, a Kingdom Statute or a Kingdom Ordinance, then a Kingdom Ordinance, while stating the legal grounds and reasons on which it is based, may determine in which manner this shall be performed.
(2) For the Netherlands, this matter is regulated, where necessary, in the Constitution.

Article 52. Country statute may confer competences with respect to country affairs, with the approval of the King, to the King as head of the Kingdom and to the Governor as an organ of the Kingdom.

Article 53. If Aruba, Curacao or Saint Martin express such wish, the independent supervision of the spending of funds in accordance with the budget of Aruba, Curacao and Saint Martin, respectively, is exercised by the General Chamber of Audit [Algemene Rekenkamer]. In that case, regulations are established after consultation with the Chamber of Audit by Kingdom Statute regarding the cooperation between the Chamber of Audit and the country involved. Thereafter, the government of the country may, upon a proposal from the representative body, appoint someone who is given the opportunity to participate in the deliberations on all matters of the country involved.

§ 5. Transitional and final provisions

Article 54. (1) In case of an amendment of the Constitution [Grondwet], Article 1, second paragraph, will be declared repealed at the moment that the position of Bonaire, Saint Eustatius and Saba within the state order of the Netherlands is provided for by the Constitution.
(2) This Article is repealed if, in accordance with the previous paragraph, Article 1, first paragraph, is declared repealed.

Article 55. (1) Amendments to this Charter are effected by Kingdom Statute.
(2) A proposal for an amendment adopted by the States-General is not approved by the King until it has been accepted by Aruba, Curacao and Saint Martin. Such acceptance is effected by country statute. Such country statute is not adopted until it has been approved by the Parliaments [Staten] in two readings. If the bill is adopted in the first reading by two-thirds of the votes cast, the adoption is effective immediately. The second reading takes place within one month after the bill has been adopted in first reading.
(3) If and in as far as a proposal for an amendment of the Charter deviates from the Constitution [Grondwet], the proposal is considered in such manner as the Constitution prescribes for proposals for an amendment of the Constitution, with the exception that both Chambers may adopt the proposed amendment in second reading by an absolute majority of votes cast.

Article 56. Authorities, binding statutes, decrees and decisions existing on the moment of the entry into force of the Charter remain in place until they are replaced by others under observance of this Charter. To the extent that the Charter itself regulates any matter differently, the regulation by the Charter applies.

Article 57. Statutes and ordinances which applied in the Netherlands Antilles have the status of Kingdom Statute or Kingdom Ordinance, respectively, with the exception that, to the extent that they may pursuant to the Charter be amended by country statute, they have the status of country statute.

Article 57a. Existing Kingdom Statutes, statutes, country statutes, Kingdom Ordinances, ordinances and other regulations which are incompatible with an amendment of the Charter remain in force until a provision for this is adopted in accordance with the Charter.

Article 58. (1) Aruba may declare by country statute that it wishes to terminate the legal order laid down by the Charter regarding Aruba.
(2) The proposal for such country statute is accompanied, when tabled, by an outline of a future constitution including at least provisions regarding fundamental rights, government, representative body, legislation and administration, judiciary and amendment of the constitution.

(3) Parliament may only adopt the proposal by a majority of two thirds of the votes of the sitting members.

Article 59. (1) Within six months after the Parliament of Aruba has adopted the proposal stipulated in Article 58 a referendum regulated by country statute is held whereby those entitled to vote may voice their opinion on the adopted proposal.
(2) The adopted proposal is adopted as country statute only if in the referendum a majority of those entitled to vote has voted in favour of the proposal.

Article 60. (1) After the adoption of the country statute in accordance with Articles 58 and 59 and the approval of the future constitution by the Parliament of Aruba by a majority of two thirds of the votes of the sitting members, by royal decree the moment of the termination of the legal order laid down by the Charter regarding Aruba is established in accordance with the wishes of the government of Aruba.
(2) That moment lies at the latest one month after the date of the adoption of the constitution. That adoption takes place at the latest one year after the date of the referendum stipulated in Article 59.

[*Articles 60a to 60c are omitted.*]

Article 61. The Charter enters into force on the moment of its ceremonial declaration, after it has been affirmed by the King.
Before the affirmation takes place, the Charter requires, for the Netherlands, approval in a manner provided by the Constitution; for Suriname and the Netherlands Antilles by a decision of the representative body.
This decision is taken by two thirds of votes cast. If such majority is not obtained, the Parliament is dissolved and it is decided by the new Parliament by an absolute majority of votes cast.

Article 62. (Repealed).

Constitution for the Kingdom of the Netherlands
[Grondwet voor het Koninkrijk der Nederlanden] of 24 August 1815, as last amended by statute of 27 June 2008 (Stb. 273).[1]

Chapter 1. Fundamental rights

Article 1. All persons in the Netherlands are treated equally in equal circumstances. Discrimination on the grounds of religion, belief, political opinion, race, sex or any other ground is not permissible.

Article 2. (1) Statute regulates who is a Dutch citizen.
(2) Statute regulates the admission and expulsion of aliens.
(3) Extradition may only be effected pursuant to a treaty. Further regulations regarding extradition are provided by statute.
(4) Everyone has the right to leave the country, save for cases provided by statute.

Article 3. All Dutch citizens are eligible for appointment in the public service on an equal footing.

Article 4. Every Dutch citizen has the equal right to elect the members of general representative bodies as well as to be elected member of these bodies, save for limitations and exceptions provided by statute.

Article 5. Everyone has the right to submit petitions in writing to the competent authorities.

Article 6. (1) Everyone has the right to freely express his religion or belief, individually or in community with others, save for everybody's responsibility according to law.
(2) Statute may, regarding the exercise of this right outside of buildings and closed locations, provide for regulations for the protection of health, in the interest of traffic and for the combat against and prevention of disorder.

Article 7. (1) No-one requires prior permission in order to publish thoughts or feelings via the press, save for everybody's responsibility according to law.
(2) Statute provides for regulations regarding radio and television. There is no supervision in advance of the content of a radio or television broadcast.
(3) For the publication of thoughts or feelings via means other than the ones stipulated in the preceding paragraphs, no-one requires prior permission regarding the content thereof, save for everybody's responsibility according to law. Statute

---

[1] Translation by Ph. Kiiver.

may regulate the rendering of displays accessible to persons younger than sixteen years of age for the protection of good morals.
(4) The preceding paragraphs do not apply to commercial advertisement.

Article 8. The right of association is recognized. By statute this right may be limited in the interest of the public order.

Article 9. (1) The right of assembly and demonstration is recognized, save for everybody's responsibility according to law.
(2) Statute may provide for regulations for the protection of health, in the interest of traffic and for the combat against and prevention of disorder.

Article 10. (1) Everyone has, save for limitations to be provided by or pursuant to statute, the right to respect for his private life.
(2) Statute provides for regulations for the protection of private life in the context of the recording and transmission of personal data.
(3) Statute provides for regulations regarding the entitlements of persons to insight into the data recorded on them and into the use made thereof, as well as to a correction of such data.

Article 11. Everyone has, save for limitations to be provided by or pursuant to statute, the right to inviolability of his body.

Article 12. (1) The entry into a home without consent of the occupant is permissible only in cases provided by or pursuant to statute, by those who are designated to that end by or pursuant to statute.
(2) An entry in accordance with the preceding paragraph requires prior identification and notification of the purpose of the entry, save for exceptions provided by statute.
(3) A written report on the entry is delivered to the occupant as soon as possible. If the entry has been effected in the interest of national security or of criminal prosecution, the delivery of the report may be postponed in accordance with regulations to be provided by statute. In cases to be provided by statute, the delivery may be omitted if the interest of national security is permanently incompatible with such delivery.

Article 13. (1) The privacy of the correspondence is inviolable except, in cases provided by statute, by order of a judge.
(2) The privacy of telephone and telegraph communications is inviolable except, in cases provided by statute, by or with the authorization of those designated to that end by statute.

Article 14. (1) Expropriation may be effected only in the general interest and for a previously guaranteed compensation, all of which in accordance with regulations to be provided by or pursuant to statute.

(2) Compensation need not be guaranteed beforehand if in a case of emergency immediate expropriation is called for.
(3) In cases provided by or pursuant to statute there is a right to compensation or partial compensation if, in the general interest, by competent authorities property is being destroyed or made unusable or the exercise of ownership rights is being limited.

Article 15. (1) Save for cases provided by or pursuant to statute, no-one may be deprived of his freedom.
(2) He who is deprived of his freedom on a basis other than upon court order may request his release to a judge. In that case he is heard by the judge within a period to be provided by statute. The judge orders immediate release if he considers the deprivation of freedom unlawful.
(3) The trial of him who is deprived of his freedom with a view thereto, takes place within reasonable time.
(4) He who is lawfully deprived of his freedom may be limited in the exercise of his fundamental rights in as far as such exercise is not compatible with the deprivation of freedom.

Article 16. No act is punishable except by virtue of a prior statutory criminal provision.

Article 17. No-one may against his will be barred from access to the judge that statute accords him.

Article 18. (1) Everyone may be aided in court and in administrative appeal.
(2) Statute provides for regulations regarding the provision of legal aid to persons of limited means.

Article 19. (1) The promotion of sufficient employment is a subject of concern for the state authority.
(2) Statute provides for regulations regarding the legal position of those who are engaged in an employment and regarding their protection therein, as well as regarding co-determination.
(3) The right of every Dutch citizen to a free choice of his occupation is recognized, save for limitations provided by or pursuant to statute.

Article 20. (1) The securing of means of subsistence of the population and the promotion of welfare is a subject of concern for the state authority.
(2) Statute provides for regulations regarding entitlements to social security.
(3) Dutch citizens in this country who cannot provide for their own subsistence have a right to state assistance to be regulated by statute.

Article 21. Concern of the state authority is directed at the habitability of the land and the protection and improvement of the environment.

Article 22. (1) State authority takes measures to promote public health.
(2) The promotion of sufficient living space is a subject of concern for the state authority.
(3) It creates conditions for social and cultural development and for leisure activity.
Article 23. (1) Education is a subject of permanent concern for the government.
(2) Teaching is free, save for state supervision and, as regards forms of education designated by statute, the monitoring of the competence and morality of those who teach, all of which is to be regulated by statute.
(3) Public education is regulated by statute with due respect to the religion or belief of everyone.
(4) In each municipality, sufficient public primary education is offered by the state in a sufficient number of public schools. In accordance with regulations to be provided by statute, deviations from this provision may be permitted as long as an opportunity to receive such education is provided, whether or not in a public school.
(5) The requirements of the appropriateness to be applied to education to be financed wholly or partly from the public purse are regulated by statute with due respect for, as far as special education [bijzonder onderwijs] is concerned, the freedom of underlying direction.
(6) These requirements are regulated for primary education in such manner that the appropriateness of special education financed wholly from the public purse and of public education is equally ensured. In the context of such regulation, in particular the freedom of special education regarding the choice of means of teaching and employment of teachers is respected.
(7) Special primary education which complies with the conditions to be provided by statute is financed from the public purse under the same criteria as public education. Statute provides the conditions under which contributions from the public purse are granted to special secondary and higher secondary education.
(8) The government reports annually to the States-General on the state of the education system.

Chapter 2. Government

§ 1. The King

Article 24. The crown is vested by hereditary succession in the lawful successors of King William I, Prince of Orange-Nassau.

Article 25. The crown passes, in the case of the death of the King, by virtue of hereditary succession to his lawful descendants, in which case the oldest child takes precedence, with further passage of the crown taking place according to the same rule. When there are no descendants of his own, the crown passes in an equal manner to the lawful descendants first of his parent, then of his grandparent, in the line of hereditary succession as long as they are blood relatives not more than thrice removed from the deceased King.

Article 26. The child which a woman carries at the moment of the death of the King is deemed already born for the purposes of hereditary succession. If it is stillborn, it is deemed never to have existed.

Article 27. Abdication leads to hereditary succession in accordance with the rules provided in the preceding Articles. Children born after the abdication, and their descendants, are excluded from hereditary succession.

Article 28. (1) The King who enters into a marriage without approval granted by statute thereby abdicates.
(2) If someone who can inherit the crown from the King enters into such marriage, then he is, together with the children born within that marriage, and their descendants, excluded from hereditary succession.
(3) The States-General deliberate and decide on a bill to grant approval in joint session.

Article 29. (1) If exceptional circumstances so require, one or more persons may be excluded from hereditary succession by statute.
(2) The bill for that purpose is submitted by or on behalf of the King. The States-General deliberate and decide on the matter in joint session. They may adopt the bill only with at least two-thirds of the number of votes cast.

Article 30. (1) If there is a prospect that there shall be no successor, he may be appointed by statute. The bill for that purpose is submitted by or on behalf of the King. After the submission of the bill, the Chambers are dissolved. The new Chambers deliberate and decide on the matter in joint session. They may adopt the bill only with at least two-thirds of the number of votes cast.
(2) If at the death of the King or at abdication there is no successor, the Chambers are dissolved. The new Chambers convene within four months after the death or abdication in joint session in order to decide on the appointment of a King. They may appoint a successor only with at least two-thirds of the number of votes cast.

Article 31. (1) An appointed King may be succeeded by hereditary succession only by his lawful descendants.
(2) The provisions regarding hereditary succession and the first paragraph of this Article apply mutatis mutandis to an appointed successor as long as he is not yet King.

Article 32. After the King has assumed the exercise of royal authority, he is as soon as possible sworn in and inaugurated in the capital city of Amsterdam in a public joint session of the States-General. He swears or promises allegiance to the Constitution and loyal exercise of his office. Statute provides further regulations.

Article 33. The King exercises royal authority only after he has attained the age of eighteen years.

Article 34. Statute regulates parental authority and guardianship over the King who is a minor and the supervision thereof. The States-General deliberate and decide on the matter in joint session.

Article 35. (1) If the council of ministers concludes that the King is incapable of exercising royal authority, it reports this, submitting the advice of the Council of State requested on the matter, to the States-General, which convene on the matter in a joint session.
(2) If the States-General share this conclusion, they declare that the King is incapable of exercising royal authority. Such declaration is published by order of the chairman of the session and enters into force immediately.
(3) As soon as the King is capable again of exercising royal authority, this is declared by statute. The States-General deliberate and decide on the matter in joint session. Immediately after the publication of this statute, the King resumes the exercise of royal authority.
(4) Statute regulates, where necessary, the supervision over the person of the King if he is declared incapable of exercising royal authority. The States-General deliberate and decide on the matter in joint session.

Article 36. The King may temporarily suspend the exercise of royal authority and resume such exercise by virtue of a statute, the bill for which is submitted by or on behalf of himself. The States-General deliberate and decide on the matter in joint session.

Article 37. (1) Royal authority is exercised by a regent:
a. as long as the King has not attained the age of eighteen years;
b. if a child not yet born can be called to take over the crown;
c. if the King has been declared incapable of exercising royal authority;
d. if the King has temporarily suspended the exercise of royal authority;
e. as long as after the death of the King or his abdication there is no successor.
(2) The regent is appointed by statute. The States-General deliberate and decide on the matter in joint session.
(3) In the cases stipulated in the first paragraph under c. and d., the descendant of the King who is his presumed successor is regent by operation of law, if he has attained the age of eighteen years.
(4) The regent swears or promises allegiance to the Constitution and loyal exercise of his office in a joint session of the States-General. Statute provides further regulations regarding regency and may provide for succession and replacement therein. The States-General deliberate and decide on the matter in joint session.
(5) Articles 35 and 36 apply to the regent mutatis mutandis.

Article 38. As long as the exercise of royal authority is not secured, it is exercised by the Council of State [Raad van State].

Article 39. Statute regulates who is a member of the royal house.

Article 40. (1) The King annually receives allowances charged to the Kingdom in accordance with rules to be provided by statute. That statute determines which other members of the royal house receive allowances charged to the Kingdom and regulates these allowances.
(2) The allowances charged to the Kingdom received by them, as well as assets which serve the exercise of their function, are exempt from personal taxation. Furthermore, what the King or his presumed successor receives from a member of the royal house by virtue of inheritance or gift, is exempt from inheritance, transfer and gift taxation. Further exemption from taxation may be granted by statute.
(3) The Chambers of the States-General may adopt bills for statutes stipulated in the preceding paragraphs only with at least two-thirds of the number of votes cast.

Article 41. The King organizes, with due respect for the public interest, his household.

§ 2. King and ministers

Article 42. (1) The government comprises the King and the ministers.
(2) The King is inviolable; the ministers are responsible.

Article 43. The Prime-Minister [minister-president] and the other ministers are appointed and dismissed by royal decree.

Article 44. (1) Ministries are established by royal decree. They are placed under the direction of a minister.
(2) Furthermore, ministers may be appointed who are not charged with directing a ministry.

Article 45. (1) The ministers together form the council of ministers [ministerraad].
(2) The Prime-Minister is chairman of the council of ministers.
(3) The council of ministers deliberates and decides on general government policy and promotes the unity of that policy.

Article 46. (1) Secretaries of state may be appointed by royal decree.
(2) A secretary of state [staatssecretaris] assumes, in the cases where the minister finds it necessary and with due regard to his instructions, his position as minister. The secretary of state is in that context responsible, notwithstanding the responsibility of the minister.

Article 47. All statutes and royal decrees are signed by the King and by one or more ministers or secretaries of state.

Article 48. The royal decree whereby a Prime-Minister is appointed, is signed also by him. The royal decrees whereby the other ministers and the secretaries of state are appointed or dismissed are signed also by the Prime-Minister.

Article 49. In a manner provided by statute, the ministers and secretaries of state, when assuming office, take an oath or make a declaration and promise before the King of their integrity, and swear or promise allegiance to the Constitution and loyal exercise of their office.

Chapter 3. States-General

§ 1. Organization and composition

Article 50. The States-General [Staten-Generaal] represent the entire Dutch people.

Article 51. (1) The States-General consist of the Second Chamber [Tweede Kamer] and the First Chamber [Eerste Kamer].
(2) The Second Chamber consists of one hundred and fifty members.
(3) The First Chamber consists of seventy-five members.
(4) In a joint session, the two Chambers are considered as one.

Article 52. (1) The term of session of both Chambers is four years.
(2) If for the provincial assemblies [provinciale staten] a term other than four years is established by statute, the term of session of the First Chamber is changed accordingly.

Article 53. (1) The members of both Chambers are elected on the basis of proportional representation within the limits to be provided by statute.
(2) Elections take place by secret ballot.

Article 54. (1) The members of the Second Chamber are elected directly by Dutch citizens who have attained the age of eighteen years, save for exceptions to be provided by statute with regard to Dutch citizens who are not residents.
(2) He who has been convicted to a prison sentence of at least one year for a criminal act so designated by statute in a final court judgment and who has at the same time been disqualified from the right to vote is excluded from the vote.

Article 55. The members of the First Chamber are elected by the members of the provincial assemblies [provinciale staten]. The elections take place, save for the event of a dissolution of the Chamber, within three months following the elections of the members of the provincial assemblies.

Article 56. In order to be able to become a member of the States-General, it is required that one be a Dutch citizen, have attained the age of eighteen years, and not be disqualified from the right to vote.

Article 57. (1) No-one may be a member of both Chambers.
(2) A member of the Second Chamber may not at the same time be a minister, secretary of state, member of the Council of State, member of the General Chamber

of Audit, National Ombudsman or substitute ombudsman, or a member of or procurator-general or advocate-general at the Supreme Court.
(3) Nevertheless a minister or secretary of state, who has tendered his resignation, may combine this office with a membership of the States-General, until a decision has been taken regarding that resignation.
(4) Statute may provide with regard to other public offices that they may not be exercised at the same time as the membership of the States-General or of one of the Chambers.

Article 57a. Statute regulates the temporary replacement of a member of the States-General because of pregnancy and delivery as well as because of illness.

Article 58. Each Chamber examines the letters patent of its newly appointed members and decides, with due regard to the regulations to be provided by statute, on disputes that arise with respect to the letters patent or the election itself.

Article 59. Everything else regarding the right to vote and the elections is regulated by statute.

Article 60. In a manner provided by statute, the members of the Chambers, when assuming their office, take an oath or make a declaration and promise in the assembly of their integrity, and swear or promise allegiance to the Constitution and loyal exercise of their office.

Article 61. (1) Each of the Chambers appoints a president from among the members.
(2) Each of the Chambers appoints a secretary. He and the other administrative staff of the Chambers may not at the same time be members of the States-General.

Article 62. The president of the First Chamber has the chairmanship over the joint session.

Article 63. Financial consideration for members and former members of the States-General and their surviving dependants are regulated by statute. The Chambers may adopt a bill on this matter only with at least two-thirds of the number of votes cast.

Article 64. (1) Each of the Chambers may be dissolved by royal decree.
(2) Each decree on such dissolution also contains an order for new elections to the dissolved Chamber and for the convention of the newly elected Chamber within three months.
(3) The dissolution takes effect on the day when the newly elected Chamber convenes.
(4) Statute determines the duration of the term of session of a Second Chamber operating after dissolution; the period may not be longer than five years. The term

of session of a First Chamber operating after dissolution ends on the moment when the term of the dissolved Chamber would have ended.

§ 2. Procedures

Article 65. Annually, on the third Tuesday of September or at an earlier moment to be determined by statute, an explanation is given by or on behalf of the King in a joint session of the States-General regarding the policies to be pursued by the government.

Article 66. (1) The meetings of the States-General are public.
(2) The doors are closed when a tenth part of the number of members present so demand or when the president deems it necessary.
(3) The Chamber or the Chambers in joint session, respectively, then decide whether they should deliberate and decide with closed doors.

Article 67. (1) The Chambers may, each separately and in joint session, deliberate and decide only if more than half of the number of members in office is present at the meeting.
(2) Decisions are taken by a majority of votes.
(3) The members vote without any instructions.
(4) Matters are voted on orally and by individual calls when one member so demands.

Article 68. The ministers and the secretaries of state provide the Chambers, separately and in joint session, orally or in writing the information demanded by one or more members, where such provision is not in conflict with the interest of the state.

Article 69. (1) The ministers and the secretaries of state have access to the meetings and may participate in deliberations.
(2) They may be invited by the Chambers, separately and in joint session, to be present at the meeting.
(3) They may be assisted at the meeting by persons designated by them for that purpose.

Article 70. Both Chambers, both separately and in joint session, have the right of inquiry [enquête] to be regulated by statute.

Article 71. The members of the States-General, the ministers, the secretaries of state and other persons who participate in deliberations may not be prosecuted or held liable for what they have said in the meetings of the States-General or in committees thereof, or for what they have submitted to them in writing.

Article 72. The Chambers, both separately and in joint session, adopt rules of procedure.

Chapter 4. Council of State, General Chamber of Audit, National Ombudsman and permanent advisory bodies

Article 73. (1) The Council of State [Raad van State] or a division of the Council is heard on bills and drafts for ordinances [algemene maatregelen van bestuur] as well as proposals for the ratification of treaties by the States-General. In cases to be provided by statute, such hearing may be omitted.
(2) The Council or a division of the Council is charged with the investigation in administrative disputes that are decided by royal decree, and proposes a decision.
(3) Statute may charge the Council or a division of the Council with deciding in administrative disputes.

Article 74. (1) The King is the president of the Council of State. The presumed successor of the King is a member of the Council by operation of law after having attained the age of eighteen years. By or pursuant to statute, other members of the royal house may be granted membership of the Council.
(2) The members of the Council are appointed for life by royal decree.
(3) They are dismissed upon their own request and because they have attained an age to be provided by statute.
(4) In cases provided by statute they may be suspended or dismissed by the Council.
(5) Statute regulates the further details of their legal position.

Article 75. (1) Statute regulates the organization, composition and competence of the Council of State.
(2) By statute, also other tasks may be assigned to the Council or a division of the Council.

Article 76. The General Chamber of Audit [Algemene Rekenkamer] is charged with investigating the revenue and expenditure of the Kingdom.

Article 77. (1) The members of the General Chamber of Audit are appointed by royal decree for life from a proposal of three persons drawn up by the Second Chamber of the States-General.
(2) They are dismissed upon their own request and because they have attained an age to be provided by statute.
(3) In cases provided by statute they may be suspended or dismissed by the Supreme Court [Hoge Raad].
(4) Statute regulates the further details of their legal position.

Article 78. (1) Statute regulates the organization, composition and competence of the General Chamber of Audit.
(2) By statute, also other tasks may be assigned to the General Chamber of Audit.

Article 78a. (1) The National Ombudsman, upon request or on his own motion, conducts investigations into the conduct of administrative authorities of the Kingdom and of other administrative authorities designated by or pursuant to statute.
(2) The National Ombudsman and a substitute ombudsman are appointed for a term to be provided by statute by the Second Chamber of the States-General. They are dismissed upon their own request and because they have attained an age to be provided by statute. In cases provided by statute they may be suspended or dismissed by the Second Chamber of the States-General. Statute regulates the further details of their legal position.
(3) Statutes regulates the competence and procedures of the National Ombudsman.
(4) By or pursuant to statute, also other tasks may be assigned to the National Ombudsman.

Article 79. (1) Permanent advisory bodies in matters of legislation and administration of the Kingdom are established by or pursuant to statute.
(2) Statute regulates the organization, composition and competence of such bodies.
(3) By or pursuant to statute, also tasks other than advisory ones may be assigned to such bodies.

Article 80. (1) The opinions of the bodies stipulated in this chapter are published in accordance with procedures to be provided by statute.
(2) Opinions given on the matter of bills which are introduced by or on behalf of the King are, save for exceptions to be provided by statute, transmitted to the States-General.

Chapter 5. Legislation and administration

§ 1. Statutes and other regulations

Article 81. Statutes [wetten] are adopted jointly by the government and the States-General.

Article 82. (1) Bills may be introduced by or on behalf of the King and by the Second Chamber of the States-General.
(2) Bills for which deliberation in the States-General in joint session is prescribed may be introduced by or on behalf of the King and, as far as the relevant Articles of Chapter 2 allow, by the joint session.
(3) Bills to be introduced by the Second Chamber or the joint session, respectively, are tabled by one or more of the members.

Article 83. Bills introduced by or on behalf of the King are transmitted to the Second Chamber or, if deliberation in the States-General in joint session is prescribed, to that assembly.

Article 84. (1) As long as a bill introduced by or on behalf of the King has not yet been adopted by the Second Chamber or the joint session, respectively, it may be amended by it, on the proposal of one or more members, and by the government.
(2) As long as the Second Chamber or the joint session, respectively, has not yet adopted a bill to be introduced by itself, it may be amended by it on the proposal of one or more members and by the member or members who have
tabled the bill.

Article 85. As soon as the Second Chamber has adopted a bill or has decided to introduce a bill, it transmits it to the First Chamber, which considers it as transmitted to it by the Second Chamber. The Second Chamber may instruct one or more of its members to defend a bill introduced by it in the First Chamber.

Article 86. (1) As long as a bill has not yet been adopted by the States-General, it may be withdrawn by or on behalf of the initiator.
(2) As long as the Second Chamber or the joint session, respectively, has not yet adopted a bill to be introduced by it, it may be withdrawn by the member or members who have tabled it.

Article 87. (1) A bill becomes a statute as soon as it has been adopted by the States-General and confirmed by the King.
(2) The King and the States-General inform each other of their decision regarding any bill.

Article 88. Statute regulates the publication and entry into force of statutes. They do not enter into force before they have been published.

Article 89. (1) Ordinances [algemene maatregelen van bestuur] are adopted by royal decree.
(2) Regulations to be enforced by sanctions are provided there only pursuant to statute. Statute regulates the sanctions to be imposed.
(3) Statute regulates the publication and entry into force of ordinances. They do not enter into force before they have been published.
(4) The second and third paragraph apply mutatis mutandis to other generally binding regulations adopted by the Kingdom.

§ 2. Further provisions

Article 90. The government promotes the development of the international legal order.

Article 91. (1) The Kingdom is not bound by treaties and they are not terminated without prior approval of the States-General. Statute provides the cases where no such approval is required.

(2) Statute provides the manner in which approval is given and may provide for tacit approval.
(3) If a treaty contains provisions which deviate from the Constitution or necessitate such deviation, the Chambers may give approval only with at least two-thirds of the number of votes cast.

Article 92. Subject, where necessary, to the provisions of Article 91 (3), legislative, executive and judicial powers may be conferred upon international organizations by or pursuant to a treaty.

Article 93. Provisions of treaties and of decisions of international organizations, which by virtue of their content can be binding upon everyone, become binding after they have been published.

Article 94. Statutory regulations in force within the Kingdom are not applicable if such application is incompatible with provisions of treaties and decisions of international organizations that are binding on everyone.

Article 95. Statute provides regulations regarding the publication of treaties and decisions of international organizations.

Article 96. (1) The Kingdom is not declared to be in a state of war unless after prior consent of the States-General.
(2) Such consent is not required when consultation with the States-General has proven to be impossible as a result of a state of war existing in fact.
(3) The States-General deliberate and decide on the matter in a joint session.
(4) The provisions of the first and the third paragraph apply mutatis mutandis to a declaration that a war has ended.

Article 97. (1) For the purposes of defence and for the protection of the interests of the Kingdom, as well as for the upholding and promotion of the international legal order, there are armed forces.
(2) The government has the supreme command over the armed forces.

Article 98. (1) The armed forces consist of volunteers and may also comprise conscripts.
(2) Statute regulates compulsory military service and the power to defer drafting into actual service.

Article 99. Statute regulates exemption from military service because of serious conscientious objections.

Article 99a. In accordance with regulations to be provided by statute, obligations may be imposed for the purposes of civil defence.

Article 100. (1) The government provides the States-General with information in advance regarding the deployment or the making available of the armed forces for the upholding and promotion of the international legal order. That includes information in advance regarding the deployment or the making available of the armed forces for humanitarian assistance in case of an armed conflict.
(2) The first paragraph does not apply if pressing reasons prevent the provision of information in advance. In that case, information is provided as soon as possible.

Articles 101 and 102. (Repealed).

Article 103. (1) Statute regulates in which cases, for the maintenance of external and internal security, a state of emergency to be designated as such by statute may be declared by royal decree; statute regulates the consequences.
(2) In that context, deviations are permissible from the constitutional provisions regarding the competences of the governments of the provinces, municipalities and water boards, from the fundamental rights regulated in Article 6, in as far as the exercise of the right stipulated in that Article outside buildings and closed locations is concerned, 7, 8, 9, 12 (2) and (3) and 13, as well as from Article 113 (1) and (3).
(3) Immediately after the declaration of a state of emergency and then, as long as it has not been lifted by royal decree, each time they consider it necessary, the States-General decide on the continuation thereof; they deliberate and decide on the matter in joint session.

Article 104. Taxes of the Kingdom are raised by virtue of a statute. Other charges of the Kingdom are regulated by statute.

Article 105. (1) The budget of the revenue and expenditure of the Kingdom is established by statute.
(2) Annually, bills for general budget statutes are introduced by or on behalf of the King on the moment provided in Article 65.
(3) Account for the revenue and expenditure of the Kingdom is given to the States-General in accordance with the provisions of statute. The accounts approved by the General Chamber of Audit are submitted to the States-General.
(4) Statute provides regulations regarding the administration of the finances of the Kingdom.

Article 106. Statute regulates the monetary system.

Article 107. (1) Statute regulates private law, criminal law and civil and criminal procedure in general codes, save for the power to regulate certain subject-matters in separate statutes.
(2) Statute provides general rules of administrative law.

Article 108. (Repealed).

Article 109. Statute regulates the legal position of civil servants. It also provides regulations regarding their protection at work and regarding co-determination.

Article 110. The state respects openness in the exercise of its tasks in accordance with regulations to be provided by statute.

Article 111. Chivalric orders are established by statute.

Chapter 6. Judiciary

Article 112. (1) The judiciary is charged with adjudicating in disputes over rights and claims of private law.
(2) Statute may assign the adjudication in disputes which did not arise from private law relations either to the judiciary or to courts which do not form part of the judiciary. Statute regulates the procedures and the consequences of decisions.

Article 113. (1) The judiciary is furthermore charged with adjudicating on criminal acts.
(2) Disciplinary jurisdiction established by the state is regulated by statute.
(3) A sentence of deprivation of freedom may be imposed only by the judiciary.
(4) For adjudication outside the Netherlands and for military criminal law, statute may provide deviating regulations.

Article 114. The death penalty may not be imposed.

Article 115. With regard to disputes stipulated in Article 112 (2), administrative appeal may be allowed.

Article 116. (1) Statute designates the courts that form part of the judiciary.
(2) Statute regulates the organization, composition and competence of the judiciary.
(3) Statute may provide that persons not belonging to the judiciary participate in the jurisprudence thereof.
(4) Statute regulates the supervision by members of the judiciary charged with jurisprudence to be exercised over the exercise of the office of such members and of persons stipulated in the preceding paragraph.

Article 117. (1) The members of the judiciary charged with jurisprudence and the procurator-general at the Supreme Court are appointed by royal decree for life.
(2) They are dismissed upon their own request and because they have attained an age to be provided by statute.
(3) In cases provided by statute they may be suspended or dismissed by a court forming part of the judiciary designated by statute.
(4) Statute regulates the further details of their legal position.

Article 118. (1) The members of the Supreme Court [Hoge Raad] of the Netherlands are appointed from a proposal of three persons drawn up by the Second Chamber of the States-General.
(2) The Supreme Court is charged, in the cases and within the boundaries provided by statute, with cassation of judicial decisions because of a violation of the law.
(3) By statute, also other tasks may be assigned to the Supreme Court.

Article 119. The members of the States-General, the ministers and the secretaries of state are prosecuted for crimes committed in office, also after their leaving office, before the Supreme Court. The order to prosecute is given by royal decree or by a decision of the Second Chamber.

Article 120. The judge does not enter into a review of the constitutionality of statutes and treaties.

Article 121. Save for cases provided by statute, trials are conducted in public and judgments contain the reasons on which they are based. The judgment is handed down in public.

Article 122. (1) Pardon is granted by royal decree after the advice of a court designated by statute and with due regard to regulations to be provided by or pursuant to statute.
(2) Amnesty is granted by or pursuant to statute.

Chapter 7. Provinces, municipalities, water boards and other public entities

Article 123. (1) By statute, provinces [provincies] and municipalities [gemeenten] may be dissolved and new ones may be established.
(2) Statute regulates the change of provincial and municipal borders.

Article 124. (1) For provinces and municipalities, the power of regulation and administration regarding their local affairs [huishouding] is left to their governments.
(2) Regulation and administration may be demanded of the governments of provinces and municipalities by or pursuant to statute.

Article 125. (1) The head of the province and the municipality is the provincial assembly [provinciale staten] and the municipal council [gemeenteraad], respectively. Their meetings are public, save for exceptions to be regulated by statute.
(2) The government [bestuur] of the province also includes the provincial executive [gedeputeerde staten] and the King's Commissioner, the government of the municipality also includes the board of burgomaster and aldermen and the burgomaster.

Article 126. Statute may provide that the King's Commissioner is charged with the execution of an official instruction given by the government.

Article 127. The provincial assembly and the municipal council adopt, save for exceptions provided by statute or by them pursuant to statute, the provincial and the municipal ordinances [verordeningen], respectively.

Article 128. Save for the cases stipulated in Article 123, the conferral of powers within the meaning of Article 124 (1) to organs other than the ones stipulated in Article 125 may be effected only by the provincial assembly and the municipal council, respectively.

Article 129. (1) The members of the provincial assembly and of the municipal council are elected directly by Dutch citizens who are at the same time residents of the province or municipality, respectively, who fulfil the conditions that apply to elections of the Second Chamber of the States-General. For membership the same conditions apply.
(2) The members are elected on the basis of proportional representation within the limits to be provided by statute.
(3) Articles 53 (2) and 59 apply. Article 57a applies mutatis mutandis.
(4) The term of session of the provincial assembly and the municipal council is four years, save for exceptions to be provided by statute.
(5) Statute provides which offices may not be exercised simultaneously with membership. Statute may provide that disqualifications derive from family relation or marriage and that the commission of acts designated by statute may lead to a loss of membership.
(6) Members vote without instructions.

Article 130. Statute may confer the right to elect the members of the municipal council and the right to be a member of the municipal council to residents who are not Dutch citizens, as long as they at least fulfil the conditions that apply to residents who are also Dutch citizens.

Article 131. The King's Commissioner and the burgomaster are appointed by royal decree.

Article 132. (1) Statute regulates the organization of provinces and municipalities as well as the composition and competence of their governments.
(2) Statute regulates supervision of these governments.
(3) Decisions of these governments may be subjected to supervision in advance only in cases to be provided by or pursuant to statute.
(4) Annulment of decisions of these governments may only be effected by royal decree because of a violation of the law or the general interest.
(5) Statute regulates provisions in case of a non-performance with regard to regulation and administration demanded by virtue of Article 124 (2). By statute, provisions in deviation from Articles 125 and 127 may be effected in case the government of a province or a municipality grossly neglects its tasks.
(6) Statute provides which taxes may be raised by the governments of provinces and municipalities and regulates their financial relation with the Kingdom.

Article 133. (1) The dissolution and establishment of water boards [waterschappen], the regulation of their tasks and organization, as well as the composition of their governing bodies is effected, in accordance with regulations to be provided by statute, by provincial ordinance, in as far as nothing is provided otherwise by or pursuant to statute.
(2) Statute regulates the regulatory and other competences of the governing bodies of water boards, as well as the public character of their meetings.
(3) Statute regulates the provincial and further supervision of these governing bodies. Annulment of decisions of these governing bodies may be effected only because of a violation of the law or the general interest.

Article 134. (1) By or pursuant to statute, public entities for professions and enterprises and other public entities may be established and dissolved.
(2) Statute regulates the tasks and the organization of these public entities, the composition and competence of their governing bodies, as well as the public character of their meetings. By or pursuant to statute, regulatory competence may be conferred upon their governing bodies.
(3) Statute regulates the supervision of these governing bodies. Annulment of decisions of these governing bodies may be effected only because of a violation of the law or the general interest.
Article 135. Statute provides regulations for provisions in cases where two or more public entities are involved. In that context, the establishment of a new public entity may be provided for, in which case Article 134 (2) and (3) applies.

Article 136. Disputes between public entities are resolved by royal decree, unless they fall under the jurisdiction of the judiciary or such resolution is assigned by statute to others.

Chapter 8. Revision of the Constitution

Article 137. (1) A statute declares that an amendment of the Constitution as it proposes shall be considered.
(2) The Second Chamber may, whether or not upon such proposal introduced by or on behalf of the King, split a bill for such a statute.
(3) After the publication of the statute stipulated in the first paragraph, the Second Chamber is dissolved.
(4) After the new Second Chamber has convened, both Chambers consider in second reading the proposal for an amendment stipulated in the first paragraph. They may adopt it only with at least two-thirds of the number of votes cast.
(5) The Second Chamber may, whether or not upon such proposal introduced by or on behalf of the King, split a proposal for an amendment with at least two-thirds of the number of votes cast.

Article 138. (1) Before the proposals for an amendment of the Constitution adopted in second reading are confirmed by the King, by statute:

a. the adopted proposals and the provisions of the Constitution left unchanged may be adjusted to one another as far as necessary;
b. the division and position of chapters, sections and Articles as well as the titles may be modified.
(2) The Chambers may adopt a bill containing provisions stipulated in the first paragraph, sub a., only with at least two-thirds of the number of votes cast.

Article 139. The amendments of the Constitution, adopted by the States-General and confirmed by the King, enter into force immediately after they have been published.

Article 140. Existing statutes and other regulations and decisions which are incompatible with an amendment of the Constitution remain in force until a provision on that matter is effected in accordance with the Constitution.

Article 141. The text of the revised Constitution is published by royal decree, in which context chapters, sections and Articles may be renumbered and references be changed accordingly.

Article 142. The Constitution may by statute be brought into line with the Charter for the Kingdom of the Netherlands [Statuut voor het Koninkrijk der Nederlanden]. Articles 139, 140 and 141 apply mutatis mutandis.

[*The supplementary provisions are omitted.*]

Elections Act

[Kieswet] of 28 September 1989, as last amended in its relevant parts by statute of 29 January 2014 (Stb. 63). Selected provisions: Articles P1, P1a, P5 to P7, P9, P10, P15, P19, P19a, U1, U2 (1), U3, U7 to U10 and U15.[1]

[*Part I is omitted.*]

Part II. The elections of the members of the Second Chamber of the States-General, of provincial assemblies and of the municipal councils

[*Chapters B to O are omitted.*]

Chapter P. The establishment of the election results by the central polling office

§ 1. General provisions

Article P 1. Immediately after the records of all main polling offices have been received, the central polling office starts carrying out the activities for the establishment and publication of the results of the elections. If elections of the municipal council or the provincial assembly of a province which forms a single polling district is concerned, the central elections office starts these activities immediately after the activities stipulated in Articles O 1 and O 2 have been concluded.

Article P1a. (1) If the central polling office makes use of software for the calculation of election results or the calculation of the allocation of seats, the central polling office announces electronically, in a generally accessible manner, which software it uses.
(2) By or pursuant to royal decree, further rules are laid down with regard to the publication of software used, determining conditions under which the central polling office can make use of software for the calculation of election results or the calculation of the allocation of seats, and determining the requirements this software must comply with.

§ 2. The allocation of seats

[*Articles P2 to P4 are omitted.*]

Article P 5. (1) The central polling office divides the sum of the number of votes of all lists by the number of seats to be allocated.
(2) The quotient thus obtained is called electoral divisor.

---

[1] Translation by Ph. Kiiver and S. Hardt.

Article P 6. A list is assigned a seat so many times as the electoral divisor is accommodated in the number of votes of that list.

Article P 7. (1) The remaining seats, which are called rest seats, are, if the number of seats to be allocated is nineteen or more, consecutively assigned to those lists which after assignment of a seat have the largest average number of votes per assigned seat. If averages are equal, the lot decides where necessary.
(2) If the election of the members of the Second Chamber is concerned, lists the number of votes of which is lower than the electoral divisor are not entitled to such assignment.

[Article P 8 is omitted.]

Article P 9. If a list which has received an absolute majority of votes cast is assigned a number of seats that is smaller than the absolute majority of seats to be allocated, that list is assigned one additional seat and, at the same time, one seat is forfeited that had been assigned to the list which had received a seat for the smallest average or the smallest remainder. If two or more lists had received a seat for the same smallest average or the smallest remainder, the lot decides.

Article P 10. If in the application of the preceding provisions a list would have to be assigned more seats than there are candidates, the remaining seat or seats pass by continued application of these provisions to one or more of the other lists on which candidates appear to whom no seat has been assigned.

[Articles P 11 to P 14 are omitted.]

§ 3. The assignment of the seats to the candidates

Article P 15. (1) In the order of the number of votes cast for them, those candidates are elected who, on the common lists on which they appear, have received a number of votes that is larger than 25% of the electoral divisor, as long as that group of lists or that list not being part of a group of lists has received sufficient seats. If numbers are equal, the lot decides where necessary.
(2) If the number of seats to be allocated in the election of members of the municipal council is lower than nineteen, then, in the application of the first paragraph, not 25% of the electoral divisor but half of the electoral divisor shall be applied.

[Articles P 16 to P 18 are omitted.]

Article P 19. (1) The central polling office ranks, with respect to each list, the candidates appearing thereon in such manner that the candidates to whom a seat is assigned by application of Article P 15 come on top, in the order in which the seats have been assigned.

(2) Subsequently, in the order of the numbers cast for them, candidates appearing on the are ranked who have, on the common lists on which they appear, received a number of votes that is larger than 25% of the electoral divisor or larger than half of the electoral divisor, respectively, but who have not been declared elected by application of Article P 15 (1) or (2), respectively. If numbers are equal, the order of the list decides.
(3) Finally, in the order of the list, the other candidates appearing on the list are ranked.
(4) Article P 18 remains inapplicable at the ranking.
(5) Save for elections in which the number of seats to be allocated is less than thirteen, the ranking shall be omitted as far as lists or numbers of identical lists are concerned on which no candidates have been declared elected and which do not form part of a combination of lists or group of lists to which one or more seats have been assigned.

Article P 19a. If a candidate is deceased, he is left out of consideration in the application of this section.

[The remainder of Chapter P is omitted.]

Part III. The election of the members of the First Chamber of the States-General

[Chapters Q to T are omitted.]

Chapter U. The establishment of the election results by the central polling office

§ 1. General provisions

Article U 1. Immediately after the records have been received, the central polling office starts carrying out the activities for the establishment and publication of the results of the elections.

Article U 2. (1) Each vote counts, depending on the province where it has been cast, as a number of votes that is equal to the number that is obtained by dividing the population number of the province by one hundred times the number of members of which the provincial assembly is composed. The quotient is thereafter rounded towards a full number upwards if a fraction is greater than 1/2 and downwards if a fraction is less than 1/2. This number is called the vote value.
[The remainder of Article U2 is omitted.]

§ 2. The allocation of seats

Article U 3. With respect to each province, the central polling office multiplies the numbers of votes cast for each candidate and the numbers of votes of the lists by the vote value that applies to that province. For the establishment of the result of the election, the products thus obtained count as the number of votes cast for each candidate or the number of votes of the lists, respectively.

[Articles U 4 to U 6 are omitted.]

Article U 7. (1) The central polling office divides the sum of the number of votes of all lists by the number of seats to be allocated.
(2) The quotient thus obtained is called electoral divisor.

Article U 8. A list is assigned a seat so many times as the electoral divisor is accommodated in the number of votes of that list.

Article U 9. The remaining seats, which are called rest seats, are consecutively assigned to those lists which after assignment of a seat have the largest average number of votes per assigned seat. If averages are equal, the lot decides where necessary.

Article U 10. If in the application of the preceding provisions a list would have to be assigned more seats than there are candidates, the remaining seat or seats pass by continued application of these provisions to one or more of the other lists on which candidates appear to whom no seat has been assigned.

[Articles U 11 to U 14 are omitted.]

§ 3. The assignment of the seats to the candidates

Article U 15. (1) Those candidates from the list are elected who are designated as such by application, mutatis mutandis, of Articles P 15 to P 18 and P 19a, save that, by means of deviation from article P15 (1), first sentence, those candidates are elected who have received a number of votes larger than or equal to the electoral divisor.
(2) The ranking of candidates is carried out in accordance with the provisions of Article P 19 (1), (3) and (4), save that the ranking is omitted as far as it concerns lists on which no candidates have been declared elected and which do not form part of a combination of lists or group of lists to which one or more seats have been assigned.

[The remainder of the Act is omitted.]

UNITED KINGDOM

Bill of Rights 1689[1]
[An Act declareing the Rights and Liberties of the Subject and Setleing the Succession of the Crowne], as amended. Selected provisions: first part.

Whereas the Lords Spirituall and Temporall and Comons assembled at Westminster lawfully fully and freely representing all the Estates of the People of this Realme did upon the thirteenth day of February in the yeare of our Lord one thousand six hundred eighty eight present unto their Majesties then called and known by the Names and Stile of William and Mary Prince and Princesse of Orange being present in their proper Persons a certaine Declaration in Writeing made by the said Lords and Comons in the Words following viz

Whereas the late King James the Second by the Assistance of diverse evill Councellors Judges and Ministers imployed by him did endeavour to subvert and extirpate the Protestant Religion and the Lawes and Liberties of this Kingdome.
By Assumeing and Exerciseing a Power of Dispensing with and Suspending of Lawes and the Execution of Lawes without Consent of Parlyament.
By Committing and Prosecuting diverse Worthy Prelates for humbly Petitioning to be excused from Concurring to the said Assumed Power.
By issueing and causeing to be executed a Commission under the Great Seale for Erecting a Court called The Court of Commissioners for Ecclesiasticall Causes.
By Levying Money for and to the Use of the Crowne by pretence of Prerogative for other time and in other manner then the same was granted by Parlyament.
By raising and keeping a Standing Army within this Kingdome in time of Peace without Consent of Parlyament and Quartering Soldiers contrary to Law.
By causing severall good Subjects being Protestants to be disarmed at the same time when Papists were both Armed and Imployed contrary to Law.

---

[1] Various publications assign the Bill of Rights to the year 1688, although it received Royal Assent on 26 December 1689.

United Kingdom: Bill of Rights 1689

By Violating the Freedome of Election of Members to serve in Parlyament.
By Prosecutions in the Court of Kings Bench for Matters and Causes cognizable onely in Parlyament and by diverse other Arbitrary and Illegall Courses.
And whereas of late yeares Partiall Corrupt and Unqualifyed Persons have beene returned and served on Juryes in Tryalls and particularly diverse Jurors in Tryalls for High Treason which were not Freeholders,
And excessive Baile hath beene required of Persons committed in Criminall Cases to elude the Benefitt of the Lawes made for the Liberty of the Subjects.
And excessive Fines have beene imposed.
And illegall and cruell Punishments inflicted.
And severall Grants and Promises made of Fines and Forfeitures before any Conviction or Judgement against the Persons upon whome the same were to be levyed. All which are utterly directly contrary to the knowne Lawes and Statutes and Freedome of this Realme.

And whereas the said late King James the Second haveing Abdicated the Government and the Throne being thereby Vacant His Hignesse the Prince of Orange (whome it hath pleased Almighty God to make the glorious Instrument of Delivering this Kingdome from Popery and Arbitrary Power) did (by the Advice of the Lords Spirituall and Temporall and diverse principall Persons of the Commons) cause Letters to be written to the Lords Spirituall and Temporall being Protestants and other Letters to the severall Countyes Cityes Universities Burroughs and Cinque Ports for the Choosing of such Persons to represent them as were of right to be sent to Parlyament to meete and sitt at Westminster upon the two and twentyeth day of January in this Yeare one thousand six hundred eighty and eight in order to such an Establishment as that their Religion Lawes and Liberties might not againe be in danger of being Subverted, Upon which Letters Elections haveing beene accordingly made.

And thereupon the said Lords Spirituall and Temporall and Commons pursuant to their respective Letters and Elections being now assembled in a full and free Representative of this Nation takeing into their most serious Consideration the best meanes for attaining the Ends aforesaid Doe in the first place (as their Auncestors in like Case have usually done) for the Vindicating and Asserting their auntient Rights and Liberties, Declare

That the pretended Power of Suspending of Laws or the Execution of Laws by Regall Authority without Consent of Parlyament is illegall.
That the pretended Power of Dispensing with Laws or the Execution of Laws by Regall Authoritie as it hath beene assumed and exercised of late is illegall.
That the Commission for erecting the late Court of Commissioners for Ecclesiasticall Causes and all other Commissions and Courts of like nature are Illegall and Pernicious.
That levying Money for or to the Use of the Crowne by pretence of Prerogative without Grant of Parlyament for longer time or in other manner then the same is or shall be granted is Illegall.

That it is the Right of the Subjects to petition the King and all Commitments and Prosecutions for such Petitioning are Illegall.

That the raising or keeping a standing Army within the Kingdome in time of Peace unlesse it be with Consent of Parlyament is against Law.

That the Subjects which are Protestants may have Arms for their Defence suitable to their Conditions and as allowed by Law.

That Election of Members of Parlyament ought to be free.

That the Freedome of Speech and Debates or Proceedings in Parlyament ought not to be impeached or questioned in any Court or Place out of Parlyament.

That excessive Baile ought not to be required nor excessive Fines imposed nor cruell and unusuall Punishments inflicted.

That Jurors ought to be duely impannelled and returned.

That all Grants and Promises of Fines and Forfeitures of particular persons before Conviction are illegall and void.

And that for Redresse of all Grievances and for the amending strengthening and preserveing of the Lawes Parlyaments ought to be held frequently.

And they doe Claime Demand and Insist upon all and singular the Premises as their undoubted Rights and Liberties and that noe Declarations Judgements Doeings or Proceedings to the Prejudice of the People in any of the said Premisses ought in any wise to be drawne hereafter into Consequence or Example. To which Demand of their Rights they are particularly encouraged by the Declaration of this Highnesse the Prince of Orange as being the onely meanes for obtaining a full Redresse and Remedy therein. Haveing therefore an intire Confidence That his said Highnesse the Prince of Orange will perfect the Deliverance soe farr advanced by him and will still preserve them from the Violation of their Rights which they have here asserted and from all other Attempts upon their Religion Rights and Liberties. The said Lords Spirituall and Temporall and Commons assembled at Westminster doe Resolve That William and Mary Prince and Princesse of Orange be and be declared King and Queene of England France and Ireland and the Dominions thereunto belonging to hold the Crowne and Royall Dignity of the said Kingdomes and Dominions to them the said Prince and Princesse dureing their Lives and the Life of the Survivour of them And that the sole and full Exercise of the Regall Power be onely in and executed by the said Prince of Orange in the Names of the said Prince and Princesse dureing their joynt Lives And after their Deceases the said Crowne and Royall Dignitie of the said Kingdoms and Dominions to be to the Heires of the Body of the said Princesse And for default of such Issue to the Princesse Anne of Denmarke and the Heires of her Body And for default of such Issue to the Heires of the Body of the said Prince of Orange. And the Lords Spirituall and Temporall and Commons doe pray the said Prince and Princesse to accept the same accordingly.

And that the Oathes hereafter mentioned be taken by all Persons of whome the Oathes of Allegiance and Supremacy might be required by Law instead of them And that the said Oathes of Allegiance and Supremacy be abrogated.

I A B doe sincerely promise and sweare That I will be faithfull and beare true Allegiance to their Majestyes King William and Queene Mary Soe helpe me God.

I A B doe sweare That I doe from my Heart Abhorr, Detest and Abjure as Impious and Hereticall this damnable Doctrine and Position That Princes Excommunicated or Deprived by the Pope or any Authority of the See of Rome may be deposed or murdered by their Subjects or any other whatsoever. And I doe declare That noe Forreigne Prince Person Prelate, State or Potentate hath or ought to have any Jurisdiction Power Superiority Preeminence or Authoritie Ecclesiasticall or Spirituall within this Realme Soe helpe me God.

Upon which their said Majestyes did accept the Crowne and Royall Dignitie of the Kingdoms of England France and Ireland and the Dominions thereunto belonging according to the Resolution and Desire of the said Lords and Commons contained in the said Declaration. And thereupon their Majestyes were pleased That the said Lords Spirituall and Temporall and Commons being the two Houses of Parlyament should continue to sitt and with their Majesties Royall Concurrence make effectuall Provision for the Setlement of the Religion Lawes and Liberties of this Kingdome soe that the same for the future might not be in danger againe of being subverted, To which the said Lords Spirituall and Temporall and Commons did agree and proceede to act accordingly.

[*The remainder is omitted.*]

United Kingdom

Parliament Act 1911
[An Act to make provision with respect to the powers of the House of Lords in relation to those of the House of Commons, and to limit the duration of Parliament] as amended by, inter alia, the Parliament Act 1949 [An Act to amend the Parliament Act 1911].

Whereas it is expedient that provision should be made for regulating the relations between the two Houses of Parliament:
And whereas it is intended to substitute for the House of Lords as it at present exists a Second Chamber constituted on a popular instead of hereditary basis, but such substitution cannot be immediately brought into operation:
And whereas provision will require hereafter to be made by Parliament in a measure effecting such substitution for limiting and defining the powers of the new Second Chamber, but it is expedient to make such provision as in this Act appears for restricting the existing powers of the House of Lords:

Section 1. (1) If a Money Bill, having been passed by the House of Commons, and sent up to the House of Lords at least one month before the end of the session, is not passed by the House of Lords without amendment within one month after it is so sent up to that House, the Bill shall, unless the House of Commons direct to the contrary, be presented to His Majesty and become an Act of Parliament on the Royal Assent being signified, notwithstanding that the House of Lords have not consented to the Bill.
(2) A Money Bill means a Public Bill which in the opinion of the Speaker of the House of Commons contains only provisions dealing with all or any of the following subjects, namely, the imposition, repeal, remission, alteration, or regulation of taxation; the imposition for the payment of debt or other financial purposes of charges on the Consolidated Fund, the National Loans Fund or on money provided by Parliament, or the variation or repeal of any such charges; supply; the appropriation, receipt, custody, issue or audit of accounts of public money; the raising or guarantee of any loan or the repayment thereof; or subordinate matters incidental to those subjects or any of them. In this subsection the expressions "taxation," "public money," and "loan" respectively do not include any taxation, money, or loan raised by local authorities or bodies for local purposes.
(3) There shall be endorsed on every Money Bill when it is sent up to the House of Lords and when it is presented to His Majesty for assent the certificate of the Speaker of the House of Commons signed by him that it is a Money Bill. Before giving his certificate the Speaker shall consult, if practicable, two members to be appointed from the Chairmen's Panel at the beginning of each Session by the Committee of Selection.

Section 2. (1) If any Public Bill (other than a Money Bill or a Bill containing any provision to extend the maximum duration of Parliament beyond five years) is passed by the House of Commons in two successive sessions (whether of the same Parliament or not), and, having been sent up to the House of Lords at least one month before the end of the session, is rejected by the House of Lords in each of those sessions, that Bill shall, on its rejection for the second time by the House of Lords, unless the House of Commons direct to the contrary, be presented to His Majesty and become an Act of Parliament on the Royal Assent being signified thereto, notwithstanding that the House of Lords have not consented to the Bill: Provided that this provision shall not take effect unless one year has elapsed between the date of the second reading in the first of those sessions of the Bill in the House of Commons and the date on which it passes the House of Commons in the second of these sessions.

(2) When a Bill is presented to His Majesty for assent in pursuance of the provisions of this section, there shall be endorsed on the Bill the certificate of the Speaker of the House of Commons signed by him that the provisions of this section have been duly complied with.

(3) A Bill shall be deemed to be rejected by the House of Lords if it is not passed by the House of Lords either without amendment or with such amendments only as may be agreed to by both Houses.

(4) A Bill shall be deemed to be the same Bill as a former Bill sent up to the House of Lords in the preceding session if, when it is sent up to the House of Lords, it is identical with the former Bill or contains only such alterations as are certified by the Speaker of the House of Commons to be necessary owing to the time which has elapsed since the date of the former Bill, or to represent any amendments which have been made by the House of Lords in the former Bill in the preceding session, and any amendments which are certified by the Speaker to have been made by the House of Lords in the second session and agreed to by the House of Commons shall be inserted in the Bill as presented for Royal Assent in pursuance of this section:

Provided that the House of Commons may, if they think fit, on the passage of such a Bill through the House in the second session, suggest any further amendments without inserting the amendments in the Bill, and any such suggested amendments shall be considered by the House of Lords, and, if agreed to by that House, shall be treated as amendments made by the House of Lords and agreed to by the House of Commons; but the exercise of this power by the House of Commons shall not affect the operation of this section in the event of the Bill being rejected by the House of Lords.

Section 3. Any certificate of the Speaker of the House of Commons given under this Act shall be conclusive for all purposes, and shall not be questioned in any court of law.

Section 4. (1) In every Bill presented to His Majesty under the preceding provisions of this Act, the words of enactment shall be as follows, that is to say:

"Be it enacted by the King's most Excellent Majesty, by and with the advice and consent of the Commons in this present Parliament assembled, in accordance with the provisions of the Parliament Acts 1911 and 1949 and by authority of the same, as follows."

(2) Any alteration of a Bill necessary to give effect to this section shall not be deemed to be an amendment of the Bill.

Section 5. In this Act the expression "Public Bill" does not include any Bill for confirming a Provisional Order.

Section 6. Nothing in this Act shall diminish or qualify the existing rights and privileges of the House of Commons.

Section 7. (Repealed by virtue of the Fixed-term Parliaments Act 2011)

Section 8. This Act may be cited as the Parliament Act 1911.

Parliament Act 1949 [An Act to amend the Parliament Act 1911].

Section 1. The Parliament Act, 1911, shall have effect, and shall be deemed to have had effect from the beginning of the session in which the Bill for this Act originated (save as regards that Bill itself), as if –
(a) there had been substituted in subsections (1) and (4) of section two thereof, for the words "in three successive sessions", "for the third time", "in the third of those sessions", "in the third session", and "in the second or third session" respectively, the words " in two successive sessions", "for the second time", "in the second of those sessions", "in the second session", and "in the second session" respectively; and
(b) there had been substituted in subsection (1) of the said section two, for the words "two years have elapsed" the words "one year has elapsed":
Provided that, if a Bill has been rejected for the second time by the House of Lords before the signification of the Royal Assent to the Bill for this Act, whether such rejection was in the same session as that in which the Royal Assent to the Bill for this Act was signified or in an earlier session, the requirement of the said section two that a Bill is to be presented to His Majesty on its rejection for the second time by the House of Lords shall have effect in relation to the Bill rejected as a requirement that it is to be presented to His Majesty as soon as the Royal Assent to the Bill for this Act has been signified, and, notwithstanding that such rejection was in an earlier session, the Royal Assent to the Bill rejected may be signified in the session in which the Royal Assent to the Bill for this Act was signified.

Section 2. (1) This Act may be cited as the Parliament Act 1949.
(2) This Act and the Parliament Act 1911, shall be construed as one and may be cited together as the Parliament Acts 1911 and 1949.

Fixed-term Parliaments Act 2011
[An Act to make provision about the dissolution of Parliament and the determination of polling days for parliamentary general elections; and for connected purposes]. Selected provisions: Sections 1–3, 6 and 7.

Section 1. (1) This section applies for the purposes of the Timetable in rule 1 in Schedule 1 to the Representation of the People Act 1983 and is subject to section 2.
(2) The polling day for the next parliamentary general election after the passing of this Act is to be 7 May 2015.
(3) The polling day for each subsequent parliamentary general election is to be the first Thursday in May in the fifth calendar year following that in which the polling day for the previous parliamentary general election fell.
(4) But, if the polling day for the previous parliamentary general election –
(a) was appointed under section 2 (7), and
(b) in the calendar year in which it fell, fell before the first Thursday in May, subsection (3) has effect as if for "fifth" there were substituted "fourth".
(5) The Prime Minister may by order made by statutory instrument provide that the polling day for a parliamentary general election in a specified calendar year is to be later than the day determined under subsection (2) or (3), but not more than two months later.
(6) A statutory instrument containing an order under subsection (5) may not be made unless a draft has been laid before and approved by a resolution of each House of Parliament.
(7) The draft laid before Parliament must be accompanied by a statement setting out the Prime Minister's reasons for proposing the change in the polling day. .

Section 2. (1) An early parliamentary general election is to take place if –
(a) the House of Commons passes a motion in the form set out in subsection (2), and
(b) if the motion is passed on a division, the number of members who vote in favour of the motion is a number equal to or greater than two thirds of the number of seats in the House (including vacant seats).
(2) The form of motion for the purposes of subsection (1) (a) is – "That there shall be an early parliamentary general election."
(3) An early parliamentary general election is also to take place if –
(a) the House of Commons passes a motion in the form set out in subsection (4), and
(b) the period of 14 days after the day on which that motion is passed ends without the House passing a motion in the form set out in subsection (5).
(4) The form of motion for the purposes of subsection (3) (a) is – "That this House has no confidence in Her Majesty's Government."
(5) The form of motion for the purposes of subsection (3) (b) is – "That this House has confidence in Her Majesty's Government."
(6) Subsection (7) applies for the purposes of the Timetable in rule 1 in Schedule 1 to the Representation of the People Act 1983.
(7) If a parliamentary general election is to take place as provided for by subsection (1) or (3), the polling day for the election is to be the day appointed by Her Majesty

by proclamation on the recommendation of the Prime Minister (and, accordingly, the appointed day replaces the day which would otherwise have been the polling day for the next election determined under section 1).

Section 3. (1) The Parliament then in existence dissolves at the beginning of the 17th working day before the polling day for the next parliamentary general election as determined under section 1 or appointed under section 2, subsection (7).
(2) Parliament cannot otherwise be dissolved.
(3) Once Parliament dissolves, the Lord Chancellor and, in relation to Northern Ireland, the Secretary of State have the authority to have the writs for the election sealed and issued (see rule 3 in Schedule 1 to the Representation of the People Act 1983).
(4) Once Parliament dissolves, Her Majesty may issue the proclamation summoning the new Parliament which may —
(a) appoint the day for the first meeting of the new Parliament;
(b) deal with any other matter which was normally dealt with before the passing of this Act by proclamations summoning new Parliaments (except a matter dealt with by subsection (1) or (3)).
(5) In this section "working day" means any day other than —
(a) a Saturday or Sunday;
(b) a Christmas Eve, Christmas Day or Good Friday;
(c) a day which is a bank holiday under the Banking and Financial Dealings Act 1971 in any part of the United Kingdom;
(d) a day appointed for public thanksgiving or mourning.
(6) But, if —
(a) on a day ("the relevant day") one or more working days are fixed or appointed as bank holidays or days for public thanksgiving or mourning, and
(b) as a result, the day for the dissolution of a Parliament would (apart from this subsection) be brought forward from what it was immediately before the relevant day to a day that is earlier than 30 days after the relevant day, the day or days in question are to continue to be treated as working days (even if the polling day is subsequently changed).

[*Sections 4 and 5 are omitted*]

Section 6. (1) This Act does not affect Her Majesty's power to prorogue Parliament.
(2) This Act does not affect the way in which the sealing of a proclamation summoning a new Parliament may be authorised; and the sealing of a proclamation to be issued under section 2 (7) may be authorised in the same way.
(3) The Schedule (which contains consequential amendments etc.) has effect.

Section 7. (1) This Act may be cited as the Fixed-term Parliaments Act 2011.
(2) This Act comes into force on the day it is passed.
(3) An amendment or repeal made by this Act has the same extent as the enactment or relevant part of the enactment to which the amendment or repeal relates.

(4) The Prime Minister must make arrangements —

(a) for a committee to carry out a review of the operation of this Act and, if appropriate in consequence of its findings, to make recommendations for the repeal or amendment of this Act, and

(b) for the publication of the committee's findings and recommendations (if any).

(5) A majority of the members of the committee are to be members of the House of Commons.

(6) Arrangements under subsection (4) (a) are to be made no earlier than 1 June 2020 and no later than 30 November 2020.

Constitutional Reform Act 2005
As last amended in its relevant parts by the Government of Wales Act 2006 (Consequential Modifications, transitional Provisions and Saving) Order 2009. Selected provisions: Part 1; Part 3, Sections 23-33, 35, 41, and 42.

Part 1: The Rule of Law

Section 1. This Act does not adversely affect —
(a) the existing principle of the rule of law, or
(b) the Lord Chancellor's existing constitutional role in relation to that principle.

[Part 2 is omitted.]

Part 3: The Supreme Court

Section 23. (1) There is to be a Supreme Court of the United Kingdom.
(2) The Court consists of 12 judges appointed by Her Majesty by letters patent.
(3) Her Majesty may from time to time by Order in Council amend subsection (2) so as to increase or further increase the number of judges of the Court.
(4) No recommendation may be made to Her Majesty in Council to make an Order under subsection (3) unless a draft of the Order has been laid before and approved by resolution of each House of Parliament.
(5) Her Majesty may by letters patent appoint one of the judges to be President and one to be Deputy President of the Court.
(6) The judges other than the President and Deputy President are to be styled "Justices of the Supreme Court".
(7) The Court is to be taken to be duly constituted despite any vacancy among the judges of the Court or in the office of President or Deputy President.

Section 24. On the commencement of section 23 —
(a) the persons who immediately before that commencement are Lords of Appeal in Ordinary become judges of the Supreme Court.
(b) the person who immediately before that commencement is the senior Lord of Appeal in Ordinary becomes the President of the Court, and
(c) the person who immediately before that commencement is the second senior Lord of Appeal in Ordinary becomes the Deputy President of the Court.

Section 25. (1) A person is not qualified to be appointed a judge of the Supreme Court unless he has (at any time) —
(a) held high judicial office for a period of at least 2 years,
(b) satisfied the judicial-appointment eligibility condition on a 15-year basis, or
(c) been a qualifying practitioner for a period of at least 15 years.
(2) A person is a qualifying practitioner for the purposes of this section at any time when —

(a) (repealed),
(b) he is an advocate in Scotland or a solicitor entitled to appear in the Court of Session and the High Court of Justiciary, or
(c) he is a member of the Bar of Northern Ireland or a solicitor of the Court of Judicature of Northern Ireland.

Section 26. (1) This section applies to a recommendation for an appointment to one of the following offices —
(a) judge of the Supreme Court;
(b) President of the Court;
(c) Deputy President of the Court.
(2) A recommendation may be made only by the Prime Minister.
(3) The Prime Minister —
(a) must recommend any person whose name is notified to him under section 29;
(b) may not recommend any other person.
(4) A person who is not a judge of the Court must be recommended for appointment as a judge if his name is notified to the Prime Minister for an appointment as President or Deputy President.
(5) If there is a vacancy in one of the offices mentioned in subsection (1), or it appears to him that there will soon be such a vacancy, the Lord Chancellor must convene a selection commission for the selection of a person to be recommended.
(6) Schedule 8 is about selection commissions.
(7) Subsection (5) is subject to Part 3 of that Schedule.
(8) Sections 27 to 31 apply where a selection commission is convened under this section.

Section 27. (1) The commission must —
(a) determine the selection process to be applied.
(b) apply the selection process, and
(c) make a selection accordingly.
(2) As part of the selection process the commission must consult each of the following —
(a) such of the senior judges as are not members of the commission and are not willing to be considered for selection;
(b) the Lord Chancellor;
(c) the First Minister in Scotland;
(d) the First Minister for Wales;
(e) the Secretary of State for Northern Ireland.
(3) If for any part of the United Kingdom no judge of the courts of that part is to be consulted under subsection (2) (a), the commission must consult as part of the selection process the most senior judge of the courts of that part who is not a member of the commission and is not willing to be considered for selection.
(4) Subsections (5) to (10) apply to any selection under this section or section 31.
(5) Selection must be on merit.
(6) A person may be selected only if he meets the requirements of section 25.
(7) A person may not be selected if he is a member of the commission.

(8) In making selections for the appointment of judges of the Court the commission must ensure that between them the judges will have knowledge of, and experience of practice in, the law of each part of the United Kingdom.
(9) The commission must have regard to any guidance given by the Lord Chancellor as to matters to be taken into account (subject to any other provision of this Act) in making a selection.
(10) Any selection must be of one person only.

Section 28. (1) After complying with section 27 the commission must submit a report to the Lord Chancellor.
(2) The report must—
(a) state who has been selected;
(b) state the senior judges consulted under section 27 (2) (a) and any judge consulted under section 27 (3);
(c) contain any other information required by the Lord Chancellor.
(3) The report must be in a form approved by the Lord Chancellor.
(4) After submitting the report the commission must provide any further information the Lord Chancellor may require.
(5) When he receives the report the Lord Chancellor must consult each of the following—
(a) the senior judges consulted under section 27 (2) (a);
(b) any judge consulted under section 27 (3);
(c) the First Minister in Scotland;
(d) the First Minister for Wales;
(e) the Secretary of State for Northern Ireland.

Section 29. (1) This section refers to the following stages—
Stage 1: where a person has been selected under section 27;
Stage 2: where a person has been selected following a rejection or reconsideration at stage 1;
Stage 3: where a person has been selected following a rejection or reconsideration at stage 2.
(2) At stage 1 the Lord Chancellor must do one of the following—
(a) notify the selection;
(b) reject the selection;
(c) require the commission to reconsider the selection.
(3) At stage 2 the Lord Chancellor must do one of the following—
(a) notify the selection;
(b) reject the selection, but only if it was made following a reconsideration at stage 1;
(c) require the commission to reconsider the selection, but only if it was made following a rejection at stage 1.
(4) At stage 3 the Lord Chancellor must notify the selection, unless subsection (5) applies and he makes a notification under it.

(5) If a person whose selection the Lord Chancellor required to be reconsidered at stage 1 or 2 was not selected again at the next stage, the Lord Chancellor may at stage 3 notify that person's name to the Prime Minister.
(6) In this Part references to the Lord Chancellor notifying a selection are references to his notifying to the Prime Minister the name of the person selected.

Section 30. (1) The power of the Lord Chancellor under section 29 to reject a selection at stage 1 or 2 is exercisable only on the grounds that, in the Lord Chancellor's opinion, the person selected is not suitable for the office concerned.
(2) The power of the Lord Chancellor under section 29 to require the commission to reconsider a selection at stage 1 or 2 is exercisable only on the grounds that, in the Lord Chancellor's opinion —
(a) there is not enough evidence that the person is suitable for the office concerned.
(b) there is evidence that the person is not the best candidate on merit, or
(c) there is not enough evidence that if the person were appointed the judges of the Court would between them have knowledge of, and experience of practice in, the law of each part of the United Kingdom.
(3) The Lord Chancellor must give the commission reasons in writing for rejecting or requiring reconsideration of a selection.

Section 31. (1) If under section 29 the Lord Chancellor rejects or requires reconsideration of a selection at stage 1 or 2, the commission must select a person in accordance with this section.
(2) If the Lord Chancellor rejects a selection, the commission —
(a) may not select the person rejected, and
(b) where the rejection is following reconsideration of a selection, may not select the person (if different) whose selection it reconsidered.
(3) If the Lord Chancellor requires a selection to be reconsidered, the commission —
(a) may select the same person or a different person, but
(b) where the requirement is following a rejection, may not select the person rejected.
(4) The commission must inform the Lord Chancellor of the person selected following a rejection or requirement to reconsider.

Section 32. (1) A person who is appointed as President of the Court must, as soon as may be after accepting office, take the required oaths in the presence of —
(a) the Deputy President, or
(b) if there is no Deputy President, the senior ordinary judge.
(2) A person who is appointed as Deputy President of the Supreme Court must, as soon as may be after accepting office, take the required oaths in the presence of —
(a) the President, or
(b) if there is no President, the senior ordinary judge.
(3) A person who is appointed as a judge of the Supreme Court must, as soon as may be after accepting office, take the required oaths in the presence of —
(a) the President, or
(b) if there is no President, the Deputy President, or

(c) if there is no President and no Deputy President, the senior ordinary judge.
(4) Subsections (1) and (2) apply whether or not the person appointed as President or Deputy President has previously taken the required oaths in accordance with this section after accepting another office.
(5) Subsection (3) does not apply where a person is first appointed as a judge of the Court upon appointment to the office of President or Deputy President.
(6) In this section "required oaths" means —
(a) the oath of allegiance, and
(b) the judicial oath,
as set out in the Promissory Oaths Act 1868.

Section 33. A judge of the Supreme Court holds that office during good behaviour, but may be removed from it on the address of both Houses of Parliament.

[Section 34 is omitted]

Section 35. (1) A judge of the Supreme Court may at any time resign that office by giving the Lord Chancellor notice in writing to that effect.
(2) The President or Deputy President of the Court may at any time resign that office (whether or not he resigns his office as a judge) by giving the Lord Chancellor notice in writing to that effect.
(3) *[omitted]*

[Sections 36-39 are omitted.]

Section 40. (1) The Supreme Court is a superior court of record.
(2) An appeal lies to the Court from any order or judgment of the Court of Appeal in England and Wales in civil proceedings.
(3) An appeal lies to the Court from any order or judgment of a court in Scotland if an appeal lay from that court to the House of Lords at or immediately before the commencement of this section.
(4) Schedule 9 —
(a) transfers other jurisdiction from the House of Lords to the Court.
(b) transfers devolution jurisdiction from the Judicial Committee of the Privy Council to the Court, and
(c) makes other amendments relating to jurisdiction.
(5) The Court has power to determine any question necessary to be determined for the purposes of doing justice in an appeal to it under any enactment.
(6) An appeal under subsection (2) lies only with the permission of the Court of Appeal or the Supreme Court; but this is subject to provision under any other enactment restricting such an appeal.

Section 41. (1) Nothing in this Part is to affect the distinctions between the separate legal systems of the parts of the United Kingdom.

(2) A decision of the Supreme Court on appeal from a court of any part of the United Kingdom, other than a decision on a devolution matter, is to be regarded as the decision of a court of that part of the United Kingdom.
(3) A decision of the Supreme Court on a devolution matter—
(a) is not binding on that Court when making such a decision;
(b) otherwise, is binding in all legal proceedings.
(4) In this section "devolution matter" means—
(a) a question referred to the Supreme Court under section 96, 99 or 112 of the Government of Wales Act 2006, section 33 of the Scotland Act 1998 or section 11 of the Northern Ireland Act 1998;
(b) a devolution issue as defined in Schedule 9 to the Government of Wales Act 2006, Schedule 6 to the Scotland Act 1998 or Schedule 10 to the Northern Ireland Act 1998.

[The remainder of the act is omitted.]

Constitutional Reform and Governance Act 2010
Selected provisions: Part 2.

[Part 1 is omitted.]

Part 2: Ratification of treaties

Section 20. (1) Subject to what follows, a treaty is not to be ratified unless—
(a) a Minister of the Crown has laid before Parliament a copy of the treaty,
(b) the treaty has been published in a way that a Minister of the Crown thinks appropriate, and
(c) period A has expired without either House having resolved, within period A, that the treaty should not be ratified.
(2) Period A is the period of 21 sitting days beginning with the first sitting day after the date on which the requirement in subsection (1) (a) is met.
(3) Subsections (4) to (6) apply if the House of Commons resolved as mentioned in subsection (1) (c) (whether or not the House of Lords also did so).
(4) The treaty may be ratified if—
(a) a Minister of the Crown has laid before Parliament a statement indicating that the Minister is of the opinion that the treaty should nevertheless be ratified and explaining why, and
(b) period B has expired without the House of Commons having resolved, within period B, that the treaty should not be ratified.
(5) Period B is the period of 21 sitting days beginning with the first sitting day after the date on which the requirement in subsection (4) (a) is met.
(6) A statement may be laid under subsection (4) (a) in relation to the treaty on more than one occasion.
(7) Subsection (8) applies if—
(a) the House of Lords resolved as mentioned in subsection (1) (c), but
(b) the House of Commons did not.
(8) The treaty may be ratified if a Minister of the Crown has laid before Parliament a statement indicating that the Minister is of the opinion that the treaty should nevertheless be ratified and explaining why.
(9) "Sitting day" means a day on which both Houses of Parliament sit.

Section 21. (1) A Minister of the Crown may, in relation to a treaty, extend the period mentioned in section 20 (1) (c) by 21 sitting days or less.
(2) The Minister does that by laying before Parliament a statement—
(a) indicating that the period is to be extended, and
(b) setting out the length of the extension.
(3) The statement must be laid before the period would have expired without the extension.
(4) The Minister must publish the statement in a way the Minister thinks appropriate.
(5) The period may be extended more than once.

Section 22. (1) Section 20 does not apply to a treaty if a Minister of the Crown is of the opinion that, exceptionally, the treaty should be ratified without the requirements of that section having been met.
(2) But a treaty may not be ratified by virtue of subsection (1) after either House has resolved, as mentioned in section 20 (1) (c), that the treaty should not be ratified.
(3) If a Minister determines that a treaty is to be ratified by virtue of subsection (1), the Minister must, either before or as soon as practicable after the treaty is ratified –
(a) lay before Parliament a copy of the treaty,
(b) arrange for the treaty to be published in a way that the Minister thinks appropriate, and
(c) lay before Parliament a statement indicating that the Minister is of the opinion mentioned in subsection (1) and explaining why.

Section 23. (1) Section 20 does not apply to –
(a) a treaty covered by section 12 of the European Parliamentary Elections Act 2002 (treaty providing for increase in European Parliament's powers not to be ratified unless approved by Act of Parliament);
(b) a treaty covered by section 5 of the European Union (Amendment) Act 2008 (treaty amending founding Treaties not to be ratified unless approved by Act of Parliament).
(2) Section 20 does not apply to a treaty in relation to which an Order in Council may be made under one or more of the following –
(a) section 158 of the Inheritance Tax Act 1984 (double taxation conventions);
(b) section 2 of the Taxation (International and Other Provisions) Act 2010 (double taxation arrangements);
(c) section 173 of the Finance Act 2006 (international tax enforcement arrangements).
(3) Section 20 does not apply to a treaty concluded (under authority given by the government of the United Kingdom) by the government of a British overseas territory, of any of the Channel Islands or of the Isle of Man.
(4) Section 20 does not apply to a treaty a copy of which is presented to Parliament by command of Her Majesty before that section comes into force.

Section 24. In laying a treaty before Parliament under this Part, a Minister shall accompany the treaty with an explanatory memorandum explaining the provisions of the treaty, the reasons for Her Majesty's Government seeking ratification of the treaty, and such other matters as the Minister considers appropriate.

Section 25. (1) In this Part "treaty" means a written agreement –
(a) between States or between States and international organisations, and
(b) binding under international law.
(2) But "treaty" does not include a regulation, rule, measure, decision or similar instrument made under a treaty (other than one that amends or replaces the treaty (in whole or in part)).
(3) In this Part a reference to ratification of a treaty is a reference to an act of a kind specified in subsection (4) which establishes as a matter of international law the United Kingdom's consent to be bound by the treaty.

(4) The acts are—
(a) deposit or delivery of an instrument of ratification, accession, approval or acceptance;
(b) deposit or delivery of a notification of completion of domestic procedures.

[*The remainder of the Act is omitted.*]

Scotland Act 1998

[An Act to provide for the establishment of a Scottish Parliament and Administration and other changes in the government of Scotland; to provide for changes in the constitution and functions of certain public authorities; to provide for the variation of the basic rate of income tax in relation to income of Scottish taxpayers in accordance with a resolution of the Scottish Parliament; to amend the law about parliamentary constituencies in Scotland; and for connected purposes] as last amended by the Treaty of Lisbon (Changes in Terminology) Order 2011. Selected provisions: Sections 1, 28 and 29; Schedule 5, Part I and Part II (Heads A and B, headlines of Heads C-L).

Part I. The Scottish Parliament

Section 1. (1) There shall be a Scottish Parliament.
(2) One member of the Parliament shall be returned for each constituency (under the simple majority system) at an election held in the constituency.
(3) Members of the Parliament for each region shall be returned at a general election under the additional member system of proportional representation provided for in this Part and vacancies among such members shall be filled in accordance with this Part.
(4) The validity of any proceedings of the Parliament is not affected by any vacancy in its membership.
(5) Schedule 1 (which makes provision for the constituencies and regions for the purposes of this Act and the number of regional members) shall have effect.

[Sections 2-27 are omitted.]

Section 28. (1) Subject to section 29, the Parliament may make laws, to be known as Acts of the Scottish Parliament.
(2) Proposed Acts of the Scottish Parliament shall be known as Bills; and a Bill shall become an Act of the Scottish Parliament when it has been passed by the Parliament and has received Royal Assent.
(3) A Bill receives Royal Assent at the beginning of the day on which Letters Patent under the Scottish Seal signed with Her Majesty's own hand signifying Her Assent are recorded in the Register of the Great Seal.
(4) The date of Royal Assent shall be written on the Act of the Scottish Parliament by the Clerk, and shall form part of the Act.
(5) The validity of an Act of the Scottish Parliament is not affected by any invalidity in the proceedings of the Parliament leading to its enactment.
(6) Every Act of the Scottish Parliament shall be judicially noticed.
(7) This section does not affect the power of the Parliament of the United Kingdom to make laws for Scotland.

Section 29. (1) An Act of the Scottish Parliament is not law so far as any provision of the Act is outside the legislative competence of the Parliament.
(2) A provision is outside that competence so far as any of the following paragraphs apply—
(a) it would form part of the law of a country or territory other than Scotland, or confer or remove functions exercisable otherwise than in or as regards Scotland,
(b) it relates to reserved matters,
(c) it is in breach of the restrictions in Schedule 4,
(d) it is incompatible with any of the Convention rights or with EU law,
(e) it would remove the Lord Advocate from his position as head of the systems of criminal prosecution and investigation of deaths in Scotland.
(3) For the purposes of this section, the question whether a provision of an Act of the Scottish Parliament relates to a reserved matter is to be determined, subject to subsection (4), by reference to the purpose of the provision, having regard (among other things) to its effect in all the circumstances.
(4) A provision which—
(a) would otherwise not relate to reserved matters, but
(b) makes modifications of Scots private law, or Scots criminal law, as it applies to reserved matters,
is to be treated as relating to reserved matters unless the purpose of the provision is to make the law in question apply consistently to reserved matters and otherwise.

[*The remainder of the Act is omitted.*]

Schedules

[*Schedules 1-4 are omitted.*]

Schedule 5. Reserved Matters

Part I. General Reservations

The Constitution

Paragraph 1. The following aspects of the constitution are reserved matters, that is—
(a) the Crown, including succession to the Crown and a regency,
(b) the Union of the Kingdoms of Scotland and England,
(c) the Parliament of the United Kingdom,
(d) the continued existence of the High Court of Justiciary as a criminal court of first instance and of appeal,
(e) the continued existence of the Court of Session as a civil court of first instance and of appeal.

Paragraph 2. (1) Paragraph 1 does not reserve—
(a) Her Majesty's prerogative and other executive functions,
(b) functions exercisable by any person acting on behalf of the Crown, or
(c) any office in the Scottish Administration.
(2) Sub-paragraph (1) does not affect the reservation by paragraph 1 of honours and dignities or the functions of the Lord Lyon King of Arms so far as relating to the granting of arms; but this sub-paragraph does not apply to the Lord Lyon King of Arms in his judicial capacity.
(3) Sub-paragraph (1) does not affect the reservation by paragraph 1 of the management (in accordance with any enactment regulating the use of land) of the Crown Estate.
(4) Sub-paragraph (1) does not affect the reservation by paragraph 1 of the functions of the Security Service, the Secret Intelligence Service and the Government Communications Headquarters.
(5) Sub-paragraph (1) does not affect the reservation by paragraph 1 of the functions exercisable through the Export Credits Guarantee Department.

Paragraph 3. (1) Paragraph 1 does not reserve property belonging to Her Majesty in right of the Crown or belonging to any person acting on behalf of the Crown or held in trust for Her Majesty for the purposes of any person acting on behalf of the Crown.
(2) Paragraph 1 does not reserve the ultimate superiority of the Crown or the superiority of the Prince and Steward of Scotland.
(3) Sub-paragraph (1) does not affect the reservation by paragraph 1 of—
(a) the hereditary revenues of the Crown, other than revenues from bona vacantia, ultimus haeres and treasure trove,
(b) the royal arms and standard,
(c) the compulsory acquisition of property held or used by a Minister of the Crown or government department.

Paragraph 4. (1) Paragraph 1 does not reserve property held by Her Majesty in Her private capacity.
(2) Sub-paragraph (1) does not affect the reservation by paragraph 1 of the subject-matter of the Crown Private Estates Acts 1800 to 1873.

Paragraph 5. Paragraph 1 does not reserve the use of the Scottish Seal.

Political parties

Paragraph 6. The registration and funding of political parties is a reserved matter but this paragraph does not reserve making payments to any political party for the purpose of assisting members of the Parliament who are connected with the party to perform their Parliamentary duties.

Foreign affairs etc.

Paragraph 7. (1) International relations, including relations with territories outside the United Kingdom, the European Union (and their institutions) and other international organisations, regulation of international trade, and international development assistance and co-operation are reserved matters.
(2) Sub-paragraph (1) does not reserve —
(a) observing and implementing international obligations, obligations under the Human Rights Convention and obligations under EU law,
(b) assisting Ministers of the Crown in relation to any matter to which that sub-paragraph applies.

Public service

Paragraph 8. (1) The Civil Service of the State is a reserved matter.
(2) Sub-paragraph (1) does not reserve the subject-matter of —
(a) Part I of the Sheriff Courts and Legal Officers (Scotland) Act 1927 (appointment of sheriff clerks and procurators fiscal etc.),
(b) Part III of the Administration of Justice (Scotland) Act 1933 (officers of the High Court of Justiciary and of the Court of Session).

Defence

Paragraph 9. (1) The following are reserved matters —
(a) the defence of the realm,
(b) the naval, military or air forces of the Crown, including reserve forces,
(c) visiting forces,
(d) international headquarters and defence organisations,
(e) trading with the enemy and enemy property.
(2) Sub-paragraph (1) does not reserve —
(a) the exercise of civil defence functions by any person otherwise than as a member of any force or organisation referred to in
sub-paragraph (1) (b) to (d) or any other force or organisation reserved by virtue of sub-paragraph (1) (a),
(b) the conferral of enforcement powers in relation to sea fishing.

Treason

Paragraph 10. Treason (including constructive treason), treason felony and misprision of treason are reserved matters.

Part II. Specific reservations

Preliminary

Paragraph 1. The matters to which any of the Sections in this Part apply are reserved matters for the purposes of this Act.

Paragraph 2. A Section applies to any matter described or referred to in it when read with any illustrations, exceptions or interpretation provisions in that Section.

Paragraph 3. Any illustrations, exceptions or interpretation provisions in a Section relate only to that Section (so that an entry under the heading "exceptions" does not affect any other Section).

Reservations

Head A – Financial and Economic Matters

A1. Fiscal, economic and monetary policy
Section A1. Fiscal, economic and monetary policy, including the issue and circulation of money, taxes and excise duties, government borrowing and lending, control over United Kingdom public expenditure, the exchange rate and the Bank of England.
Exception. Local taxes to fund local authority expenditure (for example, council tax and non-domestic rates).

A2. The currency
Section A2. Coinage, legal tender and bank notes.

A3. Financial services
Section A3. Financial services, including investment business, banking and deposit-taking, collective investment schemes and insurance.
Exception. The subject-matter of section 1 of the Banking and Financial Dealings Act 1971 (bank holidays).

A4. Financial markets
Section A4. Financial markets, including listing and public offers of securities and investments, transfer of securities and insider dealing.

A5. Money laundering
Section A5. The subject-matter of the Money Laundering Regulations 1993, but in relation to any type of business.

United Kingdom

Head B – Home Affairs

B1. Misuse of drugs
Section B1. The subject-matter of –
(a) the Misuse of Drugs Act 1971,
(b) sections 12 to 14 of the Criminal Justice (International Co-operation) Act 1990 (substances useful for manufacture of controlled drugs), and
(c) Part V of the Criminal Law (Consolidation) (Scotland) Act 1995 (drug trafficking) and, so far as relating to drug trafficking, the Proceeds of Crime (Scotland) Act 1995.

B2. Data protection
Section B2. The subject-matter of –
(a) the Data Protection Act 1998, and
(b) Council Directive 95/46/EC (protection of individuals with regard to the processing of personal data and on the free movement of such data).
Interpretation. If any provision of the Data Protection Act 1998 is not in force on the principal appointed day, it is to be treated for the purposes of this reservation as if it were.

B3. Elections
Section B3. Elections for membership of the House of Commons, the European Parliament and the Parliament, including the subject-matter of –
(a) the European Parliamentary Elections Act 2002.
(b) the Representation of the People Act 1983 and the Representation of the People Act 1985, and
(c) the Parliamentary Constituencies Act 1986,
so far as those enactments apply, or may be applied, in respect of such membership.
The franchise at local government elections.
Interpretation. Paragraph 5 (1) of Part 3 of this Schedule does not apply to the subject-matter of the European Parliamentary Elections Act 2002; and the reference to the subject-matter of that Act is to be construed as a reference to it as at the date that Act received Royal Assent.

B4. Firearms
Section B4. The subject-matter of the Firearms Acts 1968 to 1997.

B5. Entertainment
Section B5. The subject-matter of –
(a) the Video Recordings Act 1984, and
(b) sections 1 to 3 and 5 to 16 of the Cinemas Act 1985 (control of exhibitions).
The classification of films for public exhibition by reference to their suitability for viewing by persons generally or above a particular age, with or without any advice as to the desirability of parental guidance.

B6. Immigration and nationality
Section B6. Nationality; immigration, including asylum and the status and capacity of persons in the United Kingdom who are not British citizens; free movement of persons within the European Economic Area; issue of travel documents.

B7. Scientific procedures on live animals
Section B7. The subject-matter of the Animals (Scientific Procedures) Act 1986.

B8. National security, interception of communications, official secrets and terrorism
Section B8. National security.
The interception of communications; but not
(a) the interception of any communication made to or by a person detained at a place of detention, if the communication —
(i) is a written communication and is intercepted there, or
(ii) is intercepted in the course of its transmission by means of a private telecommunication system running there,
(b) the subject matter of Part III of the Police Act 1997 (authorisation to interfere with property etc.) or surveillance not involving interference with property.
The subject-matter of —
(a) the Official Secrets Acts 1911 and 1920, and
(b) the Official Secrets Act 1989, except so far as relating to any information, document or other article protected against disclosure by section 4 (2) (crime) and not by any other provision of sections 1 to 4.
Special powers, and other special provisions, for dealing with terrorism.
Interpretation. "Place of detention" means a prison, young offenders institution, remand centre or legalised police cell (as those expressions are defined for the purposes of the Prisons (Scotland) Act 1989 or a hospital (within the meaning of the given in section 329 (1) of the Mental Health (Care and Treatment) (Scotland) Act 2003; and "person detained", in relation to a hospital, means a person detained there under —
(a) section 24, 25 or 70 of the Mental Health (Scotland) Act 1984;
(b) Part 6 of the Criminal Procedure (Scotland) Act 1995;
(c) the Mental Health (Care and Treatment) (Scotland) Act 2003; or
(d) regulations under —
(i) subsection (3) of section 116B of the Army Act 1955;
(ii) subsection (3) of section 116B of the Air Force Act 1955; or
(iii) section 63B of the Naval Discipline Act 1957.
"Private telecommunication system" has the meaning given in section 2 (1) of the Regulation of Investigatory Powers Act 2000.

B9. Betting, gaming and lotteries
Section B9. Betting, gaming and lotteries.

B10. Emergency powers
Section B10. Emergency powers.

B11. Extradition
Section B11. Extradition.

B12. Lieutenancies
Section B12. The subject-matter of the Lieutenancies Act 1997.
Access to information
Public access to information held by public bodies or holders of public offices (including government departments and persons acting on behalf of the Crown).
Exception. Information held by–
(a) the Parliament,
(b) any part of the Scottish Administration,
(c) the Parliamentary corporation,
(d) any Scottish public authority with mixed functions or no reserved functions,
unless supplied by a Minister of the Crown or government department and held in confidence.

Head C – Trade and Industry

[*The provisions of Head C are omitted.*]

Head D – Energy

[*The provisions of Head D are omitted.*]

Head E – Transport

[*The provisions of Head E are omitted.*]

Head F – Social Security

[*The provisions of Head F are omitted.*]

Head G – Regulation of the Professions

[*The provisions of Head G are omitted.*]

Head H – Employment

[*The provisions of Head H are omitted.*]

Head J – Health and Medicines

[*The provisions of Head J are omitted.*]

Head K – Media and Culture

[*The provisions of Head K are omitted.*]

Head L – Miscellaneous

[*The provisions of Head L are omitted.*]

[*Schedules 6-9 are omitted.*]

Government of Wales Act 2006
As last amended by the National Assembly of Wales (Legislative Competence) (Exceptions to Matters) Order 2009. Selected provisions: Part 1, Sections 1,2,6,8 and 9; Part 3, Sections 93 and 94; Part 4, Sections 103, 107 and 108; Schedule 7 (headlines only).

Part 1: National Assembly for Wales

Section 1. (1) There is to be an Assembly for Wales to be known as the National Assembly for Wales or Cynulliad Cenedlaethol Cymru (referred to in this Act as "the Assembly").
(2) The Assembly is to consist of —
(a) one member for each Assembly constituency (referred to in this Act as "Assembly constituency members"), and
(b) members for each Assembly electoral region (referred to in this Act as "Assembly regional members").
(3) Members of the Assembly (referred to in this Act as "Assembly members") are to be returned in accordance with the provision made by and under this Act for —
(a) the holding of general elections of Assembly members (for the return of the entire Assembly), and
(b) the filling of vacancies in Assembly seats.
(4) The validity of any Assembly proceedings is not affected by any vacancy in its membership.
(5) In this Act "Assembly proceedings" means any proceedings of —
(a) the Assembly,
(b) committees of the Assembly, or
(c) sub-committees of such committees

Section 2. (1)The Assembly constituencies are the parliamentary constituencies in Wales.
(2) There are five Assembly electoral regions.
(3) The Assembly electoral regions are as specified in the Parliamentary Constituencies and Assembly Electoral Regions (Wales) Order 2006.
(4) There are four seats for each Assembly electoral region.
(5) For provision about alterations in the Assembly electoral regions and in the allocation of seats to those regions see Schedule 1.
(6) Subsections (1), (3) and (4) are subject to any Order in Council under the Parliamentary Constituencies Act 1986, as that Act has effect as extended by that Schedule.

[Sections 3-5 are omitted.]

Section 6. (1) Each person entitled to vote at a general election in an Assembly constituency has two votes.

(2) One (referred to in this Act as a "constituency vote") is a vote which may be given for a candidate to be the Assembly constituency member for the Assembly constituency.

(3) The other (referred to in this Act as an "electoral region vote") is a vote which may be given for—

(a) a registered political party which has submitted a list of candidates to be Assembly regional members for the Assembly electoral region in which the Assembly constituency is included, or

(b) an individual who is a candidate to be an Assembly regional member for that Assembly electoral region.

(4) The Assembly constituency member for the Assembly constituency is to be returned under the simple majority system.

(5) The Assembly regional members for the Assembly electoral region are to be returned under the additional member system of proportional representation provided for in this Part.

(6) In this Act "registered political party" means a party registered under Part 2 of the Political Parties, Elections and Referendums Act 2000.

[Section 7 is omitted.]

Section 8. (1) This section and section 9 are about the return of Assembly regional members for an electoral region at a general election.

(2) The person who is to be returned as the Assembly constituency member for each Assembly constituency in the Assembly electoral region is to be determined before it is determined who are to be returned as the Assembly regional members for the Assembly electoral region.

(3) For each registered political party by which a list of candidates has been submitted for the Assembly electoral region—

(a) there is to be added together the number of electoral region votes given for the party in the Assembly constituencies included in the Assembly electoral region, and

(b) the number arrived at under paragraph (a) is then to be divided by the aggregate of one and the number of candidates of the party returned as Assembly constituency members for any of those Assembly constituencies.

(4) For each individual candidate to be an Assembly regional member for the Assembly electoral region there is to be added together the number of electoral region votes given for the candidate in the Assembly constituencies included in the Assembly electoral region.

(5) The number arrived at—

(a) in the case of a registered political party, under subsection (3) (b), or

(b) in the case of an individual candidate, under subsection (4),

is referred to in this Act as the electoral region figure for that party or individual candidate.

Section 9. (1) The first seat for the Assembly electoral region is to be allocated to the party or individual candidate with the highest electoral region figure.

(2) The second and subsequent seats for the Assembly electoral region are to be allocated to the party or individual candidate with the highest electoral region figure after any recalculation required by subsection (3) has been carried out.
(3) This subsection requires a recalculation under paragraph (b) of section 8 (3) in relation to a party —
(a) for the first application of subsection (2), if the application of subsection (1) resulted in the allocation of an Assembly seat to the party, or
(b) for any subsequent application of subsection (2), if the previous application of that subsection did so,
and a recalculation is to be carried out after adding one to the aggregate mentioned in that paragraph.
(4) An individual candidate already returned as an Assembly regional member is to be disregarded.
(5) Seats for the Assembly electoral region which are allocated to a party are to be filled by the persons on the party's list in the order in which they appear on the list.
(6) Once a party's list has been exhausted by the return of persons included on it as Assembly regional members by the previous application of subsection (1) or (2), the party is to be disregarded.
(7) If (on the application of subsection (1) or any application of subsection (2)) the highest electoral region figure is the electoral region figure of two or more parties or individual candidates, the subsection applies to each of them.
(8) However, if subsection (7) would mean that more than the full number of seats for the Assembly electoral region were allocated, subsection (1) or (2) does not apply until —
(a) a recalculation has been carried out under section 8 (3) (b) after adding one to the number of votes given for each party with that electoral region figure, and
(b) one has been added to the number of votes given for each individual candidate with that electoral region figure.
(9) If, after that, the highest electoral region figure is still the electoral region figure of two or more parties or individual candidates, the regional returning officer must decide between them by lots.

Part 3: Assembly Measures

Section 93. (1) The Assembly may make laws, to be known as Measures of the National Assembly for Wales or Mesurau Cynulliad Cenedlaethol Cymru (referred to in this Act as "Assembly Measures").
(2) A proposed Assembly Measure is enacted by being passed by the Assembly and approved by Her Majesty in Council.
(3) The validity of an Assembly Measure is not affected by any invalidity in the Assembly proceedings leading to its enactment.
(4) Every Assembly Measure is to be judicially noticed.
(5) This Part does not affect the power of the Parliament of the United Kingdom to make laws for Wales.

Section 94. (1) Subject to the provisions of this Part, an Assembly Measure may make any provision that could be made by an Act of Parliament.

(2) An Assembly Measure is not law so far as any provision of the Assembly Measure is outside the Assembly's legislative competence.

(3) A provision of an Assembly Measure is within the Assembly's legislative competence only if it falls within subsection (4) or (5).

(4) A provision of an Assembly Measure falls within this subsection if —

(a) it relates to one or more of the matters specified in Part 1 of Schedule 5 and does not fall within any of the exceptions specified in paragraph A1 of Part 2 of that Schedule (whether or not the exception is under a heading corresponding to the field which includes the matter), and

(b) it neither applies otherwise than in relation to Wales nor confers, imposes, modifies or removes (or gives power to confer, impose, modify or remove) functions exercisable otherwise than in relation to Wales.

(5) A provision of an Assembly Measure falls within this subsection if —

(a) it provides for the enforcement of a provision (of that or any other Assembly Measure) which falls within subsection (4) or it is otherwise appropriate for making such a provision effective, or

(b) it is otherwise incidental to, or consequential on, such a provision.

(6) But a provision which falls within subsection (4) or (5) is outside the Assembly's legislative competence if —

(a) it breaches any of the restrictions in paragraphs 1 to 6 of Part 2 of Schedule 5, having regard to any exception in Part 3 of that Schedule from those restrictions,

(b) it extends otherwise than only to England and Wales, or

(c) it is incompatible with the Convention rights or with Community law.

(7) For the purposes of this section the question whether a provision of an Assembly Measure relates to one or more of the matters specified in Part 1 of Schedule 5 (or falls within any of the exceptions specified in paragraph A1 of Part 2 of that Schedule) is to be determined by reference to the purpose of the provision, having regard (among other things) to its effect in all the circumstances.

[*The remainder of Part 3 is omitted.*]

Part 4: Acts of the Assembly

Section 103.[1] (1) Her Majesty may by Order in Council cause a referendum to be held throughout Wales about whether the Assembly Act provisions should come into force.

(2) If the majority of the voters in a referendum held by virtue of subsection (1) vote in favour of the Assembly Act provisions coming into force, the Assembly Act provisions are to come into force in accordance with section 105.

---

[1] The referendum referred to in this Section was held on 3 March 2011. In this referendum, a majority voted in favour of extending the legislative powers of the National Assembly for Wales. Accordingly, the section referred to in subparagraph (8) (a) and (b) of this Section are not in force.

(3) But if they do not, that does not prevent the making of a subsequent Order in Council under subsection (1).
(4) No recommendation is to be made to Her Majesty in Council to make an Order in Council under subsection (1) unless a draft of the statutory instrument containing the Order in Council has been laid before, and approved by a resolution of, each House of Parliament and the Assembly.
(5) But subsection (4) is not satisfied unless the resolution of the Assembly is passed on a vote in which the number of Assembly members voting in favour of it is not less than two-thirds of the total number of Assembly seats.
(6) A draft of a statutory instrument containing an Order in Council under subsection (1) may not be laid before either House of Parliament, or the Assembly, until the Secretary of State has undertaken such consultation as the Secretary of State considers appropriate.
(7) For further provision about referendums held by virtue of subsection (1) see Schedule 6.
(8) In this Act "the Assembly Act provisions" means —
(a) sections 107 and 108, and
(b) sections 110 to 115.

[*Sections 104-106 are omitted.*]

Section 107. (1) The Assembly may make laws, to be known as Acts of the National Assembly for Wales or Deddfau Cynulliad Cenedlaethol Cymru (referred to in this Act as "Acts of the Assembly").
(2) Proposed Acts of the Assembly are to be known as Bills; and a Bill becomes an Act of the Assembly when it has been passed by the Assembly and has received Royal Assent.
(3) The validity of an Act of the Assembly is not affected by any invalidity in the Assembly proceedings leading to its enactment.
(4) Every Act of the Assembly is to be judicially noticed.
(5) This Part does not affect the power of the Parliament of the United Kingdom to make laws for Wales.

Section 108. (1) Subject to the provisions of this Part, an Act of the Assembly may make any provision that could be made by an Act of Parliament.
(2) An Act of the Assembly is not law so far as any provision of the Act is outside the Assembly's legislative competence.
(3) A provision of an Act of the Assembly is within the Assembly's legislative competence only if it falls within subsection (4) or (5).
(4) A provision of an Act of the Assembly falls within this subsection if —
(a) it relates to one or more of the subjects listed under any of the headings in Part 1 of Schedule 7 and does not fall within any of the exceptions specified in that Part of that Schedule (whether or not under that heading or any of those headings), and

(b) it neither applies otherwise than in relation to Wales nor confers, imposes, modifies or removes (or gives power to confer, impose, modify or remove) functions exercisable otherwise than in relation to Wales.

(5) A provision of an Act of the Assembly falls within this subsection if —

(a) it provides for the enforcement of a provision (of that or any other Act of the Assembly) which falls within subsection (4) or a provision of an Assembly Measure or it is otherwise appropriate for making such a provision effective, or

(b) it is otherwise incidental to, or consequential on, such a provision.

(6) But a provision which falls within subsection (4) or (5) is outside the Assembly's legislative competence if —

(a) it breaches any of the restrictions in Part 2 of Schedule 7, having regard to any exception in Part 3 of that Schedule from those restrictions,

(b) it extends otherwise than only to England and Wales, or

(c) it is incompatible with the Convention rights or with Community law.

(7) For the purposes of this section the question whether a provision of an Act of the Assembly relates to one or more of the subjects listed in Part 1 of Schedule 7 (or falls within any of the exceptions specified in that Part of that Schedule) is to be determined by reference to the purpose of the provision, having regard (among other things) to its effect in all the circumstances.

[*The remainder of the Act is omitted.*]

Schedules

[*Schedules 1-6 are omitted.*]

Schedule 7

Part 1: Subjects [*Headlines only; notes of interpretation and exceptions are omitted*]

1. Agriculture, forestry, animals, plants and rural development;
2. Ancient monuments and historic buildings;
3. Culture;
4. Economic development;
5. Education and training;
6. Environment;
7. Fire and rescue services and fire safety;
8. Food;
9. Health and health services;
10. Highways and transport;
11. Housing;
12. Local government;
13. National Assembly for Wales;
14. Public Administration;
15. Social welfare;
16. Sport and recreation;

17. Tourism;
18. Town and country planning;
19. Water and flood defence;
20. Welsh language.

[*Parts 2 and 3 of this Schedule are omitted.*]

Northern Ireland Act 1998
[An Act to make new provision for the government of Northern Ireland for the purpose of implementing the agreement reached at multi-party talks on Northern Ireland set out in Command Paper 3883] as last amended by The Northern Ireland (Miscellaneous Provisions) Act 2006. Selected provisions: Sections 4-6, 33, 34; Schedules 2 and 3.

[*Sections 1-3 are omitted.*]

Section 4. (1) In this Act—
"excepted matter" means any matter falling within a description specified in Schedule 2;
"reserved matter" means any matter falling within a description specified in Schedule 3;
"transferred matter" means any matter which is not an excepted or reserved matter.
(2) If at any time after the appointed day it appears to the Secretary of State—
(a) that any reserved matter should become a transferred matter; or
(b) that any transferred matter should become a reserved matter,
he may, subject to subsections (2A) and (3), lay before Parliament the draft of an Order in Council amending Schedule 3 so that the matter ceases to be or, as the case may be, becomes a reserved matter with effect from such date as may be specified in the Order.
(2A)The Secretary of State shall not lay before Parliament under subsection (2) the draft of an Order amending Schedule 3 so that a policing and justice matter ceases to be a reserved matter unless—
(a) a motion for a resolution praying that the matter should cease to be a reserved matter is tabled by the First Minister and the deputy First Minister acting jointly; and
(b) the resolution is passed by the Assembly with the support of a majority of the members voting on the motion, a majority of the designated Nationalists voting and a majority of the designated Unionists voting.
(3) The Secretary of State shall not lay before Parliament under subsection (2) the draft of any other Order unless the Assembly has passed with cross-community support a resolution praying that the matter concerned should cease to be or, as the case may be, should become a reserved matter.
(4) If the draft of an Order laid before Parliament under subsection (2) is approved by resolution of each House of Parliament, the Secretary of State shall submit it to Her Majesty in Council and Her Majesty in Council may make the Order.
(5) In this Act—
"the Assembly" means the New Northern Ireland Assembly, which after the appointed day shall be known as the Northern Ireland Assembly;
"cross-community support", in relation to a vote on any matter, means—
(a) the support of a majority of the members voting, a majority of the designated Nationalists voting and a majority of the designated Unionists voting; or

(b) the support of 60 per cent of the members voting, 40 per cent of the designated Nationalists voting and 40 per cent of the designated Unionists voting;
"designated Nationalist" means a member designated as a Nationalist in accordance with standing orders of the Assembly and "designated Unionist" shall be construed accordingly.
(5A) Standing orders of the Assembly shall provide that a member of the Assembly designated in accordance with the standing orders as a Nationalist, as a Unionist or as Other may change his designation only if—
(a) (being a member of a political party) he becomes a member of a different political party or he ceases to be a member of any political party;
(b) (not being a member of any political party) he becomes a member of a political party.
(6) In this section "policing and justice matter" means a matter falling within a description specified in—
(a) any of paragraphs 9 to 12, 14A to 15A and 17 of Schedule 3; or
(b) any other provision of that Schedule designated for this purpose by an order made by the Secretary of State.

Section 5. (1) Subject to sections 6 to 8, the Assembly may make laws, to be known as Acts.
(2) A Bill shall become an Act when it has been passed by the Assembly and has received Royal Assent.
(3) A Bill receives Royal Assent at the beginning of the day on which Letters Patent under the Great Seal of Northern Ireland signed with Her Majesty's own hand signifying Her Assent are notified to the Presiding Officer.
(4) The date of Royal Assent shall be written on the Act by the Presiding Officer, and shall form part of the Act.
(5) The validity of any proceedings leading to the enactment of an Act of the Assembly shall not be called into question in any legal proceedings.
(6) This section does not affect the power of the Parliament of the United Kingdom to make laws for Northern Ireland, but an Act of the Assembly may modify any provision made by or under an Act of Parliament in so far as it is part of the law of Northern Ireland.

Section 6. (1) A provision of an Act is not law if it is outside the legislative competence of the Assembly.
(2) A provision is outside that competence if any of the following paragraphs apply—
(a) it would form part of the law of a country or territory other than Northern Ireland, or confer or remove functions exercisable otherwise than in or as regards Northern Ireland;
(b) it deals with an excepted matter and is not ancillary to other provisions (whether in the Act or previously enacted) dealing with reserved or transferred matters;
(c) it is incompatible with any of the Convention rights;
(d) it is incompatible with Community law;

(e) it discriminates against any person or class of person on the ground of religious belief or political opinion;
(f) it modifies an enactment in breach of section 7.
(3) For the purposes of this Act, a provision is ancillary to other provisions if it is a provision—
(a) which provides for the enforcement of those other provisions or is otherwise necessary or expedient for making those other provisions effective; or
(b) which is otherwise incidental to, or consequential on, those provisions;
and references in this Act to provisions previously enacted are references to provisions contained in, or in any instrument made under, other Northern Ireland legislation or an Act of Parliament.
(4) Her Majesty may by Order in Council specify functions which are to be treated, for such purposes of this Act as may be specified, as being, or as not being, functions which are exercisable in or as regards Northern Ireland. .
(5) No recommendation shall be made to Her Majesty to make an Order in Council under subsection (4) unless a draft of the Order has been laid before and approved by resolution of each House of Parliament.

[Sections 7-32 are omitted.]

Section 33. (1) The members of the Assembly shall be returned for the parliamentary constituencies in Northern Ireland.
(2) Each constituency shall return six members.
(3) An Order in Council under the Parliamentary Constituencies Act 1986 changing a parliamentary constituency in Northern Ireland shall have effect for the purposes of this Act in relation to—
(a) the first election under section 31 or 32 which takes place after the Order comes into force; and
(b) later elections under that section and by-elections.

Section 34. (1) This section applies to elections of members of the Assembly, including by-elections.
(2) Each vote in the poll at an election shall be a single transferable vote.
(3) A single transferable vote is a vote—
(a) capable of being given so as to indicate the voter's order of preference for the candidates for election as members for the constituency; and
(b) capable of being transferred to the next choice when the vote is not needed to give a prior choice the necessary quota of votes or when a prior choice is eliminated from the list of candidates because of a deficiency in the number of votes given for him.
(4) The Secretary of State may by order make provision about elections or any matter relating to them.
(5) In particular, an order under subsection (4) may make—
(a) provision as to the persons entitled to vote at an election and the registration of such persons;

(b) provision for securing that no person stands as a candidate for more than one constituency at a general election;
(c) provision for determining the date of the poll at a by-election;
(d) provision about deposits.
(6) An order under subsection (4) may apply (with or without modifications) any provision of, or made under, any enactment.

[*The remainder of the Act is omitted.*]

Schedules

[*Schedule 1 is omitted.*]

Schedule 2: Excepted matters

Paragraph 1. The Crown, including the succession to the Crown and a regency, but not—
(a) functions of the First Minister and deputy First Minister, the Northern Ireland Ministers or the Northern Ireland departments, or functions in relation to Northern Ireland of any Minister of the Crown;
(b) property belonging to Her Majesty in right of the Crown or belonging to a government department or held in trust for Her Majesty for the purposes of a government department (other than property used for the purposes of the armed forces of the Crown or the Ministry of Defence Police);
(c) the foreshore or the sea bed or subsoil or their natural resources so far as vested in Her Majesty in right of the Crown.

Paragraph 2. The Parliament of the United Kingdom; parliamentary elections, including the franchise; disqualifications for membership of that Parliament.

Paragraph 3. International relations, including relations with territories outside the United Kingdom, the European Communities (and their institutions) and other international organisations and extradition, and international development assistance and co-operation, but not—
(a) (repealed)
(aa) co-operation between the Police Service of Northern Ireland and the Garda Síochána with respect to any of the following matters—
    (i) transfers, secondments, exchanges or training of officers;
    (ii) communications (including liaison and information technology);
    (iii) joint investigations;
    (iv) disaster planning;
(b) the exercise of legislative powers so far as required for giving effect to any agreement or arrangement entered into—

(i) by a Minister or junior Minister participating, by reason of any provision of section 52A or 52B, in a meeting of the North-South Ministerial Council or the British-Irish Council; or

(ii) by, or in relation to the activities of, any body established for implementing, on the basis mentioned in paragraph 11 of Strand Two of the Belfast Agreement, policies agreed in the North-South Ministerial Council;

(c) observing and implementing international obligations, obligations under the Human Rights Convention and obligations under Community law.

[Explanatory note omitted.]

Paragraph 4. The defence of the realm; trading with the enemy; the armed forces of the Crown but not any matter within paragraph 10 of Schedule 3; war pensions; the Ministry of Defence Police.

Paragraph 5. Control of nuclear, biological and chemical weapons and other weapons of mass destruction.

Paragraph 6. Dignities and titles of honour.

Paragraph 7. Treason but not powers of arrest or criminal procedure.

Paragraph 8. Nationality; immigration, including asylum and the status and capacity of persons in the United Kingdom who are not British citizens; free movement of persons within the European Economic Area; issue of travel documents.

Paragraph 9. The following matters —
(a) taxes or duties under any law applying to the United Kingdom as a whole;
(b) stamp duty levied in Northern Ireland before the appointed day; and
(c) taxes or duties substantially of the same character as those mentioned in sub-paragraph (a) or (b).

Paragraph 9A. Child Trust Funds.

Paragraph 10. The following matters —
(a) national insurance contributions;
(b) the control and management of the Northern Ireland National Insurance Fund and payments into and out of that Fund;
(c) reductions in and deductions from national insurance contributions;
(d) national insurance rebates;
(e) payments out of public money to money purchase pension schemes;
(f) contributions equivalent premiums;
(g)rights to return to the state pension scheme.
Sub-paragraph (a) includes the determination, payment, collection and return of national insurance contributions and matters incidental to those matters.

Sub-paragraph (b) does not include payments out of the Northern Ireland National Insurance Fund which relate to—
    (i) the benefits mentioned in section 143 (1) of the Social Security Administration (Northern Ireland) Act 1992, or benefits substantially of the same character as those benefits; or
    (ii) administrative expenses incurred in connection with matters not falling within sub-paragraphs (a) to (g).
Sub-paragraphs (b) and (e) do not include payments out of or into the Northern Ireland National Insurance Fund under—
    (i) section 172 (1) (b), (2) (a) or (7) (c) of the Pension Schemes (Northern Ireland) Act 1993; or
    (ii) Article 202, 227, 234 or 252 of the Employment Rights (Northern Ireland) Order 1996.
In this paragraph "contributions equivalent premium" has the meaning given by section 51 (2) of the Pension Schemes (Northern Ireland) Act 1993.

Paragraph 11. The appointment and removal of judges of the Court of Judicature of Northern Ireland, holders of offices listed in column 1 of Schedule 3 to the Judicature (Northern Ireland) Act 1978, county court judges, recorders, resident magistrates, lay magistrates, justices of the peace, members of juvenile court panels, coroners, the Chief and other Social Security Commissioners for Northern Ireland, the Chief and other Child Support Commissioners for Northern Ireland and the President and other members of the Lands Tribunal for Northern Ireland.

Paragraph 12. Elections, including the franchise, in respect of the Northern Ireland Assembly, the European Parliament and district councils.

Paragraph 13. The subject-matter of the Political Parties, Elections and Referendums Act 2000 with the exception of Part IX (political donations etc. by companies). This paragraph does not include the funding of political parties for the purpose of assisting members of the Northern Ireland Assembly connected with such parties to perform their Assembly duties.

Paragraph 14. Coinage, legal tender and bank notes.

Paragraph 15. The National Savings Bank.

Paragraph 16. The subject-matter of the Protection of Trading Interests Act 1980.

Paragraph 17. National security (including the Security Service, the Secret Intelligence Service and the Government Communications Headquarters); special powers and other provisions for dealing with terrorism or subversion; the subject-matter of—
(a) the Official Secrets Acts 1911 and 1920;

(b) Chapter I of Part I of the Regulation of Investigatory Powers Act 2000, except so far as relating to the prevention or detection of serious crime (within the meaning of that Act); and

(c) the Official Secrets Act 1989, except so far as relating to any information, document or other article protected against disclosure by section 4 (2) (crime) and not by any other provision of sections 1 to 4.

Paragraph 18. Nuclear energy and nuclear installations, including nuclear safety, security and safeguards, and liability for nuclear occurrences, but not the subject-matter of —

(a) section 3 (5) to (7) of the Environmental Protection Act 1990 (emission limits); or
(b) the Radioactive Substances Act 1993.

Paragraph 19. Regulation of sea fishing outside the Northern Ireland zone (except in relation to Northern Ireland fishing boats).

[*Explanatory note omitted.*]

Paragraph 20. Regulation of activities in outer space.

Schedule 3: Reserved Matters

Paragraph 1. The conferral of functions in relation to Northern Ireland on any Minister of the Crown.

Paragraph 2. Property belonging to Her Majesty in right of the Crown or belonging to a department of the Government of the United Kingdom or held in trust for Her Majesty for the purposes of such a department (other than property used for the purposes of the armed forces of the Crown or the Ministry of Defence Police).

Paragraph 3. Navigation, including merchant shipping, but not harbours or inland waters.

Paragraph 4. Civil aviation but not aerodromes.

Paragraph 5. The foreshore and the sea bed and subsoil and their natural resources (except so far as affecting harbours); submarine pipe-lines; submarine cables, including any land line used solely for the purpose of connecting one submarine cable with another.

Paragraph 6. Domicile.

Paragraph 7. The subject-matter of the Postal Services Act 2000.

Paragraph 8. Disqualification for membership of the Assembly; privileges, powers and immunities of the Assembly, its members and committees greater than those conferred by section 50.

Paragraph 9. The following matters —
(a) the criminal law;
(b) the creation of offences and penalties;
(c) the prevention and detection of crime and powers of arrest and detention in connection with crime or criminal proceedings;
(d) prosecutions;
(e) the treatment of offenders (including children and young persons, and mental health patients, involved in crime);
(f) (Repealed.)
(g) compensation out of public funds for victims of crime.
Sub-paragraphs (a) to (c) do not include any matter within paragraph 17 of Schedule 2.
Sub-paragraph (e) includes, in particular, prisons and other institutions for the treatment or detention of persons mentioned in that sub-paragraph.

Paragraph 10. The maintenance of public order, including the conferring of powers, authorities, privileges or immunities for that purpose on constables, members of the armed forces of the Crown and other persons (other than the Ministry of Defence Police), but not any matter within paragraph 17 of Schedule 2; the Parades Commission for Northern Ireland.

Paragraph 11. The establishment, organisation and control of the Police Service of Northern Ireland and of any other police force (other than the Ministry of Defence Police); the Northern Ireland Policing Board; traffic wardens.

Paragraph 11A. Co-operation between the Police Service of Northern Ireland and the Garda Síochána with respect to any of the following matters —
(a) transfers, secondments, exchanges or training of officers;
(b) communications (including liaison and information technology);
(c) joint investigations;
(d) disaster planning.

Paragraph 12. Firearms and explosives.

Paragraph 13. Civil defence.

Paragraph 14. The subject-matter of Part 2 of the Civil Contingencies Act 2004.

Paragraph 14A. The following matters —
(a) rights of appeal to the Supreme Court;
(b) legal aid for appeals to the Supreme Court.

Paragraph 15. All matters, other than those specified in paragraph 11 of Schedule 2, relating to the Court of Judicature of Northern Ireland, county courts, courts of summary jurisdiction (including magistrates' courts and juvenile courts) and coroners, including procedure, evidence, appeals, juries, costs, legal aid and the registration, execution and enforcement of judgments and orders but not—
(a) bankruptcy, insolvency, the winding up of corporate and unincorporated bodies or the making of arrangements or compositions with creditors;
(b) the regulation of the profession of solicitors.

Paragraph 16. The functions and procedures of the Civil Service Commissioners for Northern Ireland.

Paragraph 17. All matters (including procedure and appeals) relating to—
(a) the Chief and other Social Security Commissioners for Northern Ireland; or
(b) the Chief and other Child Support Commissioners for Northern Ireland,
but not any matter within paragraph 11 of Schedule 2.

Paragraph 18. The subject-matter of sections 149 to 151 of and Schedules 5 and 5A to the Social Security Administration (Northern Ireland) Act 1992 (Social Security Advisory Committee and Industrial Injuries Advisory Council).

Paragraph 19. The subject-matter of the Vaccine Damage Payment Scheme.

Paragraph 20. Import and export controls and trade with any place outside the United Kingdom but not—
(a) the furtherance of the trade of Northern Ireland or the protection of traders in Northern Ireland against fraud;
(b) services in connection with, or the regulation of, the quality, insurance, transport, marketing or identification of agricultural or food products, including livestock;
(c) the prevention of disease or the control of weeds and pests;
(d) aerodromes and harbours;
(e) any matter within paragraph 4 of Schedule 2.

Paragraph 21. The subject-matter of the National Minimum Wage Act 1998.

Paragraph 22. The subject-matter of the following provisions of the Pension Schemes Act 1993—
(a) section 6 (1), (2) (a) (i), (iii) and (iv) and (b), (3), (4) and (8) (registration of occupational and personal pension schemes);
(b) section 145 (Pensions Ombudsman).

Paragraph 23. The following matters—
(a) financial services, including investment business, banking and deposit-taking, collective investment schemes and insurance;

(b) financial markets, including listing and public offers of securities and investments, transfer of securities and insider dealing.
This paragraph does not include the subject-matter of—
(a) the Industrial and Provident Societies Act Northern Ireland) 1969;
(b) the Credit Unions (Northern Ireland) Order 1985;
(c) the Companies (Northern Ireland) Order 1986;
(d) the Insolvency (Northern Ireland) Order 1989;
(e) the Companies (Northern Ireland) Order 1990;
(f) the Companies (No.2) (Northern Ireland) Order 1990;
(g) the Open-Ended Investment Companies (Investment Companies with Variable Capital) Regulations (Northern Ireland) 1997.

Paragraph 24. The subject-matter of—
(a) the Building Societies Act 1986;
(b) the Friendly Societies Act 1992.

Paragraph 25. The subject-matter of the Money Laundering Regulations 2007, but in relation to any type of business.

Paragraph 25A. The subject-matter of the Transfer of Funds (Information on the Payer) Regulations 2007, but in relation to any type of business.

Paragraph 26. Regulation of anti-competitive practices and agreements; abuse of dominant position; monopolies and mergers.

Paragraph 27. Intellectual property but not the subject-matter of Parts I and II of the Plant Varieties Act 1997 (plant varieties and the Plant Varieties and Seeds Tribunal).

Paragraph 28. Units of measurement and United Kingdom primary standards.

Paragraph 29. Telecommunications; wireless telegraphy; the provision of programme services (within the meaning of the Broadcasting Act 1990); internet services; electronic encryption; the subject matter of Part II of the Wireless Telegraphy Act 1949 (electromagnetic disturbance).

Paragraph 30. The National Lottery (except in so far as any matter within Schedule 2 is concerned).

Paragraph 31. Xenotransplantation.

Paragraph 32. Surrogacy arrangements, within the meaning of the Surrogacy Arrangements Act 1985, including the subject-matter of that Act.

Paragraph 33. The subject-matter of the Human Fertilisation and Embryology Act 1990.

Paragraph 34. Human genetics.

Paragraph 35. Research Councils within the meaning of the Science and Technology Act 1965.

Paragraph 35A. The Arts and Humanities Research Council (as defined by section 1 of the Higher Education Act 2004).

Paragraph 36. Areas in which industry may qualify for assistance under Part III of the Industrial Development Act 1982.

Paragraph 37. Consumer safety in relation to goods.

Paragraph 38. Technical standards and requirements in relation to products in pursuance of an obligation under Community law but not standards and requirements in relation to food, agricultural or horticultural produce, fish or fish products, seeds, animal feeding stuffs, fertilisers or pesticides.

Paragraph 39. The subject-matter of section 3 (5) to (7) of the Environmental Protection Act 1990 (emission limits); the environmental protection technology scheme for research and development in the United Kingdom.

Paragraph 40. The subject-matter of —
(a) the Data Protection Act 1984;
(b) the Data Protection Act 1998; and
(c) Council Directive 95/46/EC (protection of individuals with regard to the processing of personal data and free movement of such data).

Paragraph 41. Oaths and declarations (including all undertakings and affirmations, by whatever name) other than those within section 77 (3).

Paragraph 42. Any matter with which a provision of this Act falling within the following sub-paragraphs solely or mainly deals —
(a) in Part III, sections 19, 20, 28, 28A and 28B;
(b) in Part VII, sections 73, 74 (3) and (4), 75 and 77 (1), (2) and (4) to (8) and Schedules 8 and 9;
(c) in Part VIII, sections 90 to 93 and Schedule 11.
This paragraph does not apply to —
> (i) any matter in respect of which it is stated by this Act that provision may be made by Act of the Assembly; or
> (ii) any matter to which a description specified in this Schedule or Schedule 2 is stated not to apply.

[*The remaining Schedules are omitted.*]

Human Rights Act 1998

[An Act to give further effect to rights and freedoms guaranteed under the European Convention on Human Rights; to make provision with respect to holders of certain judicial offices who become judges of the European Court of Human Rights; and for connected purposes] as last amended by the Constitutional Reform Act 2005 (Commencement No. 11) Order 2009. Selected provisions: Sections 1-10; Schedule 2.

Section 1. (1) In this Act "the Convention rights" means the rights and fundamental freedoms set out in—
(a) Articles 2 to 12 and 14 of the Convention,
(b) Articles 1 to 3 of the First Protocol, and
(c) Article 1 of the Thirteenth Protocol,
as read with Articles 16 to 18 of the Convention.
(2) Those Articles are to have effect for the purposes of this Act subject to any designated derogation or reservation (as to which see sections 14 and 15).
(3) The Articles are set out in Schedule 1.
(4) The Secretary of State may by order make such amendments to this Act as he considers appropriate to reflect the effect, in relation to the United Kingdom, of a protocol.
(5) In subsection (4) "protocol" means a protocol to the Convention—
(a) which the United Kingdom has ratified; or
(b) which the United Kingdom has signed with a view to ratification.
(6) No amendment may be made by an order under subsection (4) so as to come into force before the protocol concerned is in force in relation to the United Kingdom.

Section 2. (1) A court or tribunal determining a question which has arisen in connection with a Convention right must take into account any—
(a) judgment, decision, declaration or advisory opinion of the European Court of Human Rights,
(b) opinion of the Commission given in a report adopted under Article 31 of the Convention,
(c) decision of the Commission in connection with Article 26 or 27 (2) of the Convention, or
(d) decision of the Committee of Ministers taken under Article 46 of the Convention, whenever made or given, so far as, in the opinion of the court or tribunal, it is relevant to the proceedings in which that question has arisen.
(2) Evidence of any judgment, decision, declaration or opinion of which account may have to be taken under this section is to be given in proceedings before any court or tribunal in such manner as may be provided by rules.
(3) In this section "rules" means rules of court or, in the case of proceedings before a tribunal, rules made for the purposes of this section—
(a) by the Lord Chancellor or the Secretary of State, in relation to any proceedings outside Scotland;
(b) by the Secretary of State, in relation to proceedings in Scotland; or

(c) by a Northern Ireland department, in relation to proceedings before a tribunal in Northern Ireland —
  (i) which deals with transferred matters; and
  (ii) for which no rules made under paragraph (a) are in force.

Section 3. (1) So far as it is possible to do so, primary legislation and subordinate legislation must be read and given effect in a way which is compatible with the Convention rights.
(2) This section —
(a) applies to primary legislation and subordinate legislation whenever enacted;
(b) does not affect the validity, continuing operation or enforcement of any incompatible primary legislation; and
(c) does not affect the validity, continuing operation or enforcement of any incompatible subordinate legislation if (disregarding any possibility of revocation) primary legislation prevents removal of the incompatibility.

Section 4. (1) Subsection (2) applies in any proceedings in which a court determines whether a provision of primary legislation is compatible with a Convention right.
(2) If the court is satisfied that the provision is incompatible with a Convention right, it may make a declaration of that incompatibility.
(3) Subsection (4) applies in any proceedings in which a court determines whether a provision of subordinate legislation, made in the exercise of a power conferred by primary legislation, is compatible with a Convention right.
(4) If the court is satisfied —
(a) that the provision is incompatible with a Convention right, and
(b) that (disregarding any possibility of revocation) the primary legislation concerned prevents removal of the incompatibility,
it may make a declaration of that incompatibility.
(5) In this section "court" means —
(a) the Supreme Court;
(b) the Judicial Committee of the Privy Council;
(c) the Court Martial Appeal Court;
(d) in Scotland, the High Court of Justiciary sitting otherwise than as a trial court or the Court of Session;
(e) in England and Wales or Northern Ireland, the High Court or the Court of Appeal.
(f) the Court of Protection, in anz matter being dealt with by the President of the Family Division, the Vice-Chancellor or a puisne judge on the High Court.
(6) A declaration under this section ("a declaration of incompatibility") —
(a) does not affect the validity, continuing operation or enforcement of the provision in respect of which it is given; and
(b) is not binding on the parties to the proceedings in which it is made.

Section 5. (1) Where a court is considering whether to make a declaration of incompatibility, the Crown is entitled to notice in accordance with rules of court.
(2) In any case to which subsection (1) applies —

(a) a Minister of the Crown (or a person nominated by him),
(b) a member of the Scottish Executive,
(c) a Northern Ireland Minister,
(d) a Northern Ireland department,
is entitled, on giving notice in accordance with rules of court, to be joined as a party to the proceedings.
(3) Notice under subsection (2) may be given at any time during the proceedings.
(4) A person who has been made a party to criminal proceedings (other than in Scotland) as the result of a notice under subsection (2) may, with leave, appeal to the Supreme Court against any declaration of incompatibility made in the proceedings.
(5) In subsection (4) —
"criminal proceedings" includes all proceedings before the Court Martial Appeal Court; and
"leave" means leave granted by the court making the declaration of incompatibility or by the Supreme Court.

Section 6. (1) It is unlawful for a public authority to act in a way which is incompatible with a Convention right.
(2) Subsection (1) does not apply to an act if —
(a) as the result of one or more provisions of primary legislation, the authority could not have acted differently; or
(b) in the case of one or more provisions of, or made under, primary legislation which cannot be read or given effect in a way which is compatible with the Convention rights, the authority was acting so as to give effect to or enforce those provisions.
(3) In this section "public authority" includes —
(a) a court or tribunal, and
(b) any person certain of whose functions are functions of a public nature,
but does not include either House of Parliament or a person exercising functions in connection with proceedings in Parliament.
(4) (Repealed).
(5) In relation to a particular act, a person is not a public authority by virtue only of subsection (3) (b) if the nature of the act is private.
(6) "An act" includes a failure to act but does not include a failure to —
(a) introduce in, or lay before, Parliament a proposal for legislation; or
(b) make any primary legislation or remedial order.

Section 7. (1) A person who claims that a public authority has acted (or proposes to act) in a way which is made unlawful by section 6, subsection (1), may —
(a) bring proceedings against the authority under this Act in the appropriate court or tribunal, or
(b) rely on the Convention right or rights concerned in any legal proceedings,
but only if he is (or would be) a victim of the unlawful act.

(2) In subsection (1) (a) "appropriate court or tribunal" means such court or tribunal as may be determined in accordance with rules; and proceedings against an authority include a counterclaim or similar proceeding.
(3) If the proceedings are brought on an application for judicial review, the applicant is to be taken to have a sufficient interest in relation to the unlawful act only if he is, or would be, a victim of that act.
(4) If the proceedings are made by way of a petition for judicial review in Scotland, the applicant shall be taken to have title and interest to sue in relation to the unlawful act only if he is, or would be, a victim of that act.
(5) Proceedings under subsection (1) (a) must be brought before the end of—
(a) the period of one year beginning with the date on which the act complained of took place; or
(b) such longer period as the court or tribunal considers equitable having regard to all the circumstances,
but that is subject to any rule imposing a stricter time limit in relation to the procedure in question.
(6) In subsection (1) (b) "legal proceedings" includes—
(a) proceedings brought by or at the instigation of a public authority; and
(b) an appeal against the decision of a court or tribunal.
(7) For the purposes of this section, a person is a victim of an unlawful act only if he would be a victim for the purposes of Article 34 of the Convention if proceedings were brought in the European Court of Human Rights in respect of that act.
(8) Nothing in this Act creates a criminal offence.
(9) In this section "rules" means—
(a) in relation to proceedings before a court or tribunal outside Scotland, rules made by the Lord Chancellor or the Secretary of State for the purposes of this section or rules of court,
(b) in relation to proceedings before a court or tribunal in Scotland, rules made by the Secretary of State for those purposes,
(c) in relation to proceedings before a tribunal in Northern Ireland—
    (i) which deals with transferred matters; and
    (ii) for which no rules made under paragraph (a) are in force,
    rules made by a Northern Ireland department for those purposes,
    and includes provision made by order under section 1 of the Courts and Legal Services Act 1990.
(10) In making rules, regard must be had to section 9.
(11) The Minister who has power to make rules in relation to a particular tribunal may, to the extent he considers it necessary to ensure that the tribunal can provide an appropriate remedy in relation to an act (or proposed act) of a public authority which is (or would be) unlawful as a result of section 6 (1), by order add to—
(a) the relief or remedies which the tribunal may grant; or
(b) the grounds on which it may grant any of them.
(12) An order made under subsection (11) may contain such incidental, supplemental, consequential or transitional provision as the Minister making it considers appropriate.
(13) "The Minister" includes the Northern Ireland department concerned.

Section 8. (1) In relation to any act (or proposed act) of a public authority which the court finds is (or would be) unlawful, it may grant such relief or remedy, or make such order, within its powers as it considers just and appropriate.
(2) But damages may be awarded only by a court which has power to award damages, or to order the payment of compensation, in civil proceedings.
(3) No award of damages is to be made unless, taking account of all the circumstances of the case, including —
(a) any other relief or remedy granted, or order made, in relation to the act in question (by that or any other court), and
(b) the consequences of any decision (of that or any other court) in respect of that act,
the court is satisfied that the award is necessary to afford just satisfaction to the person in whose favour it is made.
(4) In determining —
(a) whether to award damages, or
(b) the amount of an award,
the court must take into account the principles applied by the European Court of Human Rights in relation to the award of compensation under Article 41 of the Convention.
(5) A public authority against which damages are awarded is to be treated —
(a) in Scotland, for the purposes of section 3 of the Law Reform (Miscellaneous Provisions) (Scotland) Act 1940 as if the award were made in an action of damages in which the authority has been found liable in respect of loss or damage to the person to whom the award is made;
(b) for the purposes of the Civil Liability (Contribution) Act 1978 as liable in respect of damage suffered by the person to whom the award is made.
(6) In this section —
"court" includes a tribunal;
"damages" means damages for an unlawful act of a public authority; and
"unlawful" means unlawful under section 6 (1).

Section 9. (1) Proceedings under section 7 (1) (a) in respect of a judicial act may be brought only —
(a) by exercising a right of appeal;
(b) on an application (in Scotland a petition) for judicial review; or
(c) in such other forum as may be prescribed by rules.
(2) That does not affect any rule of law which prevents a court from being the subject of judicial review.
(3) In proceedings under this Act in respect of a judicial act done in good faith, damages may not be awarded otherwise than to compensate a person to the extent required by Article 5 (5) of the Convention.
(4) An award of damages permitted by subsection (3) is to be made against the Crown; but no award may be made unless the appropriate person, if not a party to the proceedings, is joined.
(5) In this section —

"appropriate person" means the Minister responsible for the court concerned, or a person or government department nominated by him;
"court" includes a tribunal;
"judge" includes a member of a tribunal, a justice of the peace (or, in Northern Ireland, a lay magistrate) and a clerk or other officer entitled to exercise the jurisdiction of a court;
"judicial act" means a judicial act of a court and includes an act done on the instructions, or on behalf, of a judge; and
"rules" has the same meaning as in section 7 (9).

Section 10. (1) This section applies if—
(a) a provision of legislation has been declared under section 4 to be incompatible with a Convention right and, if an appeal lies—
    (i) all persons who may appeal have stated in writing that they do not intend to do so;
    (ii) the time for bringing an appeal has expired and no appeal has been brought within that time; or
    (iii) an appeal brought within that time has been determined or abandoned; or
(b) it appears to a Minister of the Crown or Her Majesty in Council that, having regard to a finding of the European Court of Human Rights made after the coming into force of this section in proceedings against the United Kingdom, a provision of legislation is incompatible with an obligation of the United Kingdom arising from the Convention.
(2) If a Minister of the Crown considers that there are compelling reasons for proceeding under this section, he may by order make such amendments to the legislation as he considers necessary to remove the incompatibility.
(3) If, in the case of subordinate legislation, a Minister of the Crown considers—
(a) that it is necessary to amend the primary legislation under which the subordinate legislation in question was made, in order to enable the incompatibility to be removed, and
(b) that there are compelling reasons for proceeding under this section,
he may by order make such amendments to the primary legislation as he considers necessary.
(4) This section also applies where the provision in question is in subordinate legislation and has been quashed, or declared invalid, by reason of incompatibility with a Convention right and the Minister proposes to proceed under paragraph 2 (b) of Schedule 2.
(5) If the legislation is an Order in Council, the power conferred by subsection (2) or (3) is exercisable by Her Majesty in Council.
(6) In this section "legislation" does not include a Measure of the Church Assembly or of the General Synod of the Church of England.
(7) Schedule 2 makes further provision about remedial orders.

[*The remainder of the Act and Schedule 1 are omitted.*]

Schedule 2 (Remedial Orders)

Paragraph 1. (1) A remedial order may —
(a) contain such incidental, supplemental, consequential or transitional provision as the person making it considers appropriate;
(b) be made so as to have effect from a date earlier than that on which it is made;
(c) make provision for the delegation of specific functions;
(d) make different provision for different cases.
(2) The power conferred by sub-paragraph (1) (a) includes —
(a) power to amend primary legislation (including primary legislation other than that which contains the incompatible provision); and
(b) power to amend or revoke subordinate legislation (including subordinate legislation other than that which contains the incompatible provision).
(3) A remedial order may be made so as to have the same extent as the legislation which it affects.
(4) No person is to be guilty of an offence solely as a result of the retrospective effect of a remedial order.

Paragraph 2. No remedial order may be made unless —
(a) a draft of the order has been approved by a resolution of each House of Parliament made after the end of the period of 60 days beginning with the day on which the draft was laid; or
(b) it is declared in the order that it appears to the person making it that, because of the urgency of the matter, it is necessary to make the order without a draft being so approved.

Paragraph 3. (1) No draft may be laid under paragraph 2 (a) unless —
(a) the person proposing to make the order has laid before Parliament a document which contains a draft of the proposed order and the required information; and
(b) the period of 60 days, beginning with the day on which the document required by this sub-paragraph was laid, has ended.
(2) If representations have been made during that period, the draft laid under paragraph 2 (a) must be accompanied by a statement containing —
(a) a summary of the representations; and
(b) if, as a result of the representations, the proposed order has been changed, details of the changes.

Paragraph 4. (1) If a remedial order ("the original order") is made without being approved in draft, the person making it must lay it before Parliament, accompanied by the required information, after it is made.
(2) If representations have been made during the period of 60 days beginning with the day on which the original order was made, the person making it must (after the end of that period) lay before Parliament a statement containing —
(a) a summary of the representations; and

(b) if, as a result of the representations, he considers it appropriate to make changes to the original order, details of the changes.
(3) If sub-paragraph (2) (b) applies, the person making the statement must—
(a) make a further remedial order replacing the original order; and
(b) lay the replacement order before Parliament.
(4) If, at the end of the period of 120 days beginning with the day on which the original order was made, a resolution has not been passed by each House approving the original or replacement order, the order ceases to have effect (but without that affecting anything previously done under either order or the power to make a fresh remedial order).

Paragraph 5. In this Schedule—
"representations" means representations about a remedial order (or proposed remedial order) made to the person making (or proposing to make) it and includes any relevant Parliamentary report or resolution; and
"required information" means—
(a) an explanation of the incompatibility which the order (or proposed order) seeks to remove, including particulars of the relevant declaration, finding or order; and
(b) a statement of the reasons for proceeding under section 10 and for making an order in those terms.

Paragraph 6. In calculating any period for the purposes of this Schedule, no account is to be taken of any time during which—
(a) Parliament is dissolved or prorogued; or
(b) both Houses are adjourned for more than four days.

Paragraph 7. (1) This paragraph applies in relation to—
(a) any remedial order made, and any draft of such an order proposed to be made,—
    (i) by the Scottish Ministers; or
    (ii) within devolved competence (within the meaning of the Scotland Act 1998) by Her Majesty in Council; and
(b) any document or statement to be laid in connection with such an order (or proposed order).
(2) This Schedule has effect in relation to any such order (or proposed order), document or statement subject to the following modifications.
(3) Any reference to Parliament, each House of Parliament or both Houses of Parliament shall be construed as a reference to the Scottish Parliament.
(4) Paragraph 6 does not apply and instead, in calculating any period for the purposes of this Schedule, no account is to be taken of any time during which the Scottish Parliament is dissolved or is in recess for more than four days.

[*The remaining Schedules are omitted.*]

EUROPEAN FUNDAMENTAL RIGHTS

Convention for the Protection of Human Rights and Fundamental Freedoms
Rome, 4 November 1950, as last amended by Protocol 14 (1 June 2010).

Preamble
The governments signatory hereto, being members of the Council of Europe,
Considering the Universal Declaration of Human Rights proclaimed by the General Assembly of the United Nations on 10 December 1948;
Considering that this Declaration aims at securing the universal and effective recognition and observance of the Rights therein declared;
Considering that the aim of the Council of Europe is the achievement of greater unity between its members and that one of the methods by which that aim is to be pursued is the maintenance and further realisation of human rights and fundamental freedoms;
Reaffirming their profound belief in those fundamental freedoms which are the foundation of justice and peace in the world and are best maintained on the one hand by an effective political democracy and on the other by a common understanding and observance of the human rights upon which they depend;
Being resolved, as the governments of European countries which are likeminded and have a common heritage of political traditions, ideals, freedom and the rule of law, to take the first steps for the collective enforcement of certain of the rights stated in the Universal Declaration,
Have agreed as follows:

Article 1. The High Contracting Parties shall secure to everyone within their jurisdiction the rights and freedoms defined in Section I of this Convention.

Section I. Rights and freedoms

Article 2. (1) Everyone's right to life shall be protected by law. No one shall be deprived of his life intentionally save in the execution of a sentence of a court following his conviction of a crime for which this penalty is provided by law.
(2) Deprivation of life shall not be regarded as inflicted in contravention of this Article when it results from the use of force which is no more than absolutely necessary:
(a) in defence of any person from unlawful violence;
(b) in order to effect a lawful arrest or to prevent the escape of a person lawfully detained;
(c) in action lawfully taken for the purpose of quelling a riot or insurrection.

Article 3. No one shall be subjected to torture or to inhuman or degrading treatment or punishment.

Article 4. (1) No one shall be held in slavery or servitude.
(2) No one shall be required to perform forced or compulsory labour.
(3) For the purpose of this Article the term "forced or compulsory labour" shall not include:
(a) any work required to be done in the ordinary course of detention imposed according to the provisions of Article 5 of this Convention or during conditional release from such detention;
(b) any service of a military character or, in case of conscientious objectors in countries where they are recognised, service exacted instead of compulsory military service;
(c) any service exacted in case of an emergency or calamity threatening the life or well-being of the community;
(d) any work or service which forms part of normal civic obligations.

Article 5. (1) Everyone has the right to liberty and security of person. No one shall be deprived of his liberty save in the following cases and in accordance with a procedure prescribed by law:
(a) the lawful detention of a person after conviction by a competent court;
(b) the lawful arrest or detention of a person for non-compliance with the lawful order of a court or in order to secure the fulfilment of any obligation prescribed by law;
(c) the lawful arrest or detention of a person effected for the purpose of bringing him before the competent legal authority on reasonable suspicion of having committed an offence or when it is reasonably considered necessary to prevent his committing an offence or fleeing after having done so;
(d) the detention of a minor by lawful order for the purpose of educational supervision or his lawful detention for the purpose of bringing him before the competent legal authority;
(e) the lawful detention of persons for the prevention of the spreading of infectious diseases, of persons of un-sound mind, alcoholics or drug addicts or vagrants;

(f) the lawful arrest or detention of a person to prevent his effecting an unauthorised entry into the country or of a person against whom action is being taken with a view to deportation or extradition.
(2) Everyone who is arrested shall be informed promptly, in a language which he understands, of the reasons for his arrest and of any charge against him.
(3) Everyone arrested or detained in accordance with the provisions of paragraph 1 (c) of this Article shall be brought promptly before a judge or other officer authorised by law to exercise judicial power and shall be entitled to trial within a reasonable time or to release pending trial. Release may be conditioned by guarantees to appear for trial.
(4) Everyone who is deprived of his liberty by arrest or detention shall be entitled to take proceedings by which the lawfulness of his detention shall be decided speedily by a court and his release ordered if the detention is not lawful.
(5) Everyone who has been the victim of arrest or detention in contravention of the provisions of this Article shall have an enforceable right to compensation.

Article 6. (1) In the determination of his civil rights and obligations or of any criminal charge against him, everyone is entitled to a fair and public hearing within a reasonable time by an independent and impartial tribunal established by law. Judgment shall be pronounced publicly but the press and public may be excluded from all or part of the trial in the interests of morals, public order or national security in a democratic society, where the interests of juveniles or the protection of the private life of the parties so require, or to the extent strictly necessary in the opinion of the court in special circumstances where publicity would prejudice the interests of justice.
(2) Everyone charged with a criminal offence shall be presumed innocent until proved guilty according to law.
(3) Everyone charged with a criminal offence has the following minimum rights:
(a) to be informed promptly, in a language which he understands and in detail, of the nature and cause of the accusation against him;
(b) to have adequate time and facilities for the preparation of his defence;
(c) to defend himself in person or through legal assistance of his own choosing or, if he has not sufficient means to pay for legal assistance, to be given it free when the interests of justice so require;
(d) to examine or have examined witnesses against him and to obtain the attendance and examination of witnesses on his behalf under the same conditions as witnesses against him;
(e) to have the free assistance of an interpreter if he cannot understand or speak the language used in court.

Article 7. (1) No one shall be held guilty of any criminal offence on account of any act or omission which did not constitute a criminal offence under national or international law at the time when it was committed. Nor shall a heavier penalty be imposed than the one that was applicable at the time the criminal offence was committed.

(2) This Article shall not prejudice the trial and punishment of any person for any act or omission which, at the time when it was committed, was criminal according to the general principles of law recognised by civilised nations.

Article 8. (1) Everyone has the right to respect for his private and family life, his home and his correspondence.
(2) There shall be no interference by a public authority with the exercise of this right except such as is in accordance with the law and is necessary in a democratic society in the interests of national security, public safety or the economic well-being of the country, for the prevention of disorder or crime, for the protection of health or morals, or for the protection of the rights and freedoms of others.

Article 9. (1) Everyone has the right to freedom of thought, conscience and religion; this right includes freedom to change his religion or belief and freedom, either alone or in community with others and in public or private, to manifest his religion or belief, in worship, teaching, practice and observance.
(2) Freedom to manifest one's religion or beliefs shall be subject only to such limitations as are prescribed by law and are necessary in a democratic society in the interests of public safety, for the protection of public order, health or morals, or for the protection of the rights and freedoms of others.

Article 10. (1) Everyone has the right to freedom of expression. This right shall include freedom to hold opinions and to receive and impart information and ideas without interference by public authority and regardless of frontiers. This Article shall not prevent States from requiring the licensing of broadcasting, television or cinema enterprises.
(2) The exercise of these freedoms, since it carries with it duties and responsibilities, may be subject to such formalities, conditions, restrictions or penalties as are prescribed by law and are necessary in a democratic society, in the interests of national security, territorial integrity or public safety, for the prevention of disorder or crime, for the protection of health or morals, for the protection of the reputation or rights of others, for preventing the disclosure of information received in confidence, or for maintaining the authority and impartiality of the judiciary.

Article 11. (1) Everyone has the right to freedom of peaceful assembly and to freedom of association with others, including the right to form and to join trade unions for the protection of his interests.
(2) No restrictions shall be placed on the exercise of these rights other than such as are prescribed by law and are necessary in a democratic society in the interests of national security or public safety, for the prevention of disorder or crime, for the protection of health or morals or for the protection of the rights and freedoms of others. This Article shall not prevent the imposition of lawful restrictions on the exercise of these rights by members of the armed forces, of the police or of the administration of the State.

Article 12. Men and women of marriageable age have the right to marry and to found a family, according to the national laws governing the exercise of this right.

Article 13. Everyone whose rights and freedoms as set forth in this Convention are violated shall have an effective remedy before a national authority notwithstanding that the violation has been committed by persons acting in an official capacity.

Article 14. The enjoyment of the rights and freedoms set forth in this Convention shall be secured without discrimination on any ground such as sex, race, colour, language, religion, political or other opinion, national or social origin, association with a national minority, property, birth or other status.

Article 15. (1) In time of war or other public emergency threatening the life of the nation any High Contracting Party may take measures derogating from its obligations under this Convention to the extent strictly required by the exigencies of the situation, provided that such measures are not inconsistent with its other obligations under international law.
(2) No derogation from Article 2, except in respect of deaths resulting from lawful acts of war, or from Articles 3, 4 § 1 and 7 shall be made under this provision.
(3) Any High Contracting Party availing itself of this right of derogation shall keep the Secretary General of the Council of Europe fully informed of the measures which it has taken and the reasons therefor. It shall also inform the Secretary General of the Council of Europe when such measures have ceased to operate and the provisions of the Convention are again being fully executed.

Article 16. Nothing in Articles 10, 11 and 14 shall be regarded as preventing the High Contracting Parties from imposing restrictions on the political activity of aliens.

Article 17. Nothing in this Convention may be interpreted as implying for any State, group or person any right to engage in any activity or perform any act aimed at the destruction of any of the rights and freedoms set forth herein or at their limitation to a greater extent than is provided for in the Convention.

Article 18. The restrictions permitted under this Convention to the said rights and freedoms shall not be applied for any purpose other than those for which they have been prescribed.

Section II. European Court of Human Rights

Article 19. To ensure the observance of the engagements undertaken by the High Contracting Parties in the Convention and the Protocols thereto, there shall be set up a European Court of Human Rights, hereinafter referred to as "the Court". It shall function on a permanent basis.

Article 20. The Court shall consist of a number of judges equal to that of the High Contracting Parties.

Article 21. (1) The judges shall be of high moral character and must either possess the qualifications required for appointment to high judicial office or be jurisconsults of recognised competence.
(2) The judges shall sit on the Court in their individual capacity.
(3) During their term of office the judges shall not engage in any activity which is incompatible with their independence, impartiality or with the demands of a full-time office; all questions arising from the application of this paragraph shall be decided by the Court.

Article 22. The judges shall be elected by the Parliamentary Assembly with respect to each High Contracting Party by a majority of votes cast from a list of three candidates nominated by the High Contracting Party.

Article 23. (1) The judges shall be elected for a period of nine years. They may not be re-elected.
(2) The terms of office of judges shall expire when they reach the age of 70.
(3) The judges shall hold office until replaced. They shall, however, continue to deal with such cases as they already have under consideration.
(4) No judge may be dismissed from office unless the other judges decide by a majority of two-thirds that that judge has ceased to fulfil the required conditions.

Article 24. (1) The Court shall have a Registry, the functions and organisation of which shall be laid down in the rules of the Court.
(2) When sitting in a single-judge formation, the Court shall be assisted by rapporteurs who shall function under the authority of the President of the Court. They shall form part of the Court's Registry.

Article 25. The plenary Court shall
(a) elect its President and one or two Vice-Presidents for a period of three years; they may be re-elected;
(b) set up Chambers, constituted for a fixed period of time;
(c) elect the Presidents of the Chambers of the Court; they may be re-elected;
(d) adopt the rules of the Court;
(e) elect the Registrar and one or more Deputy Registrars;
(f) make any request under Article 26 § 2.

Article 26. (1) To consider cases brought before it, the Court shall sit in a single-judge formation, in Committees of three judges, in Chambers of seven judges and in a Grand Chamber of seventeen judges. The Court's Chambers shall set up Committees for a fixed period of time.

(2) At the request of the plenary Court, the Committee of Ministers may, by a unanimous decision and for a fixed period, reduce to five the number of judges of the Chambers.
(3) When sitting as a single judge, a judge shall not examine any application against the High Contracting Party in respect of which that judge has been elected.
(4) There shall sit as an ex officio member of the Chamber and the Grand Chamber the judge elected in respect of the High Contracting Party concerned. If there is none or if that judge is unable to sit, a person chosen by the President of the Court from a list submitted in advance by that Party shall sit in the capacity of judge.
(5) The Grand Chamber shall also include the President of the Court, the Vice-Presidents, the Presidents of the Chambers and other judges chosen in accordance with the rules of the Court. When a case is referred to the Grand Chamber under Article 43, no judge from the Chamber which rendered the judgment shall sit in the Grand Chamber, with the exception of the President of the Chamber and the judge who sat in respect of the High Contracting Party concerned.

Article 27. (1) A single judge may declare inadmissible or strike out of the Court's list of cases an application submitted under Article 34, where such a decision can be taken without further examination.
(2) The decision shall be final.
(3) If the single judge does not declare an application inadmissible or strike it out, that judge shall forward it to a Committee or to a Chamber for further examination.

Article 28. (1) In respect of an application sub-mitted under Article 34, a Committee may, by a unanimous vote,
(a) declare it inadmissible or strike it out of its list of cases, where such decision can be taken without further examination; or
(b) declare it admissible and render at the same time a judgment on the merits, if the underlying question in the case, concerning the interpretation or the application of the Convention or the Protocols thereto, is already the subject of well-established case-law of the Court.
(2) Decisions and judgments under paragraph 1 shall be final.
(3) If the judge elected in respect of the High Contracting Party concerned is not a member of the Committee, the Committee may at any stage of the proceedings invite that judge to take the place of one of the members of the Committee, having regard to all relevant factors, including whether that Party has contested the application of the procedure under paragraph 1 (b).

Article 29. (1) If no decision is taken under Article 27 or 28, or no judgment rendered under Article 28, a Chamber shall decide on the admissibility and merits of individual applications submitted under Article 34. The decision on admissibility may be taken separately.
(2) A Chamber shall decide on the admissibility and merits of inter-State applications submitted under Article 33. The decision on admissibility shall be taken separately unless the Court, in exceptional cases, decides otherwise.

Article 30. Where a case pending before a Chamber raises a serious question affecting the interpretation of the Convention or the Protocols thereto, or where the resolution of a question before the Chamber might have a result inconsistent with a judgment previously delivered by the Court, the Chamber may, at any time before it has rendered its judgment, relinquish jurisdiction in favour of the Grand Chamber, unless one of the parties to the case objects.

Article 31. The Grand Chamber shall
(a) determine applications submitted either under Article 33 or Article 34 when a Chamber has relinquished jurisdiction under Article 30 or when the case has been referred to it under Article 43;
(b) decide on issues referred to the Court by the Committee of Ministers in accordance with Article 46 § 4; and
(c) consider requests for advisory opinions submitted under Article 47.

Article 32. (1) The jurisdiction of the Court shall extend to all matters concerning the interpretation and application of the Convention and the Protocols thereto which are referred to it as provided in Articles 33, 34, 46 and 47.
(2) In the event of dispute as to whether the Court has jurisdiction, the Court shall decide.

Article 33. Any High Contracting Party may refer to the Court any alleged breach of the provisions of the Convention and the Protocols thereto by another High Contracting Party.

Article 34. The Court may receive applications from any person, non-governmental organisation or group of individuals claiming to be the victim of a violation by one of the High Contracting Parties of the rights set forth in the Convention or the Protocols thereto. The High Contracting Parties undertake not to hinder in any way the effective exercise of this right.

Article 35. (1) The Court may only deal with the matter after all domestic remedies have been exhausted, according to the generally recognised rules of inter-national law, and within a period of six months from the date on which the final decision was taken.
(2) The Court shall not deal with any application submitted under Article 34 that
(a) is anonymous; or
(b) is substantially the same as a matter that has already been examined by the Court or has already been submitted to another procedure of international investigation or settlement and contains no relevant new information.
(3) The Court shall declare inadmissible any individual application submitted under Article 34 if it considers that:
(a) the application is incompatible with the provisions of the Convention or the Protocols thereto, manifestly ill-founded, or an abuse of the right of individual application; or

(b) the applicant has not suffered a significant disadvantage, unless respect for human rights as defined in the Convention and the Protocols thereto requires an examination of the application on the merits and provided that no case may be rejected on this ground which has not been duly considered by a domestic tribunal.
(4) The Court shall reject any application which it considers inadmissible under this Article. It may do so at any stage of the proceedings.

Article 36. (1) In all cases before a Chamber or the Grand Chamber, a High Contracting Party one of whose nationals is an applicant shall have the right to submit written comments and to take part in hearings.
(2) The President of the Court may, in the interest of the proper administration of justice, invite any High Contracting Party which is not a party to the proceedings or any person concerned who is not the applicant to submit written comments or take part in hearings.
(3) In all cases before a Chamber or the Grand Chamber, the Council of Europe Commissioner for Human Rights may submit written comments and take part in hearings.

Article 37. (1) The Court may at any stage of the proceedings decide to strike an application out of its list of cases where the circumstances lead to the conclusion that
(a) the applicant does not intend to pursue his application; or
(b) the matter has been resolved; or
(c) for any other reason established by the Court, it is no longer justified to continue the examination of the application.
However, the Court shall continue the examination of the application if respect for human rights as defined in the Convention and the Protocols thereto so requires.
(2) The Court may decide to restore an application to its list of cases if it considers that the circumstances justify such a course.

Article 38. The Court shall examine the case together with the representatives of the parties and, if need be, undertake an investigation, for the effective conduct of which the High Contracting Parties concerned shall furnish all necessary facilities.

Article 39. (1) At any stage of the proceedings, the Court may place itself at the disposal of the parties concerned with a view to securing a friendly settlement of the matter on the basis of respect for human rights as defined in the Convention and the Protocols thereto.
(2) Proceedings conducted under para-graph 1 shall be confidential.
(3) If a friendly settlement is effected, the Court shall strike the case out of its list by means of a decision which shall be confined to a brief statement of the facts and of the solution reached.
(4) This decision shall be transmitted to the Committee of Ministers, which shall supervise the execution of the terms of the friendly settlement as set out in the decision.

Article 40. (1) Hearings shall be in public unless the Court in exceptional circumstances decides otherwise.
(2) Documents deposited with the Registrar shall be accessible to the public unless the President of the Court decides otherwise.

Article 41. If the Court finds that there has been a violation of the Convention or the Protocols thereto, and if the internal law of the High Contracting Party concerned allows only partial reparation to be made, the Court shall, if necessary, afford just satisfaction to the injured party.

Article 42. Judgments of Chambers shall become final in accordance with the provisions of Article 44 § 2.

Article 43. (1) Within a period of three months from the date of the judgment of the Chamber, any party to the case may, in exceptional cases, request that the case be referred to the Grand Chamber.
(2) A panel of five judges of the Grand Chamber shall accept the request if the case raises a serious question affecting the interpretation or application of the Convention or the Protocols thereto, or a serious issue of general importance.
(3) If the panel accepts the request, the Grand Chamber shall decide the case by means of a judgment.

Article 44. (1) The judgment of the Grand Chamber shall be final.
(2) The judgment of a Chamber shall become final
(a) when the parties declare that they will not request that the case be referred to the Grand Chamber; or
(b) three months after the date of the judgment, if reference of the case to the Grand Chamber has not been requested; or
(c) when the panel of the Grand Chamber rejects the request to refer under Article 43.
(3) The final judgment shall be published.

Article 45. (1) Reasons shall be given for judgments as well as for decisions declaring applications admissible or inadmissible.
(2) If a judgment does not represent, in whole or in part, the unanimous opinion of the judges, any judge shall be entitled to deliver a separate opinion.

Article 46. (1). The High Contracting Parties under-take to abide by the final judgment of the Court in any case to which they are parties.
(2) The final judgment of the Court shall be transmitted to the Committee of Ministers, which shall supervise its execution.
(3) If the Committee of Ministers considers that the supervision of the execution of a final judgment is hindered by a problem of interpretation of the judgment, it may refer the matter to the Court for a ruling on the question of interpretation. A referral

decision shall require a majority vote of two thirds of the representatives entitled to sit on the Committee.

(4) If the Committee of Ministers considers that a High Contracting Party refuses to abide by a final judgment in a case to which it is a party, it may, after serving formal notice on that Party and by decision adopted by a majority vote of two-thirds of the representatives entitled to sit on the Committee, refer to the Court the question whether that Party has failed to fulfil its obligation under paragraph 1.

(5) If the Court finds a violation of paragraph 1, it shall refer the case to the Committee of Ministers for consideration of the measures to be taken. If the Court finds no violation of paragraph 1, it shall refer the case to the Committee of Ministers, which shall close its examination of the case.

Article 47. (1) The Court may, at the request of the Committee of Ministers, give advisory opinions on legal questions concerning the interpretation of the Convention and the Protocols thereto.

(2) Such opinions shall not deal with any question relating to the content or scope of the rights or freedoms defined in Section I of the Convention and the Protocols thereto, or with any other question which the Court or the Committee of Ministers might have to consider in consequence of any such proceedings as could be instituted in accordance with the Convention.

(3) Decisions of the Committee of Ministers to request an advisory opinion of the Court shall require a majority vote of the representatives entitled to sit on the Committee.

Article 48. The Court shall decide whether a request for an advisory opinion submitted by the Committee of Ministers is within its competence as defined in Article 47.

Article 49. (1) Reasons shall be given for advisory opinions of the Court.

(2) If the advisory opinion does not represent, in whole or in part, the unanimous opinion of the judges, any judge shall be entitled to deliver a separate opinion.

(3) Advisory opinions of the Court shall be communicated to the Committee of Ministers.

Article 50. The expenditure on the Court shall be borne by the Council of Europe.

Article 51. The judges shall be entitled, during the exercise of their functions, to the privileges and immunities provided for in Article 40 of the Statute of the Council of Europe and in the agreements made thereunder.

Article 52. On receipt of a request from the Secretary General of the Council of Europe any High Contracting Party shall furnish an explanation of the manner in which its internal law ensures the effective implementation of any of the provisions of the Convention.

Article 53. Nothing in this Convention shall be construed as limiting or derogating from any of the human rights and fundamental freedoms which may be ensured under the laws of any High Contracting Party or under any other agreement to which it is a party.

Article 54. Nothing in this Convention shall prejudice the powers conferred on the Committee of Ministers by the Statute of the Council of Europe.

Article 55. The High Contracting Parties agree that, except by special agreement, they will not avail themselves of treaties, conventions or declarations in force between them for the purpose of submitting, by way of petition, a dispute arising out of the interpretation or application of this Convention to a means of settlement other than those provided for in this Convention.

Article 56. (1) Any State may at the time of its ratification or at any time thereafter declare by notification addressed to the Secretary General of the Council of Europe that the present Convention shall, subject to paragraph 4 of this Article, extend to all or any of the territories for whose international relations it is responsible.
(2) The Convention shall extend to the territory or territories named in the notification as from the thirtieth day after the receipt of this notification by the Secretary General of the Council of Europe.
(3) The provisions of this Convention shall be applied in such territories with due regard, however, to local requirements.
(4) Any State which has made a declaration in accordance with paragraph 1 of this Article may at any time thereafter declare on behalf of one or more of the territories to which the declaration relates that it accepts the competence of the Court to receive applications from individuals, non-governmental organisations or groups of individuals as provided by Article 34 of the Convention.

Article 57. (1) Any State may, when signing this Convention or when depositing its instrument of ratification, make a reservation in respect of any particular provision of the Convention to the extent that any law then in force in its territory is not in conformity with the provision. Reservations of a general character shall not be permitted under this Article.
(2) Any reservation made under this Article shall contain a brief statement of the law concerned.

Article 58. (1) A High Contracting Party may denounce the present Convention only after the expiry of five years from the date on which it became a party to it and after six months' notice contained in a notification addressed to the Secretary General of the Council of Europe, who shall inform the other High Contracting Parties.
(2) Such a denunciation shall not have the effect of releasing the High
Contracting Party concerned from its obligations under this Convention in respect of any act which, being capable of constituting a violation of such obligations, may

have been performed by it before the date at which the denunciation became effective.

(3) Any High Contracting Party which shall cease to be a member of the Council of Europe shall cease to be a party to this Convention under the same conditions.

(4) The Convention may be denounced in accordance with the provisions of the preceding paragraphs in respect of any territory to which it has been declared to extend under the terms of Article 56.

Article 59. (1) This Convention shall be open to the signature of the members of the Council of Europe. It shall be ratified. Ratifications shall be deposited with the Secretary General of the Council of Europe.

(2) The European Union may accede to this Convention.

(3) The present Convention shall come into force after the deposit of ten instruments of ratification.

(4) As regards any signatory ratifying subsequently, the Convention shall come into force at the date of the deposit of its instrument of ratification.

(5) The Secretary General of the Council of Europe shall notify all the members of the Council of Europe of the entry into force of the Convention, the names of the High Contracting Parties who have ratified it, and the deposit of all instruments of ratification which may be effected subsequently.

Protocol (No. 1) to the Convention for the Protection of Human Rights and Fundamental Freedoms. Paris, 20 March 1952.

The governments signatory hereto, being members of the Council of Europe,
Being resolved to take steps to ensure the collective enforcement of certain rights and freedoms other than those already included in Section I of the Convention for the Protection of Human Rights and Fundamental Freedoms signed at Rome on 4 November 1950 (hereinafter referred to as 'the Convention'),
Have agreed as follows:

Article 1. Every natural or legal person is entitled to the peaceful enjoyment of his possessions. No one shall be deprived of his possessions except in the public interest and subject to the conditions provided for by law and by the general principles of international law.
The preceding provisions shall not, however, in any way impair the right of a State to enforce such laws as it deems necessary to control the use of property in accordance with the general interest or to secure the payment of taxes or other contributions or penalties.

Article 2. No person shall be denied the right to education. In the exercise of any functions which it assumes in relation to education and to teaching, the State shall respect the right of parents to ensure such education and teaching in conformity with their own religious and philosophical convictions.

Article 3. The High Contracting Parties undertake to hold free elections at reasonable intervals by secret ballot, under conditions which will ensure the free expression of the opinion of the people in the choice of the legislature.

[*Articles 4-6 are omitted.*]

Protocol No. 4 to the Convention for the Protection of Human Rights and Fundamental Freedoms securing certain rights and freedoms other than those already included in the Convention and in the first Protocol thereto. Strasbourg, 16 September 1963.

[*The Preamble is omitted.*]

Article 1. No one shall be deprived of his liberty merely on the ground of inability to fulfil a contractual obligation.

Article 2. (1) Everyone lawfully within the territory of a State shall, within that territory, have the right to liberty of movement and freedom to choose his residence.
(2) Everyone shall be free to leave any country, including his own.
(3) No restrictions shall be placed on the exercise of these rights other than such as are in accordance with law and are necessary in a democratic society in the interests

of national security or public safety, for the maintenance of ordre public, for the prevention of crime, for the protection of health or morals, or for the protection of the rights and freedoms of others.
(4) The rights set forth in paragraph 1 may also be subject, in particular areas, to restrictions imposed in accordance with law and justified by the public interest in a democratic society.

Article 3. (1) No one shall be expelled, by means either of an individual or of a collective measure, from the territory of the State of which he is a national.
(2) No one shall be deprived of the right to enter the territory of the state of which he is a national.

Article 4. Collective expulsion of aliens is prohibited.

[Articles 5-7 are omitted.]

Protocol No. 6 to the Convention for the Protection of Human Rights and Fundamental Freedoms concerning the abolition of the death penalty. Strasbourg, 28 April 1983.

[The Preamble is omitted.]

Article 1. The death penalty shall be abolished. No-one shall be condemned to such penalty or executed.

Article 2. A State may make provision in its law for the death penalty in respect of acts committed in time of war or of imminent threat of war; such penalty shall be applied only in the instances laid down in the law and in accordance with its provisions. The State shall communicate to the Secretary General of the Council of Europe the relevant provisions of that law.

[Articles 3-9 are omitted.]

Protocol No. 7 to the Convention for the Protection of Human Rights and Fundamental Freedoms. Strasbourg, 22 November 1984.

[The Preamble is omitted.]

Article 1. (1) An alien lawfully resident in the territory of a State shall not be expelled therefrom except in pursuance of a decision reached in accordance with law and shall be allowed:
a. to submit reasons against his expulsion,
b. to have his case reviewed, and
c. to be represented for these purposes before the competent authority or a person or persons designated by that authority.

(2) An alien may be expelled before the exercise of his rights under paragraph 1.a, b and c of this Article, when such expulsion is necessary in the interests of public order or is grounded on reasons of national security.

Article 2. (1) Everyone convicted of a criminal offence by a tribunal shall have the right to have his conviction or sentence reviewed by a higher tribunal. The exercise of this right, including the grounds on which it may be exercised, shall be governed by law.
(2) This right may be subject to exceptions in regard to offences of a minor character, as prescribed by law, or in cases in which the person concerned was tried in the first instance by the highest tribunal or was convicted following an appeal against acquittal.

Article 3. When a person has by a final decision been convicted of a criminal offence and when subsequently his conviction has been reversed, or he has been pardoned, on the ground that a new or newly discovered fact shows conclusively that there has been a miscarriage of justice, the person who has suffered punishment as a result of such conviction shall be compensated according to the law or the practice of the State concerned, unless it is proved that the non-disclosure of the unknown fact in time is wholly or partly attributable to him.

Article 4. (1) No one shall be liable to be tried or punished again in criminal proceedings under the jurisdiction of the same State for an offence for which he has already been finally acquitted or convicted in accordance with the law and penal procedure of that State.
(2) The provisions of the preceding paragraph shall not prevent the reopening of the case in accordance with the law and penal procedure of the State concerned, if there is evidence of new or newly discovered facts, or if there has been a fundamental defect in the previous proceedings, which could affect the outcome of the case.
(3) No derogation from this Article shall be made under Article 15 of the Convention.

Article 5. Spouses shall enjoy equality of rights and responsibilities of a private law character between them, and in their relations with their children, as to marriage, during marriage and in the event of its dissolution. This Article shall not prevent States from taking such measures as are necessary in the interests of the children.

[*Articles 6-10 are omitted.*]

Protocol No. 12 to the Convention for the Protection of Human Rights and Fundamental Freedoms. Rome, 4 November 2000.

[*The Preamble is omitted.*]

Article 1. (1) The enjoyment of any right set forth by law shall be secured without discrimination on any ground such as sex, race, colour, language, religion, political or other opinion, national or social origin, association with a national minority, property, birth or other status.
(2) No one shall be discriminated against by any public authority on any ground such as those mentioned in paragraph 1.

[Articles 2-6 are omitted.]

Protocol No. 13 to the Convention for the Protection of Human Rights and Fundamental Freedoms Concerning the abolition of the death penalty in all circumstances. Vilnius, 3 May 2002.

[The Preamble is omitted.]

Article 1. The death penalty shall be abolished. No one shall be condemned to such penalty or executed.

[Articles 2-8 are omitted.]

Charter of Fundamental Rights of the European Union

Preamble

The peoples of Europe, in creating an ever closer union among them, are resolved to share a peaceful future based on common values.

Conscious of its spiritual and moral heritage, the Union is founded on the indivisible, universal values of human dignity, freedom, equality and solidarity; it is based on the principles of democracy and the rule of law. It places the individual at the heart of its activities, by establishing the citizenship of the Union and by creating an area of freedom, security and justice.

The Union contributes to the preservation and to the development of these common values while respecting the diversity of the cultures and traditions of the peoples of Europe as well as the national identities of the Member States and the organisation of their public authorities at national, regional and local levels; it seeks to promote balanced and sustainable development and ensures free movement of persons, services, goods and capital, and the freedom of establishment.

To this end, it is necessary to strengthen the protection of fundamental rights in the light of changes in society, social progress and scientific and technological developments by making those rights more visible in a Charter.

This Charter reaffirms, with due regard for the powers and tasks of the Union and for the principle of subsidiarity, the rights as they result, in particular, from the constitutional traditions and international obligations common to the Member States, the European Convention for the Protection of Human Rights and Fundamental Freedoms, the Social Charters adopted by the Union and by the Council of Europe and the case-law of the Court of Justice of the European Union and of the European Court of Human Rights. In this context the Charter will be interpreted by the courts of the Union and the Member States with due regard to the explanations prepared under the authority of the Praesidium of the Convention which drafted the Charter and updated under the responsibility of the Praesidium of the European Convention.

Enjoyment of these rights entails responsibilities and duties with regard to other persons, to the human community and to future generations.

The Union therefore recognises the rights, freedoms and principles set out hereafter.

Title I: Dignity

Article 1. Human dignity is inviolable. It must be respected and protected.

Article 2. (1) Everyone has the right to life.
(2) No one shall be condemned to the death penalty, or executed.

Article 3. (1) Everyone has the right to respect for his or her physical and mental integrity.
(2) In the fields of medicine and biology, the following must be respected in particular:
(a) the free and informed consent of the person concerned, according to the procedures laid down by law;
(b) the prohibition of eugenic practices, in particular those aiming at the selection of persons;
(c) the prohibition on making the human body and its parts as such a source of financial gain;
(d) the prohibition of the reproductive cloning of human beings.

Article 4. No one shall be subjected to torture or to inhuman or degrading treatment or punishment.

Article 5. (1) No one shall be held in slavery or servitude.
(2) No one shall be required to perform forced or compulsory labour.
(3) Trafficking in human beings is prohibited.

Title II: Freedoms

Article 6. Everyone has the right to liberty and security of person.

Article 7. Everyone has the right to respect for his or her private and family life, home and communications.

Article 8. (1) Everyone has the right to the protection of personal data concerning him or her.
(2) Such data must be processed fairly for specified purposes and on the basis of the consent of the person concerned or some other legitimate basis laid down by law. Everyone has the right of access to data which has been collected concerning him or her, and the right to have it rectified.
(3) Compliance with these rules shall be subject to control by an independent authority.

Article 9. The right to marry and the right to found a family shall be guaranteed in accordance with the national laws governing the exercise of these rights.

Article 10. (1) Everyone has the right to freedom of thought, conscience and religion. This right includes freedom to change religion or belief and freedom, either alone or in community with others and in public or in private, to manifest religion or belief, in worship, teaching, practice and observance.

(2) The right to conscientious objection is recognised, in accordance with the national laws governing the exercise of this right.

Article 11. (1) Everyone has the right to freedom of expression. This right shall include freedom to hold opinions and to receive and impart information and ideas without interference by public authority and regardless of frontiers.
(2) The freedom and pluralism of the media shall be respected.

Article 12. (1) Everyone has the right to freedom of peaceful assembly and to freedom of association at all levels, in particular in political, trade union and civic matters, which implies the right of everyone to form and to join trade unions for the protection of his or her interests.
(2) Political parties at Union level contribute to expressing the political will of the citizens of the Union.

Article 13. The arts and scientific research shall be free of constraint. Academic freedom shall be respected.

Article 14. (1) Everyone has the right to education and to have access to vocational and continuing training.
(2) This right includes the possibility to receive free compulsory education.
(3) The freedom to found educational establishments with due respect for democratic principles and the right of parents to ensure the education and teaching of their children in conformity with their religious, philosophical and pedagogical convictions shall be respected, in accordance with the national laws governing the exercise of such freedom and right.

Article 15. (1) Everyone has the right to engage in work and to pursue a freely chosen or accepted occupation.
(2) Every citizen of the Union has the freedom to seek employment, to work, to exercise the right of establishment and to provide services in any Member State.
(3) Nationals of third countries who are authorised to work in the territories of the Member States are entitled to working conditions equivalent to those of citizens of the Union.

Article 16. The freedom to conduct a business in accordance with Union law and national laws and practices is recognised.

Article 17. (1) Everyone has the right to own, use, dispose of and bequeath his or her lawfully acquired possessions. No one may be deprived of his or her possessions, except in the public interest and in the cases and under the conditions provided for by law, subject to fair compensation being paid in good time for their loss. The use of property may be regulated by law in so far as is necessary for the general interest.
(2) Intellectual property shall be protected.

Article 18. The right to asylum shall be guaranteed with due respect for the rules of the Geneva Convention of 28 July 1951 and the Protocol of 31 January 1967 relating to the status of refugees and in accordance with the Treaty on European Union and the Treaty on the Functioning of the European Union (hereinafter referred to as 'the Treaties').

Article 19. (1) Collective expulsions are prohibited.
(2) No one may be removed, expelled or extradited to a State where there is a serious risk that he or she would be subjected to the death penalty, torture or other inhuman or degrading treatment or punishment.

Title III: Equality

Article 20. Everyone is equal before the law.

Article 21. (1) Any discrimination based on any ground such as sex, race, colour, ethnic or social origin, genetic features, language, religion or belief, political or any other opinion, membership of a national minority, property, birth, disability, age or sexual orientation shall be prohibited.
(2) Within the scope of application of the Treaties and without prejudice to any of their specific provisions, any discrimination on grounds of nationality shall be prohibited.

Article 22. The Union shall respect cultural, religious and linguistic diversity.

Article 23. Equality between women and men must be ensured in all areas, including employment, work and pay.
The principle of equality shall not prevent the maintenance or adoption of measures providing for specific advantages in favour of the under-represented sex.

Article 24. (1) Children shall have the right to such protection and care as is necessary for their well-being. They may express their views freely. Such views shall be taken into consideration on matters which concern them in accordance with their age and maturity.
(2) In all actions relating to children, whether taken by public authorities or private institutions, the child's best interests must be a primary consideration.
(3) Every child shall have the right to maintain on a regular basis a personal relationship and direct contact with both his or her parents, unless that is contrary to his or her interests.

Article 25. The Union recognises and respects the rights of the elderly to lead a life of dignity and independence and to participate in social and cultural life.

Article 26. The Union recognises and respects the right of persons with disabilities to benefit from measures designed to ensure their independence, social and occupational integration and participation in the life of the community.

Title IV: Solidarity

Article 27. Workers or their representatives must, at the appropriate levels, be guaranteed information and consultation in good time in the cases and under the conditions provided for by Union law and national laws and practices.

Article 28. Workers and employers, or their respective organisations, have, in accordance with Union law and national laws and practices, the right to negotiate and conclude collective agreements at the appropriate levels and, in cases of conflicts of interest, to take collective action to defend their interests, including strike action.

Article 29. Everyone has the right of access to a free placement service.

Article 30. Every worker has the right to protection against unjustified dismissal, in accordance with Union law and national laws and practices.

Article 31. (1) Every worker has the right to working conditions which respect his or her health, safety and dignity.
(2) Every worker has the right to limitation of maximum working hours, to daily and weekly rest periods and to an annual period of paid leave.

Article 32. The employment of children is prohibited. The minimum age of admission to employment may not be lower than the minimum school-leaving age, without prejudice to such rules as may be more favourable to young people and except for limited derogations.
Young people admitted to work must have working conditions appropriate to their age and be protected against economic exploitation and any work likely to harm their safety, health or physical, mental, moral or social development or to interfere with their education.

Article 33. (1) The family shall enjoy legal, economic and social protection.
(2) To reconcile family and professional life, everyone shall have the right to protection from dismissal for a reason connected with maternity and the right to paid maternity leave and to parental leave following the birth or adoption of a child.

Article 34. (1) The Union recognises and respects the entitlement to social security benefits and social services providing protection in cases such as maternity, illness, industrial accidents, dependency or old age, and in the case of loss of employment, in accordance with the rules laid down by Union law and national laws and practices.

(2) Everyone residing and moving legally within the European Union is entitled to social security benefits and social advantages in accordance with Union law and national laws and practices.
(3) In order to combat social exclusion and poverty, the Union recognises and respects the right to social and housing assistance so as to ensure a decent existence for all those who lack sufficient resources, in accordance with the rules laid down by Union law and national laws and practices.

Article 35. Everyone has the right of access to preventive health care and the right to benefit from medical treatment under the conditions established by national laws and practices. A high level of human health protection shall be ensured in the definition and implementation of all the Union's policies and activities.

Article 36. The Union recognises and respects access to services of general economic interest as provided for in national laws and practices, in accordance with the Treaties, in order to promote the social and territorial cohesion of the Union.

Article 37. A high level of environmental protection and the improvement of the quality of the environment must be integrated into the policies of the Union and ensured in accordance with the principle of sustainable development.

Article 38. Union policies shall ensure a high level of consumer protection.

Title V: Citizens' Rights

Article 39. (1) Every citizen of the Union has the right to vote and to stand as a candidate at elections to the European Parliament in the Member State in which he or she resides, under the same conditions as nationals of that State.
(2) Members of the European Parliament shall be elected by direct universal suffrage in a free and secret ballot.

Article 40. Every citizen of the Union has the right to vote and to stand as a candidate at municipal elections in the Member State in which he or she resides under the same conditions as nationals of that State.

Article 41. (1) Every person has the right to have his or her affairs handled impartially, fairly and within a reasonable time by the institutions, bodies, offices and agencies of the Union.
(2) This right includes:
(a) the right of every person to be heard, before any individual measure which would affect him or her adversely is taken;
(b) the right of every person to have access to his or her file, while respecting the legitimate interests of confidentiality and of professional and business secrecy;
(c) the obligation of the administration to give reasons for its decisions.

(3) Every person has the right to have the Union make good any damage caused by its institutions or by its servants in the performance of their duties, in accordance with the general principles common to the laws of the Member States.
(4) Every person may write to the institutions of the Union in one of the languages of the Treaties and must have an answer in the same language.

Article 42. Any citizen of the Union, and any natural or legal person residing or having its registered office in a Member State, has a right of access to documents of the institutions, bodies, offices and agencies of the Union, whatever their medium.

Article 43. Any citizen of the Union and any natural or legal person residing or having its registered office in a Member State has the right to refer to the European Ombudsman cases of maladministration in the activities of the institutions, bodies, offices or agencies of the Union, with the exception of the Court of Justice of the European Union acting in its judicial role.

Article 44. Any citizen of the Union and any natural or legal person residing or having its registered office in a Member State has the right to petition the European Parliament.

Article 45. (1) Every citizen of the Union has the right to move and reside freely within the territory of the Member States.
(2) Freedom of movement and residence may be granted, in accordance with the Treaties, to nationals of third countries legally resident in the territory of a Member State.

Article 46. Every citizen of the Union shall, in the territory of a third country in which the Member State of which he or she is a national is not represented, be entitled to protection by the diplomatic or consular authorities of any Member State, on the same conditions as the nationals of that Member State.

Title VI: Justice

Article 47. Everyone whose rights and freedoms guaranteed by the law of the Union are violated has the right to an effective remedy before a tribunal in compliance with the conditions laid down in this Article.
Everyone is entitled to a fair and public hearing within a reasonable time by an independent and impartial tribunal previously established by law. Everyone shall have the possibility of being advised, defended and represented.
Legal aid shall be made available to those who lack sufficient resources in so far as such aid is necessary to ensure effective access to justice.

Article 48. (1) Everyone who has been charged shall be presumed innocent until proved guilty according to law.

(2) Respect for the rights of the defence of anyone who has been charged shall be guaranteed.

Article 49. (1) No one shall be held guilty of any criminal offence on account of any act or omission which did not constitute a criminal offence under national law or international law at the time when it was committed. Nor shall a heavier penalty be imposed than the one that was applicable at the time the criminal offence was committed. If, subsequent to the commission of a criminal offence, the law provides for a lighter penalty, that penalty shall be applicable.
(2) This Article shall not prejudice the trial and punishment of any person for any act or omission which, at the time when it was committed, was criminal according to the general principles recognised by the community of nations.
(3) The severity of penalties must not be disproportionate to the criminal offence.

Article 50. No one shall be liable to be tried or punished again in criminal proceedings for an offence for which he or she has already been finally acquitted or convicted within the Union in accordance with the law.

Title VII: General Provisions Governing the Interpretation and Application of the Charter

Article 51. (1) The provisions of this Charter are addressed to the institutions, bodies, offices and agencies of the Union with due regard for the principle of subsidiarity and to the Member States only when they are implementing Union law. They shall therefore respect the rights, observe the principles and promote the application thereof in accordance with their respective powers and respecting the limits of the powers of the Union as conferred on it in the Treaties.
(2) The Charter does not extend the field of application of Union law beyond the powers of the Union or establish any new power or task for the Union, or modify powers and tasks as defined in the Treaties.

Article 52. (1) Any limitation on the exercise of the rights and freedoms recognised by this Charter must be provided for by law and respect the essence of those rights and freedoms. Subject to the principle of proportionality, limitations may be made only if they are necessary and genuinely meet objectives of general interest recognised by the Union or the need to protect the rights and freedoms of others.
(2) Rights recognised by this Charter for which provision is made in the Treaties shall be exercised under the conditions and within the limits defined by those Treaties.
(3) In so far as this Charter contains rights which correspond to rights guaranteed by the Convention for the Protection of Human Rights and Fundamental Freedoms, the meaning and scope of those rights shall be the same as those laid down by the said Convention. This provision shall not prevent Union law providing more extensive protection.

(4) In so far as this Charter recognises fundamental rights as they result from the constitutional traditions common to the Member States, those rights shall be interpreted in harmony with those traditions.
(5) The provisions of this Charter which contain principles may be implemented by legislative and executive acts taken by institutions, bodies, offices and agencies of the Union, and by acts of Member States when they are implementing Union law, in the exercise of their respective powers. They shall be judicially cognisable only in the interpretation of such acts and in the ruling on their legality.
(6) Full account shall be taken of national laws and practices as specified in this Charter.
(7) The explanations drawn up as a way of providing guidance in the interpretation of this Charter shall be given due regard by the courts of the Union and of the Member States.

Article 53. Nothing in this Charter shall be interpreted as restricting or adversely affecting human rights and fundamental freedoms as recognised, in their respective fields of application, by Union law and international law and by international agreements to which the Union or all the Member States are party, including the European Convention for the Protection of Human Rights and Fundamental Freedoms, and by the Member States' constitutions.

Article 54. Nothing in this Charter shall be interpreted as implying any right to engage in any activity or to perform any act aimed at the destruction of any of the rights and freedoms recognised in this Charter or at their limitation to a greater extent than is provided for herein.

www.ingramcontent.com/pod-product-compliance
Ingram Content Group UK Ltd.
Pitfield, Milton Keynes, MK11 3LW, UK
UKHW051849210426
5322IPUK00025B/631